LEGENDARY LOCALS

OF

AURORA

INDIANA

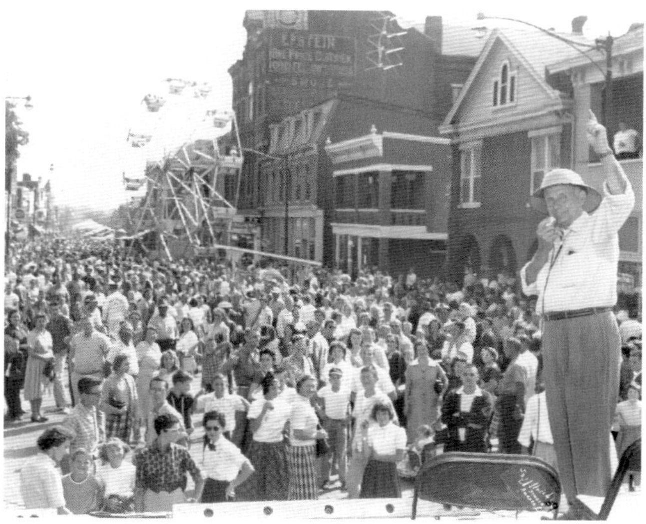

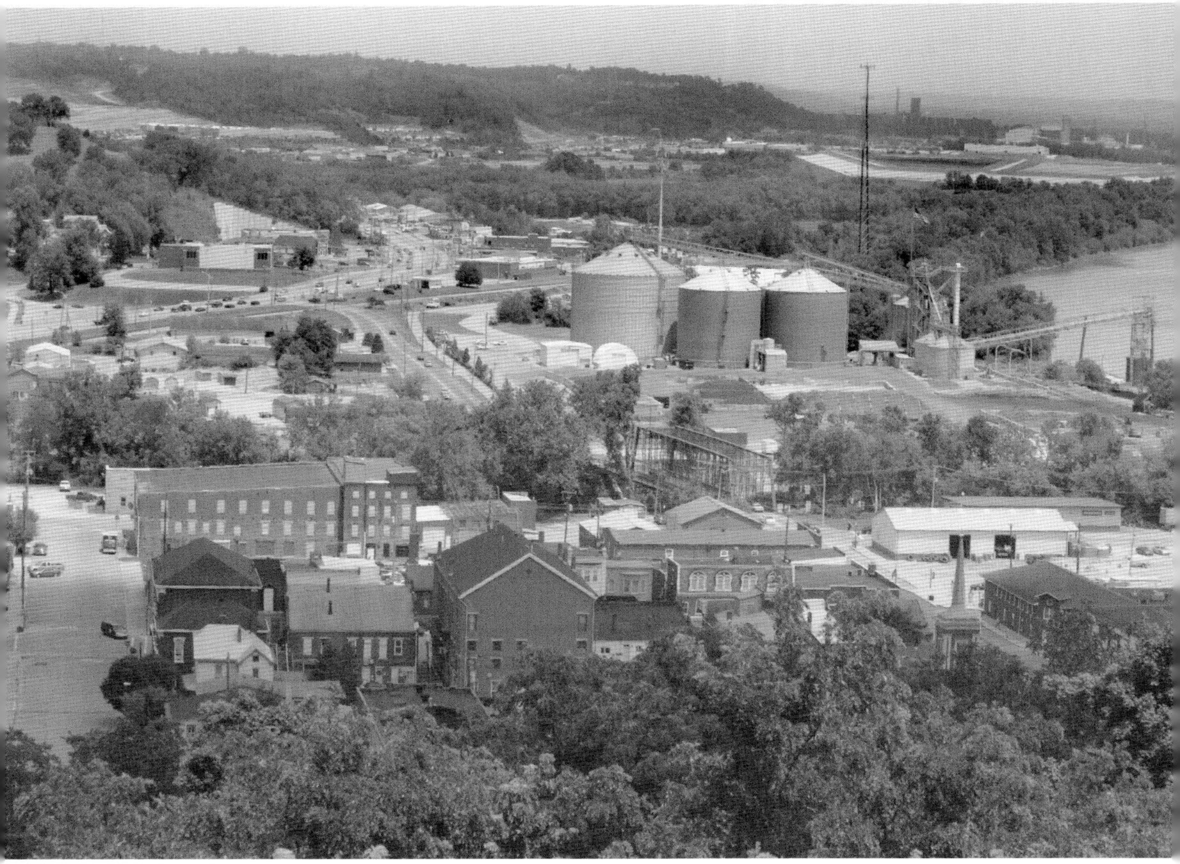

Dearborn County Historical Society

The Dearborn County Historical Society, formed in 1984, is the sole repository of historical materials related to Dearborn County, Indiana. The society is located in the historic 1818 Vance-Tousey House, home of Samuel C. Vance, Lawrenceburg's founder. The house, set apart by its soaring spiral staircase and grand riverfront façade, is considered one of the finest examples of Federal architecture in Indiana. Additionally, the society is steward to the 1820 Angevine Log Cabin, located in the society's Pioneer Homestead across the street. (Courtesy of McKenna Murray.)

Page 1: Earl Huffman

Earl Francis Huffman was considered a promoter extraordinaire. Much can be and has been written about him. No one person has done more to document the history of Aurora in his lifetime than Earl. He was born in 1896 and spent his whole life working and volunteering in Aurora. In this photograph, he stands on stage at the Aurora Farmers' Fair, with the crowd in the background. His favorite saying on stage was, "Folks, you ain't seen nothing yet!" (Courtesy of Ullrich Studios.)

LEGENDARY LOCALS

OF

AURORA

INDIANA

JENNY AWAD
FOR THE DEARBORN COUNTY HISTORICAL SOCIETY

LEGENDARY LOCALS

ISBN 978-1-4671-0057-1

Legendary Locals is an imprint of Arcadia Publishing
Charleston, South Carolina

Printed in the United States of America

Library of Congress Control Number: 2012947946

For all general information, please contact Arcadia Publishing:
Telephone 843-853-2070
Fax 843-853-0044
E-mail sales@arcadiapublishing.com
For customer service and orders:
Toll-Free 1-888-313-2665

Visit us on the Internet at www.arcadiapublishing.com

Dedication
The idea of neighbor helping neighbor has been one of the distinguishing marks of our town. To all of the extraordinary people of Aurora who never realize what legends they are.

On the Cover: From left to right:
(TOP ROW) Anthony Meyer (Courtesy of the Meyer Family, page 54); Anna Langtree Burton (Courtesy of Steven Lawsongatch, page 41); Ellsworth Haynes (Courtesy of Steven Lawsongatch, page 19); Luella Roppers (Courtesy of Louella Roppers, page 50); Dink Carter (Courtesy of DCHS, page 74).
(MIDDLE ROW) Curtis Chipman (Courtesy of Larry Moses, page 72); Quacky the Clown (Courtesy of DCHS, page 87); Samuel Langtree (Courtesy of Steve Lawsongatch, page 20); Judge Lester Baker (Courtesy of the Baker family, page 84); Jim Lee (Courtesy of Jenny Awad, page 113).
(BOTTOM ROW) John Hamilton (Courtesy of DCHS, page 14); Irene Peters (Courtesy of the Peters family, page 111); Emery Nocks (Courtesy of the Nocks Family, page 60); Louisa Plummer Haynes (Courtesy of Steven Lawsongatch, page 18); John Shattuck (Courtesy of Adena Charlton, page 23).

CONTENTS

ACKNOWLEDGMENTS

On behalf of the Dearborn County Historical Society (DCHS), I would like to thank everyone for their support of this project. The society is the sole repository of historical materials and photographs pertaining to all people, in all times, of Dearborn County's past. Also, thanks to the DCHS board, for "protecting the past for the future."

The Internet has become one of the greatest tools for genealogy research, which has reached a new level with the vast amounts of information available now. I have met so many people through the Facebook page "Lost Aurora and Center Township." Local history buff Milt Masing monitors this page, where people are invited to share photographs and memories of the past. The Aurora Public Library has moved their genealogy department to the old B&O Railroad depot. The beautifully renovated building is also a repository of Aurora history. Aurora historian Roy Lambert developed a "Talk about Aurora" program held at the depot. His monthly program invites the public to join in and discuss various Aurora topics. Another person to thank is my cousin Larry Moses. Without a second thought, he jumped in to help collect history, scan family photographs, or just go "fetch" for me. Thank you to our Dearborn County historian, Chris McHenry, for writing the introduction and for all the time she has dedicated to our "local legend" history.

INTRODUCTION

The first settlers in the Aurora area arrived in the 1790s. Revolutionary War veterans Isaac Morrison, Adam Flake, and George Cheek had been here years before the area was officially opened for settlement. They were looking for a new start for their families on what was then the frontier of the United States, attracted by the fertile soil and the location along the main east-west route.

Aurora grew slowly, officially becoming a town in 1819. By the late 1830s, two bridges had been built across Hogan Creek, allowing for fairly easy travel to the north and west, and a newspaper had been established. In some years, as many as 100 flatboats were launched, carrying goods to the south. With river travel the accustomed way of getting around, there was more connection between Aurora and Petersburg, Kentucky, than with many nearby Indiana locations. Thomas Gaff's brother James had come to town a year or so ahead of him, and so the family already had begun to make contacts and friendships with the movers and shakers of the day. James Gaff had also become acquainted with a Rising Sun industrialist named Nathan Stedman. In 1849, the two Gaffs bought into the business and moved it to Aurora.

Aurora was growing rapidly. The 1850 census revealed a population of 2,000, a huge increase in only 10 years. That year, more than 100 houses were built, along with additions to the Gaff mill and distillery. There were also two churches, 10 warehouses, four blacksmiths, and four cooper shops. Barrels were used in those days to ship whiskey, flour, pork, and other goods down the river. The whole town celebrated the arrival of the newest Gaff riverboat, the *Forest Queen*. The boat could achieve a speed of 10 miles per hour, even going upstream. The winter of 1851–1852 was exceptionally cold and by December, river traffic was brought to a halt by ice that remained until February, causing a major disruption with no way to obtain or ship goods that usually traveled by river.

Just two years later, the newspaper reported that there were now two newspapers and almost 3,000 people, and it bragged that houses cost from $9,000 up to as much as $15,000 to build. The population estimate may have been slightly exaggerated, since the official 1860 census recorded 3,000 people. In 1852, the first telegraph lines were installed, serving only Lawrenceburg, Aurora, and Rising Sun. It was expanded to include service from Cincinnati to St. Louis when the long-awaited railroad came through a couple of years later. The railroad established car shops in Cochran, providing plenty of employment for the burgeoning population of Irish railroad workers.

With the arrival of so many new people of different faiths, churches were needed. In 1849, a meeting had already been held to consider forming a Roman Catholic congregation, and in 1857, the Catholics built their first church. St. John Lutheran Church was founded in 1856. By the late 1850s, the prospect of civil war loomed. There was an active portion of the population that opposed slavery; another, made up mainly of people who had come from the South, thought the decision should be left to individual states. During this heady time, Petersburg, Kentucky, and Aurora, Indiana, had become well connected. People from Petersburg worked in Aurora, and many attended school here. All were appalled when the Civil War began, and they vowed not to let it ruin their friendly relationships. Leaders of the two towns got together and proposed an agreement, often referred to as the Friendly Pact. In it, they promised that—no matter what happened—the people of the two towns would remain friends forever. Once war was declared and volunteers were needed, Aurora mayor Frederick Slater resigned his position and raised an entire company of soldiers, mostly from Aurora and Boone County, Kentucky. They found themselves assigned to the 11th Kentucky Regiment. They fought throughout the war, and several of them died in Confederate prisons. Two members of the group, Edward H. Green and Louis Beinkamp, were later elected mayors of Aurora. Robert Q. Terrill was also a member of this company. Born in Petersburg, Kentucky, he was living in Aurora when the war started. He and his brother found themselves fighting on opposite sides and, after a couple of years, decided to opt out of the senseless fight. Both resigned their positions.

The Gaff brothers supplied transports for Union troops during the war. Their ships, *Diana* and *Forest Queen*, ran the Confederate batteries sensationally at Vicksburg.

Aurora continued to grow and prosper in spite of the war, and in 1861, the first street lamps were installed, probably fueled by kerosene. Gas lamps did not arrive until 1874. By 1863, the school system had grown with the addition of the Southside School. The first graduating class in 1865 had two students; a year later, there were three. A new form of entertainment, baseball, arrived not long after the Civil War and became all the rage in the 1870s. Every small town and factory had its own team, and rivalries were intense. Games were usually played on Sunday afternoons. If that was not enough to upset many churchgoers, the contests also usually involved large amounts of beer and sometimes ended in knockdown brawls. For those with more refined tastes, the Grand Opera House was built in 1878.

Communication moved into the forefront when the first telephone was installed in the Gaffs' office in 1879. It connected with only one other phone, that of H.W. Smith in Cincinnati. Smith was, at the time, the secretary and treasurer of the Aurora Distilling Company. As the 1880s began, Aurora City Hall was built and the Northside School was completed. This latter facility, along with the schools at St. John's and St. Mary's churches, provided ample opportunity for education. Railroad service and the ever-present Ohio River drew several thriving industries to Aurora in the late 1800s, manufacturing everything from bricks to foundry products. At one time, there were no less than four chair and furniture factories. The Aurora Coffin Co., later known as the Aurora Casket Co., was founded in the 1890s by John J. Backman and remained a family-owned industry for more than 100 years. Still in business, the company has been sold to outside interests.

Like many small towns today, Aurora no longer has the booming distilleries and furniture companies it once did. The city can brag that there are many family-owned businesses celebrating over 100 years of success, all descendants of some of the very first families. In 1908, one of Aurora's signature events, the annual Farmers' Fair, held its first session. It continues to this day, serving as a homecoming for thousands of people each year. As always, Aurora continues its love-hate relationship with the Ohio River, enduring frequent floods and undertaking recoveries but also calling attention to the river, with its pleasure-boat marinas, riverside park, the annual A Roar of Thunder powerboat races, and the Firecracker Festival on the riverfront.

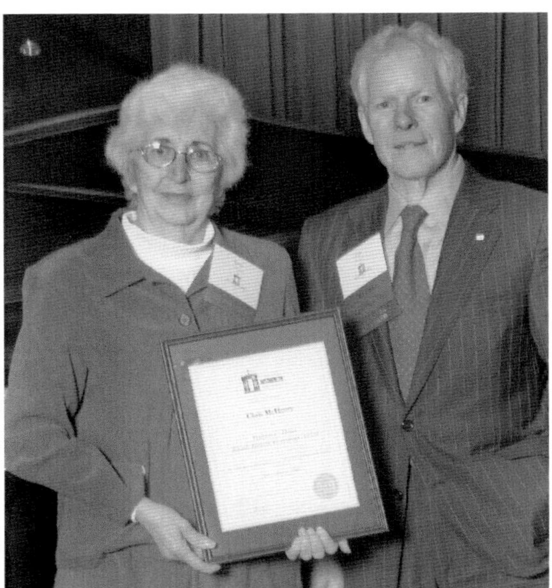

Chris McHenry
Among her many honors, Chris McHenry, (left) was presented the 2010 Willard C. Heiss Family History/Genealogy Award by Thomas Hoback, Indiana Historical Society Board Trustee Chair. McHenry is the acknowledged leading history expert in Dearborn County. (Courtesy of IHS.)

CHAPTER ONE

Early Times

When Jesse Holman, his wife, Elizabeth, and their two-month-old baby stepped on the shores of Aurora in 1811, it was snowing and turning nightfall. Holman's account conveys his loneliness and his desperation in bringing a young wife and child to the wilderness. In his diary, he wrote:

> We persevered in our journey. In fact, there was little prospect of our doing better, as there were very few families living on the road, and not much promise of accommodation in any of them. When we reached our cabin, we were cold, hungry, and fatigued; and what a prospect was presented! The eye of civilized woman scarcely ever looked upon a more lonely, dreary, desolate habitation. But we were thankful for it—after which I read a chapter in the Bible, and we for the first time in our lives, as a worshiping family, knelt down together and gave thanks to God for the mercies we had enjoyed, and committed ourselves to his paternal care. There is not much of this world's goods that are absolutely necessary to happiness, and we laid down that night on our very humble couch with feelings as cheerful as we had ever enjoyed when surrounded with all the comforts, the luxuries, and the splendors of life.

The area was unknown and wild. The Indians visited trading posts where travelers gathered, and, in time, conversed with white men, asking of where they came.

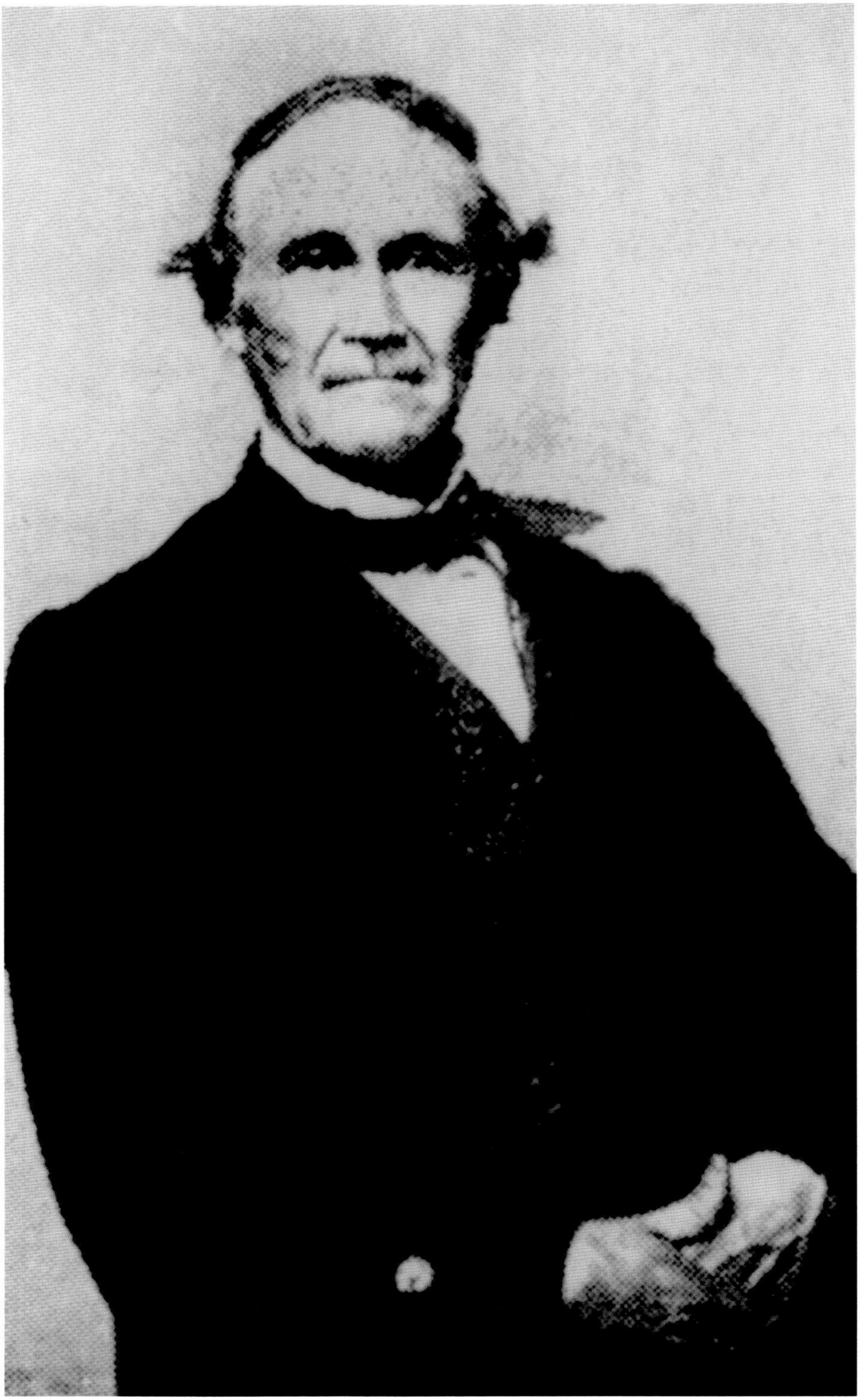

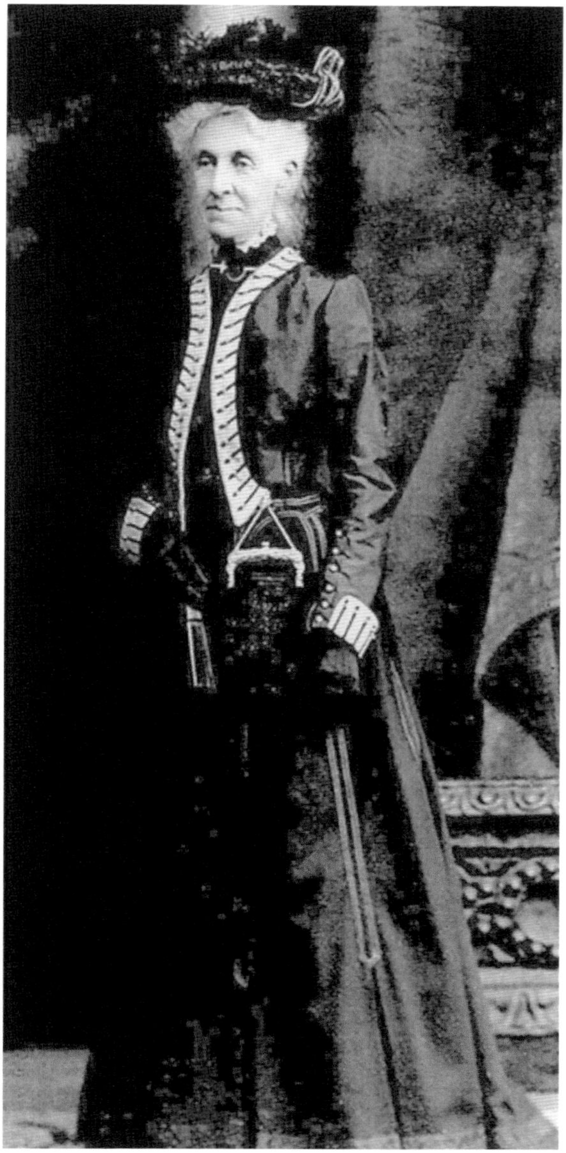

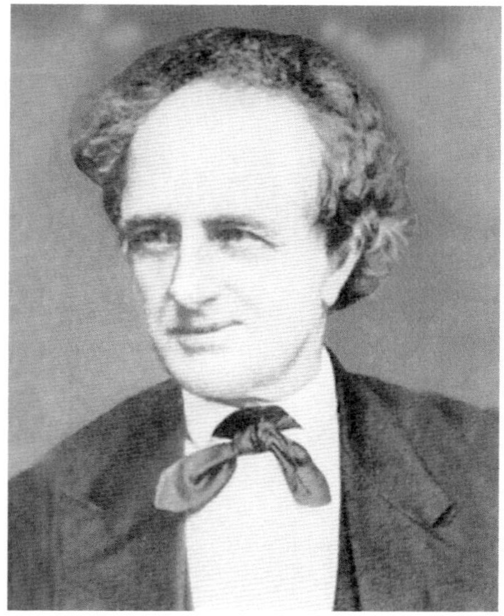

George Sutton, MD
Dr. Sutton began his practice in the spring of 1836. In the summer of 1849, cholera made its appearance. His eldest son passed within a few hours of displaying symptoms. Sutton believed he knew what was causing cholera, and wrote a paper on it. Physicians across the United States used his informational pamphlet for their own practice. Sutton was the seventh mayor, elected three times in succession. (Courtesy of DCHS.)

Georgiana Sutton
Georgiana Sutton was the daughter of Dr. George Sutton. In her will, Georgiana bequeathed the town a public library. She set aside $10,000 for the purpose, as a memorial in loving remembrance of her father and mother. The building was completed in 1914. (Courtesy of Hillforest Foundation.)

Samuel Morrison (OPPOSITE PAGE)
When Ephraim Morrison moved his family to this area, they resided in a deserted Indian hut at the mouth of Hogan Creek and the Ohio River. Here was the birthplace of Samuel Morrison. Samuel was the first white child born in the county, on March 1, 1798. The family lived in the hut until better housing could be built. His mother died in 1803 in Dearborn County and his father, Ephraim, in 1806, after moving the family to Dayton, Ohio. Samuel (1798–1888) was a gifted historian, artist, and inventor. As a mapmaker during the Civil War, he drew a map of the Vicksburg area, which he sent to Gen. Ulysses S. Grant.

When Samuel was three, squirrels plagued Aurora. In 1801, the pesky critters moved along the river with nothing to check their march. It was said that one woman killed over 300 squirrels with her "clothes beater" while washing on the river's shore. (Courtesy of DCHS.)

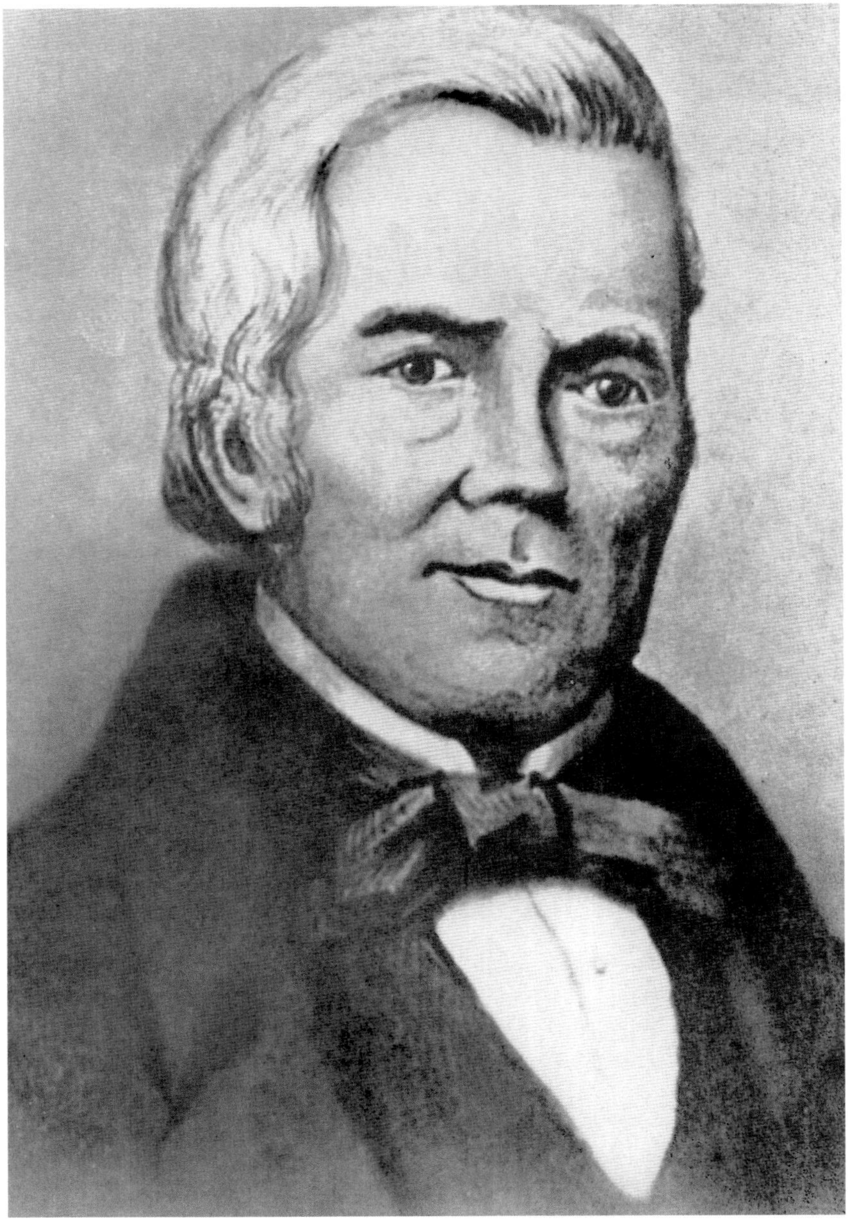

Jesse Holman
In his diary, Holman (1784–1842) relates how he crossed the river from Kentucky to Aurora with his wife and two-month-old baby in 1811. He was appointed by Gov. William Henry Harrison, of Indiana Territory, to be prosecuting attorney and, within a year of his settlement, qualified as an attorney in Dearborn County and began serving his appointment. Just two years after that, he became a member of Indiana's Territorial Legislature, appointed circuit court judge. When Indiana became a state in 1816, he was one of the first three state supreme court judges. He remained on the court for 14 years. By 1832, he had been named superintendent of schools for Dearborn County and, in 1834, he became a US district judge, a post he held until his death in 1842. (Courtesy of DCHS.)

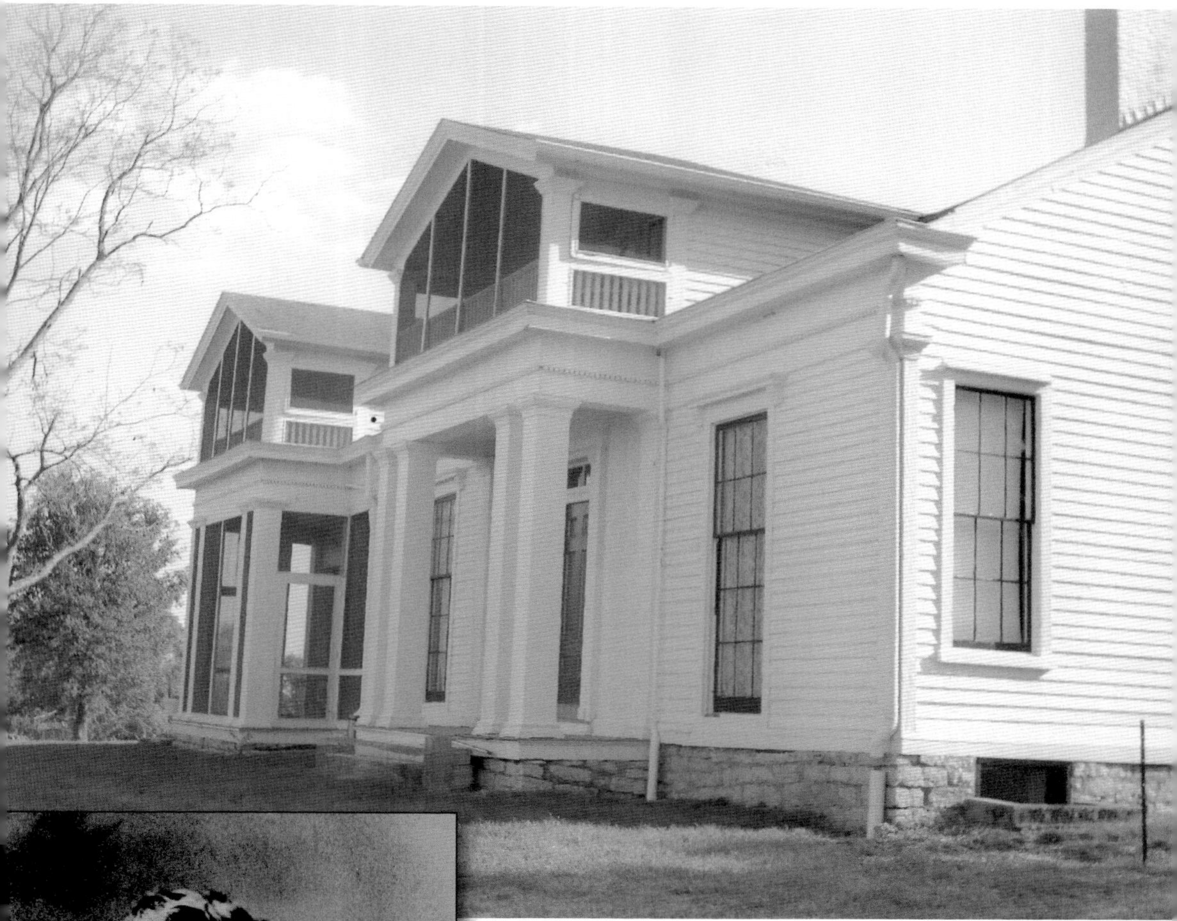

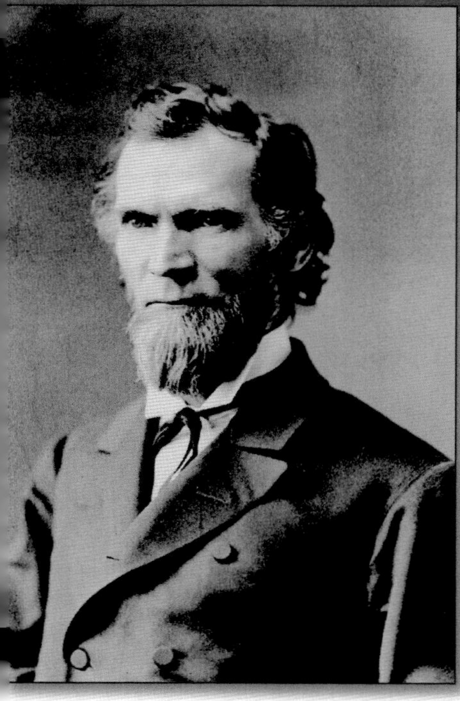

Jesse and Elizabeth Holman
When the Holmans left Kentucky for their new cabin, Jesse chose a hilltop with a commanding view of the Ohio River and the Kentucky hills. There, he built Veraestau. In 2004, Indiana Landmarks received the 116-acre property as a gift from the Cornelius and Anna Cook O'Brien Foundation. Veraestau serves as Indiana Landmarks's southeast field office. (Courtesy of Indiana Landmarks.)

William Steele Holman
William Steele Holman (1822–1897), the son of Jesse L. Holman, was a lawyer, judge, and politician from Aurora. He was a member of the Democratic party, who served several terms as a US representative (1859–1865, 1867–1877, 1881–1895, and 1897). In 1842, William married Abigail Knapp. They had one son, William S. Holman Jr. The senior Holman is buried at Riverview Cemetery. (Courtesy of Hillforest Foundation.)

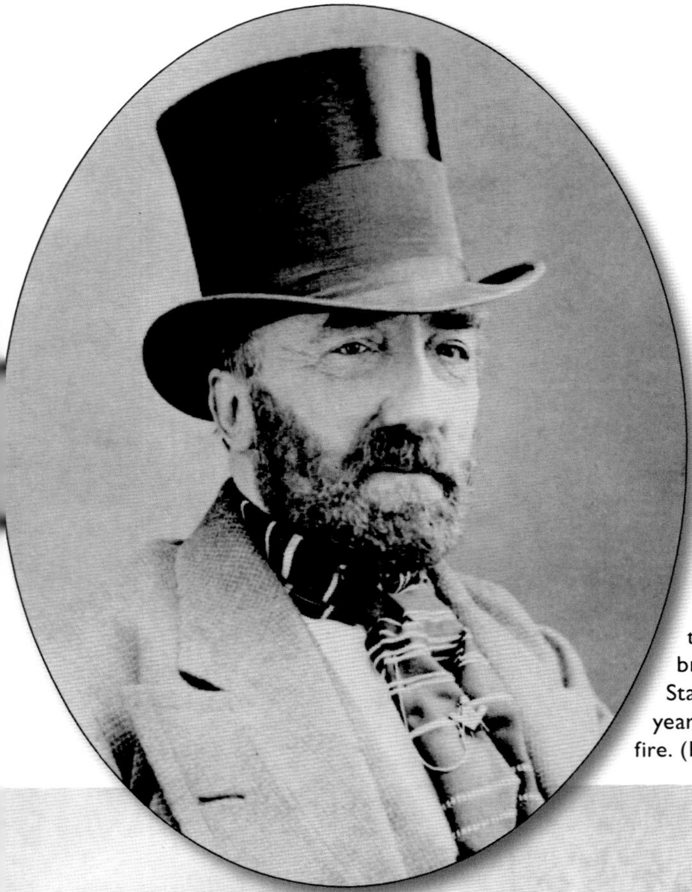

The Eagle Hotel

When John Hamilton (left) owned the Eagle Hotel, riverboats regularly docked nearby. The hotel (below, left of center) stood facing the river and was located opposite the mouth of Hogan Creek. It had a large porch extending across the front where guests sat and watched the river. Behind the hotel were a three-story brick building and the George Taylor Livery Stable. The Eagle Hotel operated for about 50 years. It, along with the livery, was destroyed by fire. (Both courtesy of DCHS.)

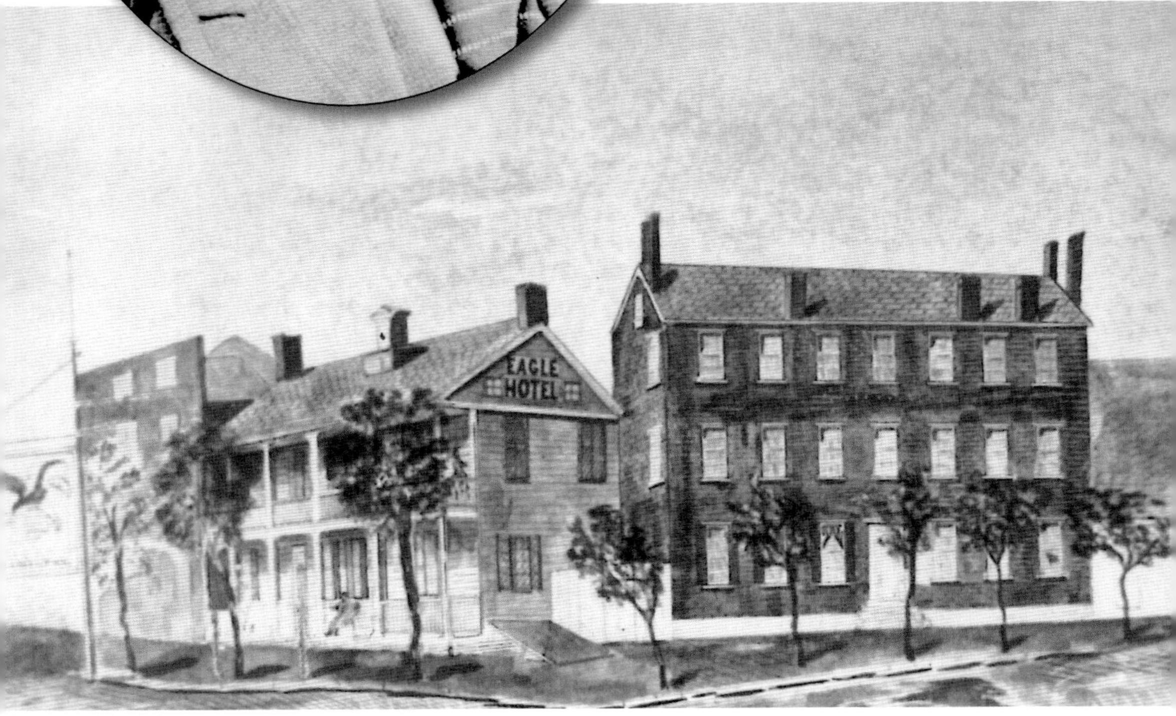

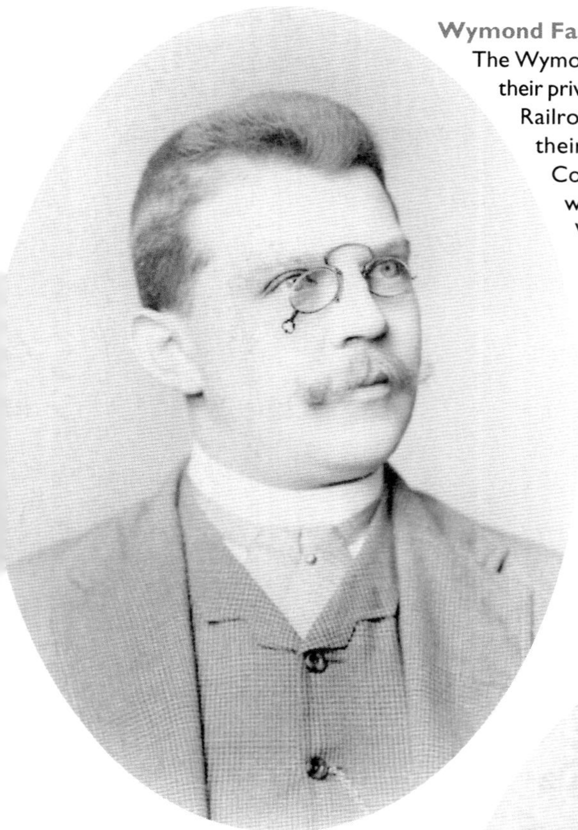

Wymond Family

The Wymond family included well-known industrialists, but, in their private lives, they were conductors on the Underground Railroad. They hid escaped slaves in a secret room at their farmhouse, which later became the Dearborn Country Club. In the late 1850s, two escaped slaves were caught as they tried to make their way to the Wymond property. Their captors took them to the Eagle Hotel, where they tied them up securely and proceeded to celebrate with large amounts of alcohol. The two slave captors lay down across the doorways to their room and fell sound asleep. Wymond went to John Milburn, who then went to his teenage nephew John Hope to rescue the slaves. As soon as the captors were drunk, Hope climbed a tree next to the balcony of the hotel, stepped over the man at the door, untied the slaves, and led them back down the tree to safety. R.J. Wymond is shown left. Below is Mabel Wymond. (Both courtesy of DCHS.)

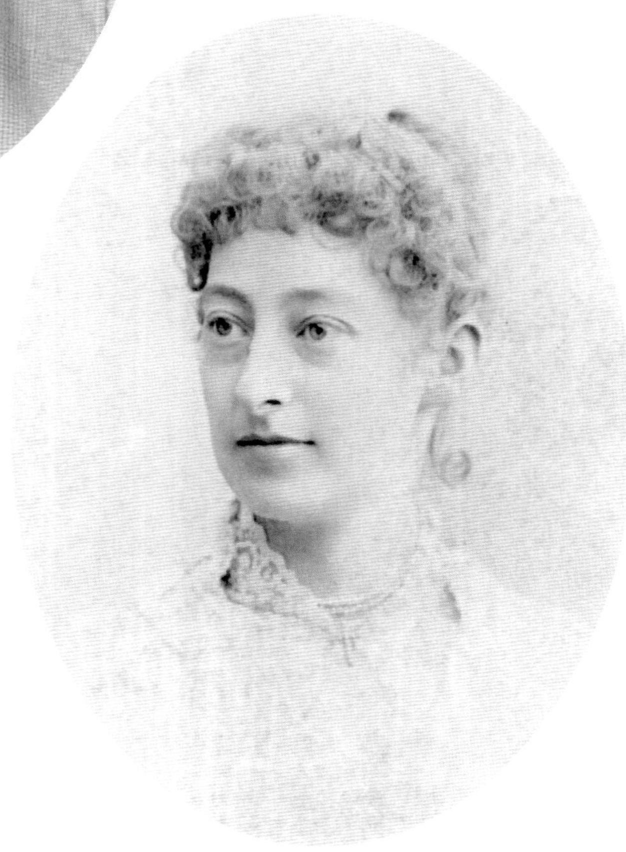

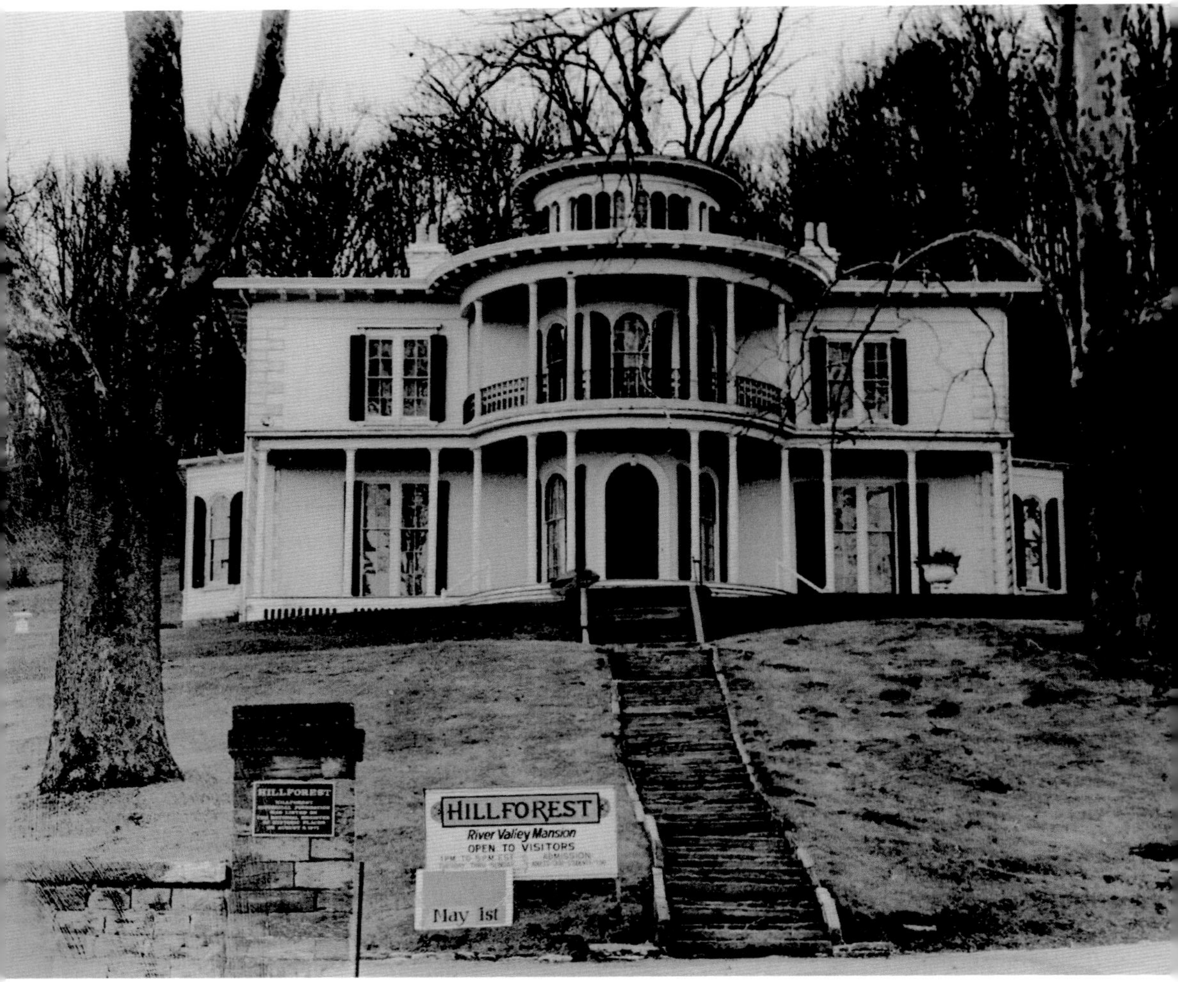

Thomas Gaff

Hillforest was the home of the Thomas Gaff family. There are no known photographs of Thomas Gaff (1808–1884). Besides their many business ventures, the Gaff brothers were heavily involved in civic affairs, backing the town's first utility company, the Aurora Gas & Coke Company, and founding the First National Bank of Aurora in 1856, for which Thomas served as president. He also helped organize Aurora's school system, served on the city council with his brother James (brother John Gaff was mayor), incorporated Riverview Cemetery, and, with his brothers, bought a fire engine and town clock. With their heavy reliance on the Ohio River for shipping, the Gaff brothers also owned a fleet of steamboats with which they transported their distillery and brewery products. During the Civil War, the Gaffs furnished these steamboats and other supplies to the Union cause. One of their steamboats, the *Forest Queen*, became headquarters for Gen. William Tecumseh Sherman during the Siege of Vicksburg. The steamboat, under the command of Capt. C.D. Conway of Aurora, successfully ran the Vicksburg blockade but was burned by Confederates in St. Louis, Missouri.

The beautiful Hillforest overlooks the Ohio River and was the family residence between 1855 and 1891. The Italian Renaissance structure is listed in the National Register of Historic Places and was designated a National Historic Landmark in 1992. The mansion is open for tours by volunteer docents, who often dress in period costumes. (Courtesy of DCHS.)

The James Gaff Home

This rare photograph is of Linden Terrace, once the home of the James Gaff family. It was located at the corner of Fourth and Main Streets and was named for the Linden trees Gaff imported from Germany. Linden Terrace was said to equal the beauty of Hillforest Mansion. The bearded man on the corner may be James Gaff. (Courtesy of Telford Walker and Ullrich Studio.)

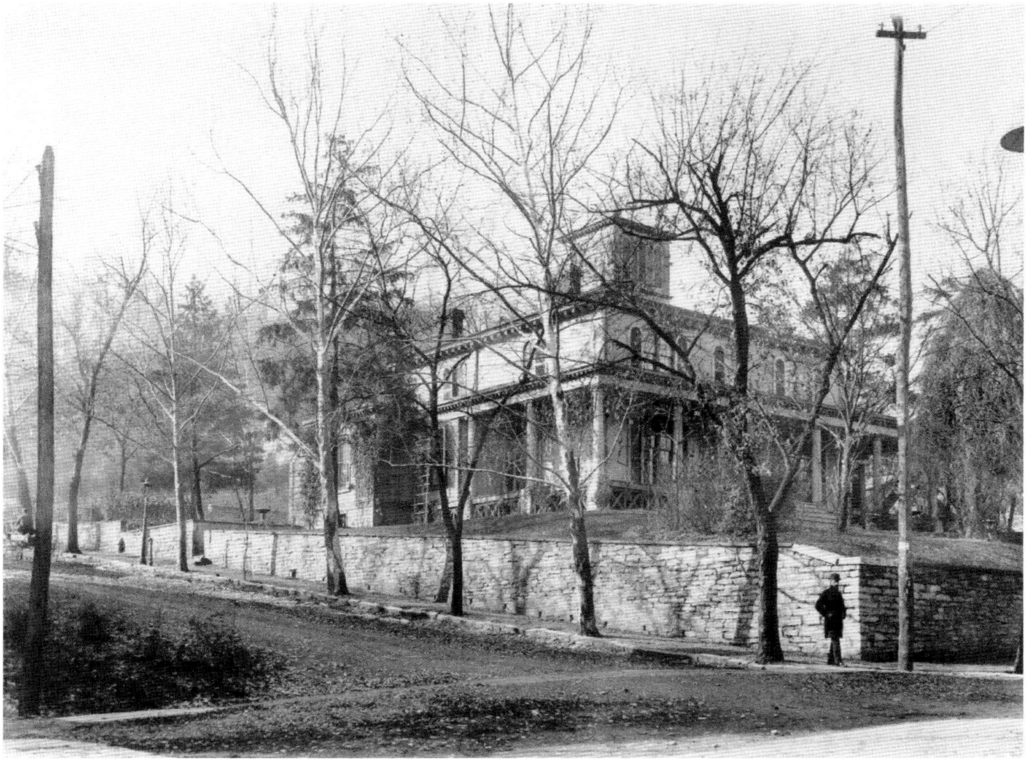

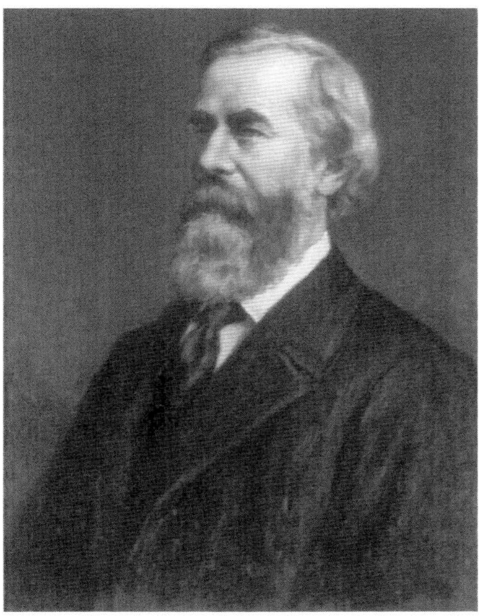

James Gaff

James Gaff (1808–1884) learned papermaking from his father and the distillery business from his uncle Charles Wilson. With his brothers, John and Thomas, he opened a distillery in Philadelphia in the 1830s. The Gaffs moved their business to Aurora in 1843, reestablishing it as the T & J.W. Gaff & Company Distillery. They produced bourbon, rye, and Thistle Dew Scotch whiskey. Gaff died in Cincinnati, Ohio, in 1884, at the age of 75. (Courtesy of Hillforest Foundation.)

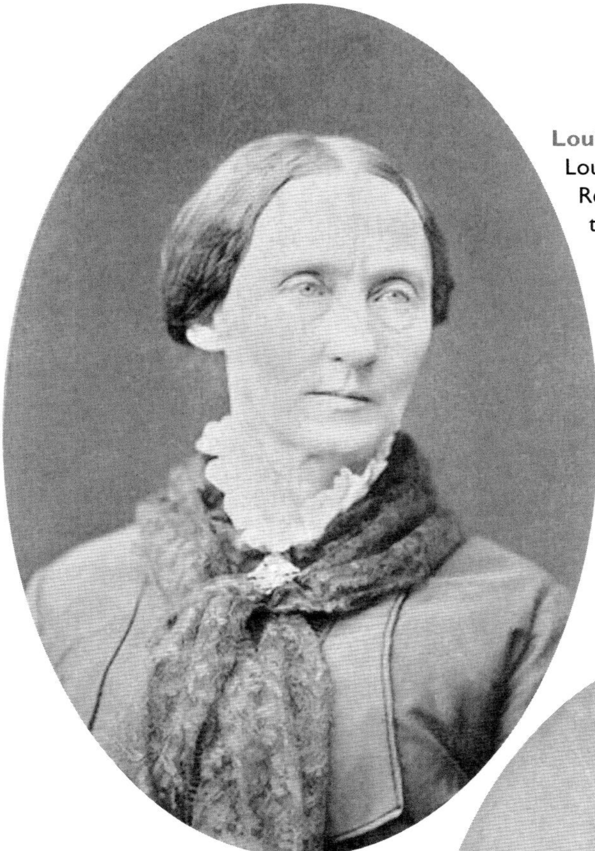

Louisa Plummer Haynes (1823–1885)
Louisa was the daughter of pioneer parents the Reverend Daniel and Lucy Plummer. She was the wife of John Douglas Haynes, and they had six children: Ellsworth, Sarah, Anna, Heber, William, and Katie. (Courtesy of Steven Lawsongatch.)

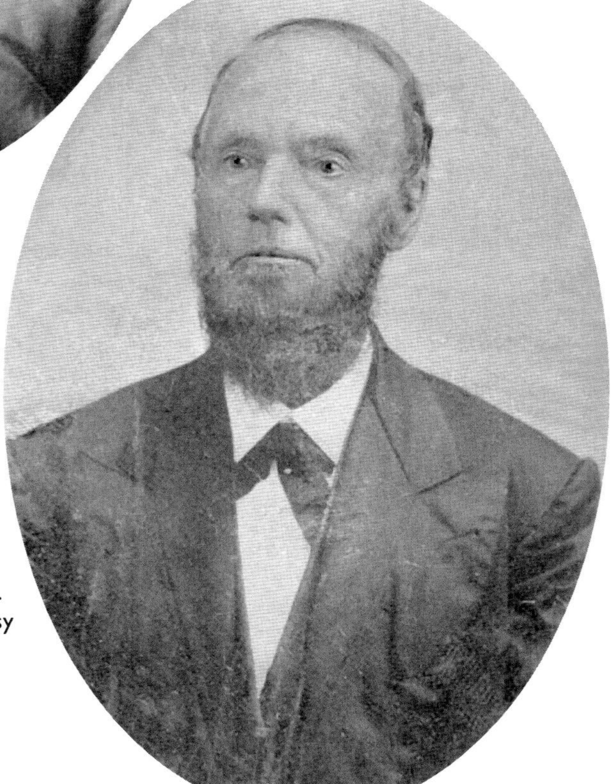

John Douglas Haynes
Haynes (1812–1886), a native of New York State, was the first mayor of Aurora (1848–1851). He was an attorney and partner in the law firm of Holman & Haynes. In 1859, he had an office on Second Street, west of Judiciary Street. Haynes married Louisa Plummer in 1840. Later in life, he became a judge. (Courtesy of Steven Lawsongatch.)

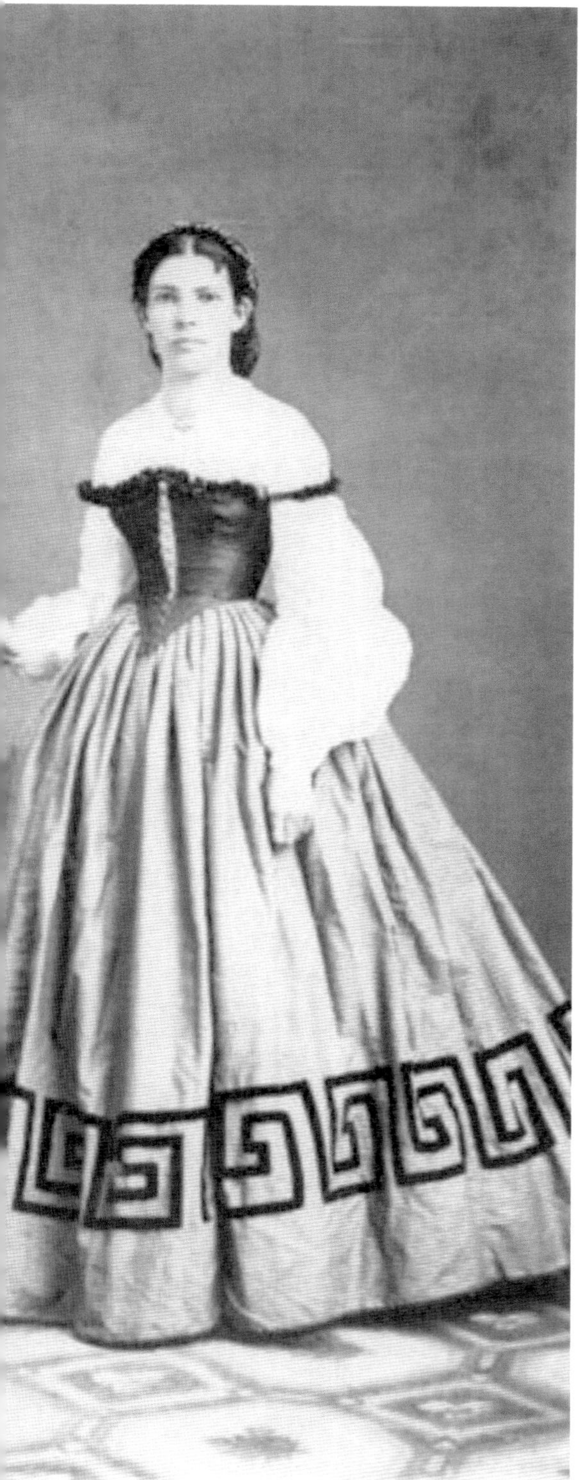

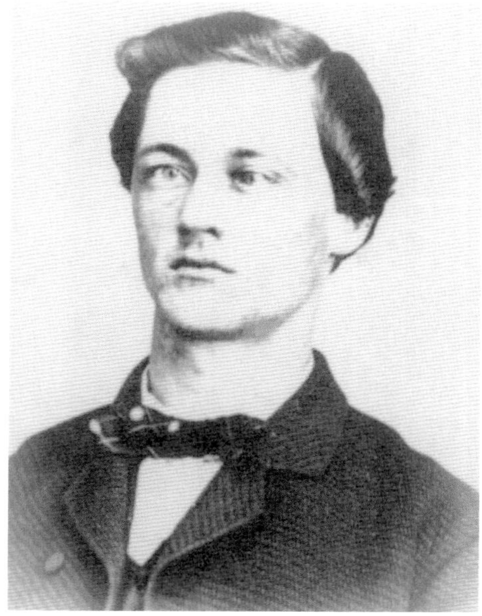

Ellsworth Haynes
Ellsworth Haynes (1845–1920) had an eye condition that may have kept him from volunteering for the Union army. However, he did belong to the Aurora local militia. The group was armed and ready for Morgan's Raiders as they made their way across Indiana. Early on, Haynes was in business with Samuel Langtree, his brother-in-law. Haynes and his wife, Katherine, moved to Claremont County, Ohio, where he worked for an insurance company. (Courtesy of Steven Lawsongatch.)

Katherine Langtree Haynes
Katherine (1844–1911) was a beauty. Her husband, Ellsworth, and her brother, Samuel Langtree, established a store on the corner of Bridgeway and Third Streets. They were married on May 5, 1867 and had four children together. (Courtesy of Steven Lawsongatch.)

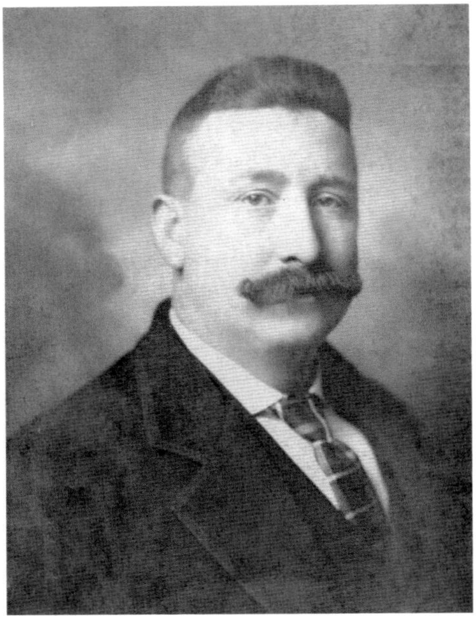

John Ullrich
The Ullriches were German immigrants and coopers by trade. John's parents, Frank and Anna, emigrated from Bavaria through New Orleans in 1854, arriving in Aurora in 1861. When John was 23, he purchased the building on Second and Main Streets from Dr. Hubert Marshall and started the German Drug Store. John married Helena Nees, daughter of hotel keeper John Nees. Ullrich's Drug Store became the meeting place for local businessmen and politicians. They would gather out on the corner in the evenings and, inside, around the potbellied stove. John (1860–1918) was elected clerk of the circuit court in 1898 and served for eight years. He died in 1918 after a six-month illness. (Courtesy of Richard Ullrich.)

Samuel D. Langtree
When Langtree (1839–1888) was 19 years of age, he opened a retail grocery in Aurora with his brother-in-law Ellsworth Haynes. In 1865, he began to ship produce to New Orleans, and in five years, shipped 135 boatloads of produce and plantation supplies to that market. In 1872, he and J.W. Gaff purchased the old Union Brewery property and called it the Crescent Brewery. The brewery produced a daily average of 600 kegs of beer. Langtree married Louisa R. Conwell. (Courtesy of Steven Lawsongatch.)

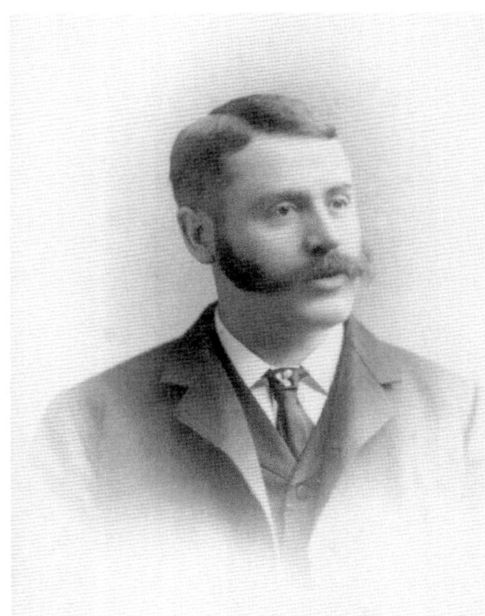

Early & Daniel Warehouse (OPPOSITE PAGE)
The Gaffs, Langtrees, Williams, and Cobbs bought, sold, and shipped from this major port on the river. The Early & Daniel Co. warehouse (top) was located near Market and Decatur Streets. Indiana hay was in high demand in the south. Hay-buyer A.F. Howe purchased 800 tons of hay, which filled four flat boats, at a cost of about $12 a ton. Once in New Orleans, it was sold for about $20 a ton. Large warehouses once stood along the river, storing product until good prices could be had.

To this day, it is not if the river floods, but when the river floods. Melting snows and heavy rains beginning in January have always brought chaos to the city. The bottom photograph shows the same building as above during one of many floods. (Both courtesy of DCHS.)

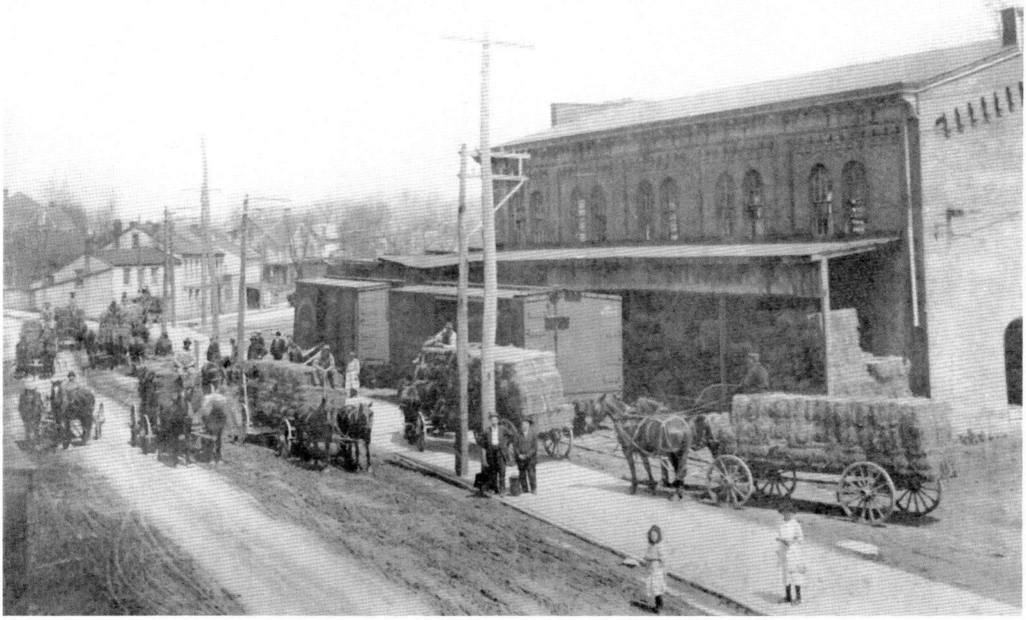

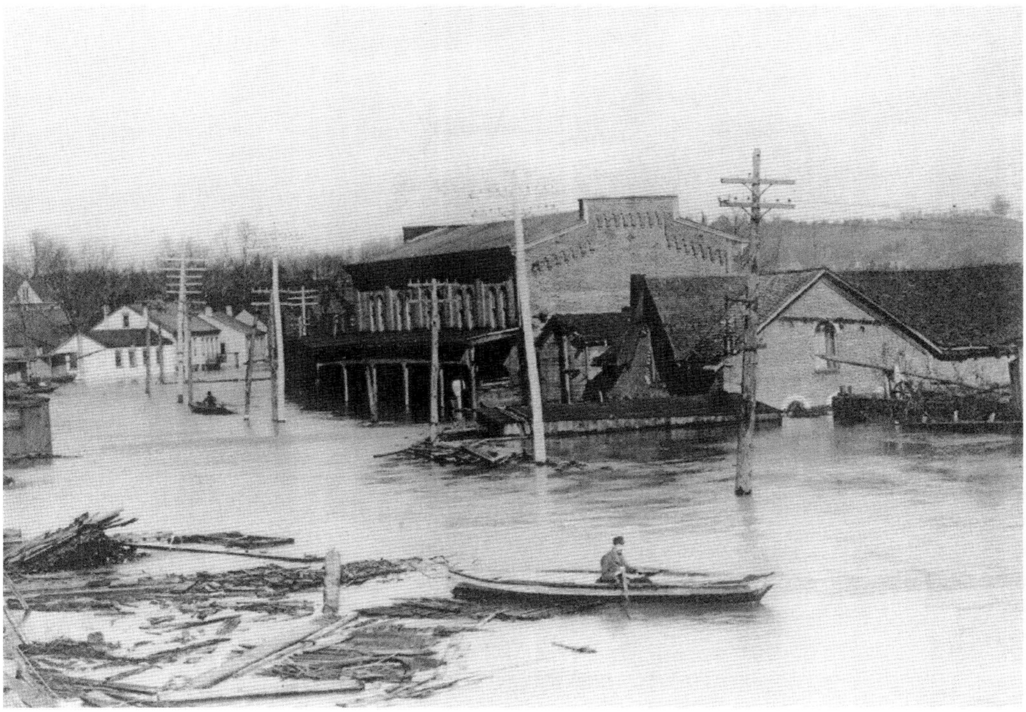

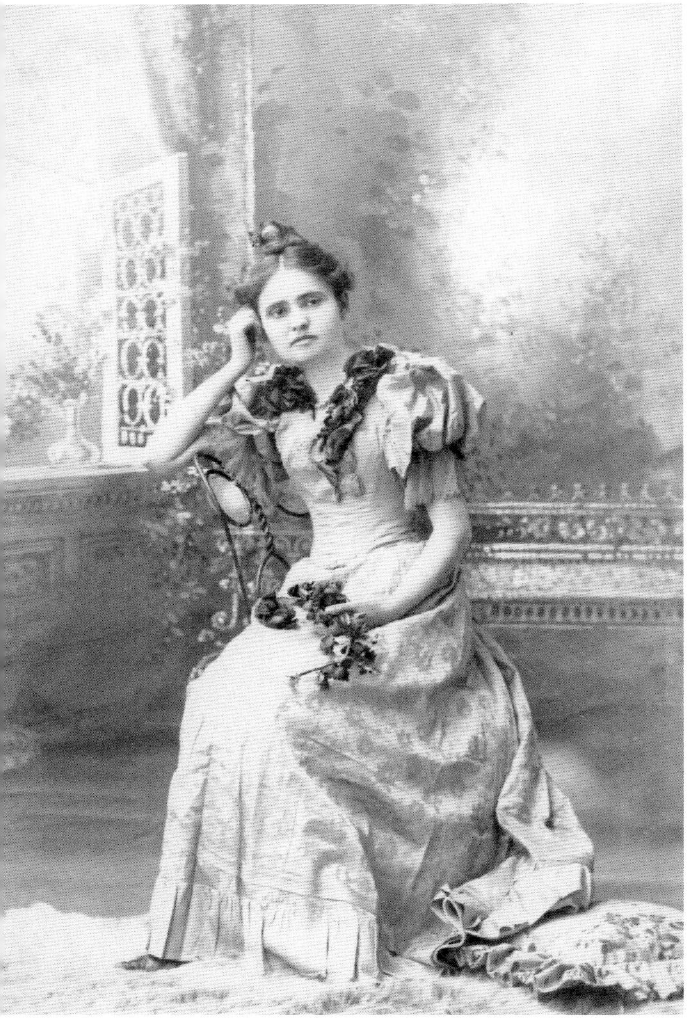

Inez Cobb
In 1873, Louis Cobb became owner and editor of the *Dearborn Independent* newspaper. He employed his children Mack and Inez. Inez (1856–1957)worked for the newspaper and was known as an excellent columnist. In 1926, employee William Fehrman purchased the newspaper interests from the family. (Courtesy of DCHS.)

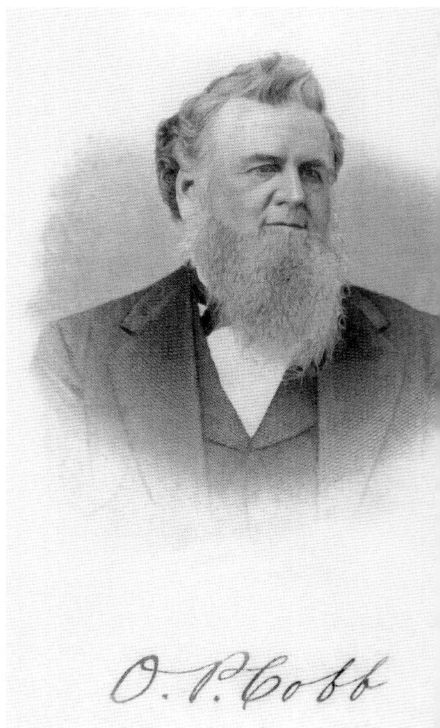

Oliver Perry Cobb
Cobb (1817–1891) was president of the Aurora Iron & Nail Company, where he invented and held several patents. He was also engaged in the shipping of hay and pork to the South. During the Civil War, Cobb was named by the Union government to furnish forage to the South. At one point, a large order was shipped to New Orleans. Once there, the order was refused by a government agent. Cobb, at one time a wealthy man, died penniless after several bad investments. (Courtesy of DCHS.)

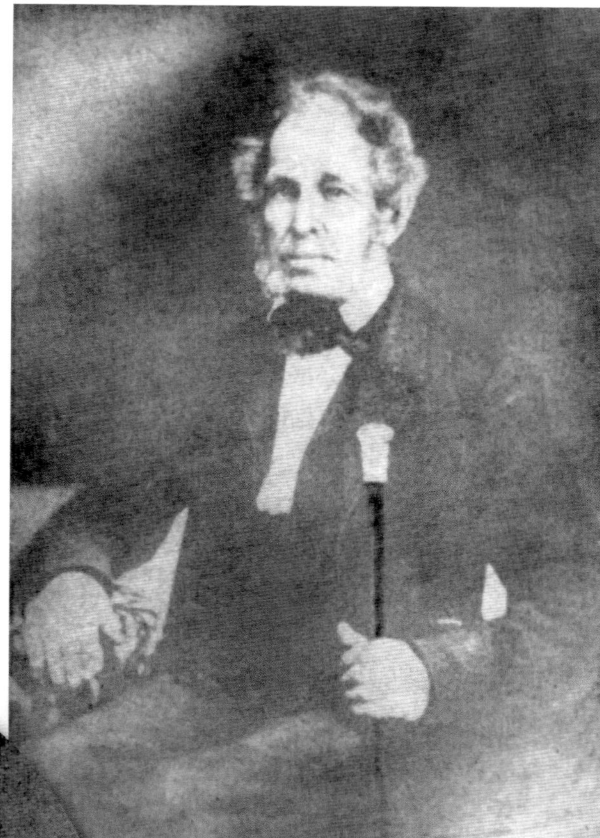

Asa Shattuck
Born in Massachusetts on July 8, 1789, Shattuck settled in Aurora on January 1, 1820, as a schoolteacher. He became a master builder and fine plasterer and was responsible for the fine plasterwork at Hillforest, which was made from molds imported from Italy. Shattuck also worked as a bricklayer. He died in 1867 after falling from a building. (Courtesy of Adena Charlton.)

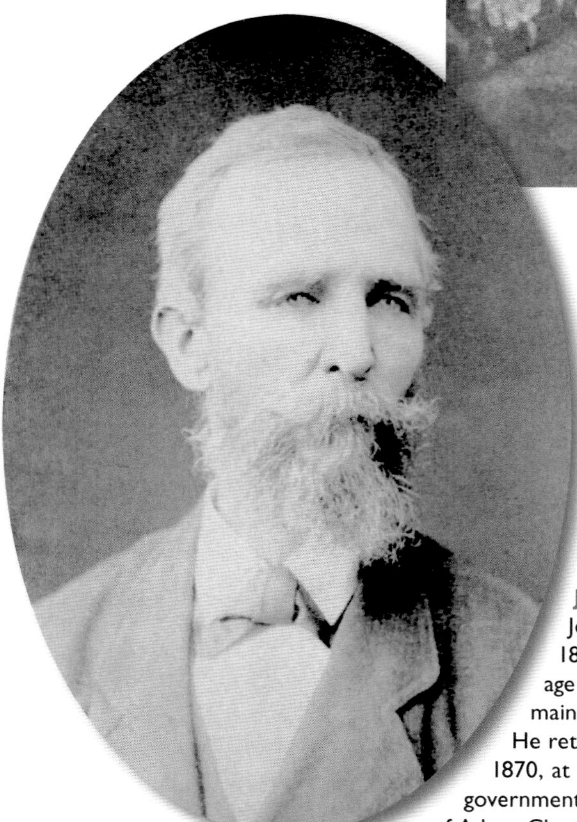

John Sobieskie Shattuck
John was born to Asa and Prudence Shattuck in 1821. He began learning the plastering trade at the age of 15. In 1856, he engaged in the drug business and maintained the telegraph and Adams Express offices. He retained the telegraph and express positions until 1870, at which time he was appointed "gauger" by the government. He married Sarah Ann Hill in 1847. (Courtesy of Adena Charlton.)

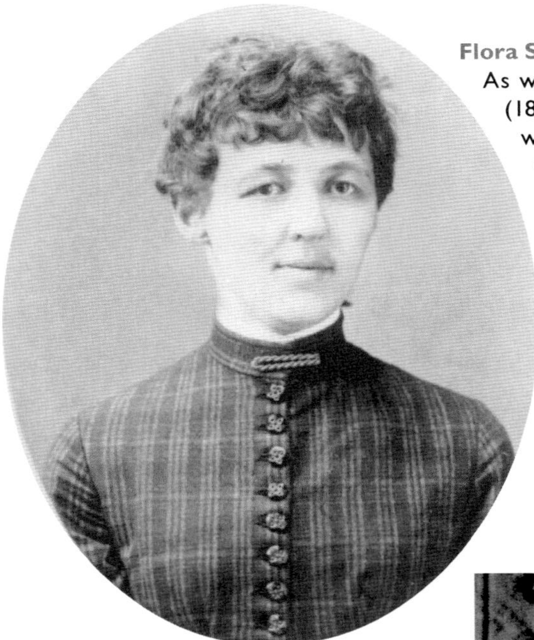

Flora Shattuck

As were her ancestors, Flora (1856–1918) was a pioneer woman in the business world. She was one of seven children born to John and Sara Shattuck. Flora attended business schools in Cincinnati and New York City and worked for many years at the H.W. Smith Furniture Co. in Aurora. (Courtesy of Adena Charlton.)

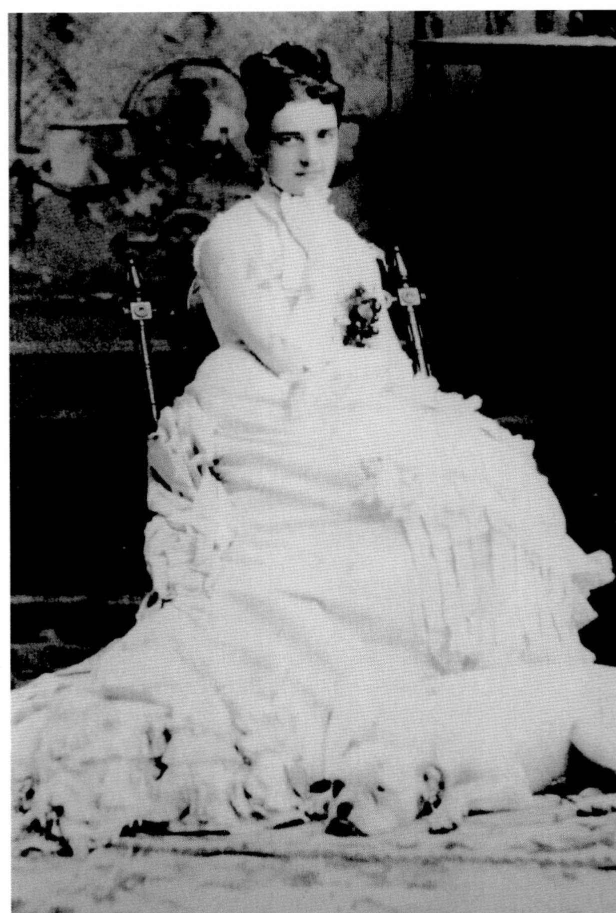

Alexina Gaff Mitchell

Alexina was the youngest daughter of Thomas and Sarah (Darling) Gaff. Hillforest's archives contain love letters between Alexina Gaff Mitchell and her husband, Robert Charlton Mitchell, during the Civil War era. One letter reads: "Hush little one? I am home sick or love sick, which? It does not seem possible to me that it was only last Sunday that I parted with you—away from you, the time drags slowly, very slowly and warily along, while with you it flies only too rapidly. —to be treated with all frankness, and to be thoroughly advised as to all that interests me, no less than yourself. In other words I would have to be to me all that I understand the word 'wife' to mean—the dearest partner of all my pleasures—my duty should be, and I trust will be, to shield and protect you from all trouble, and to make your life a happy one. —Charlton" (Courtesy of Hillforest.)

CHAPTER TWO

Building an Ohio River Town

What does it take to build a river town? At one time, the Aurora port was one of the busiest on the river. The fertile lands of southeastern Indiana attracted immigrants and businesses. As the roads were dirt and the creeks hard to cross, the Ohio River was at times the best route. French explorer Rene Robert Cavelier Sieur de La Salle was so taken with the Ohio River when he first laid eyes on it in 1669 that he christened it La Belle Riviere (the Beautiful River). "Ohio" derives from an Iroquois Indian word, *oheo*, which is traditionally interpreted to mean "beautiful river," in agreement with the opinion of the Frenchman.

The Gaffs were from Scotland. Arriving from Germany were craftsmen and beer-makers. When the railroad was being built, the Irish arrived. All brought with them skills, knowledge, and various religions that would aid in the building of Aurora.

The early settlers were definitely put to the test. Aurora is steeped in history and has always had to adapt to economic challenges. Despite yearly flooding, the natural beauty of the city's location, on a graceful curve of the river, is rarely surpassed. Today, the view of the church spires and buildings is mesmerizing.

Robert Clark Mattox

Mattox (1859–1937) became a partner in the Aurora Lumber Co. yard in the 1890s with L.G. Hurlbert & Son, the founder of the lumber company in 1848. The company handled upwards of one million feet of lumber and produced almost 1.5 million shingles annually. Mattox became full owner in 1906, and he sold the yard in the 1920s to Midland Building Industries. He married Fannie Barnhart in 1887. In 1966, Del Hizer, manager of the Aurora yard since 1953, bought the yard from liquidators. He was joined in the business by son-in-law Carl Petty and daughter Janet. In 1972, Carl's brother Larry joined the business. The firm was incorporated and added several buildings to handle its growing inventory. In 1988, David Hizer came on board and Carl assumed the responsibilities of running the operation. In 2000, a new, 8,000-square-foot store replaced the 3,000-square-foot store from 1954. Carl and Janet's son John also joined the operation. The Aurora Lumber Co. is the oldest lumberyard in the state of Indiana and will celebrate 165 years of continuous business. (Courtesy of DCHS.)

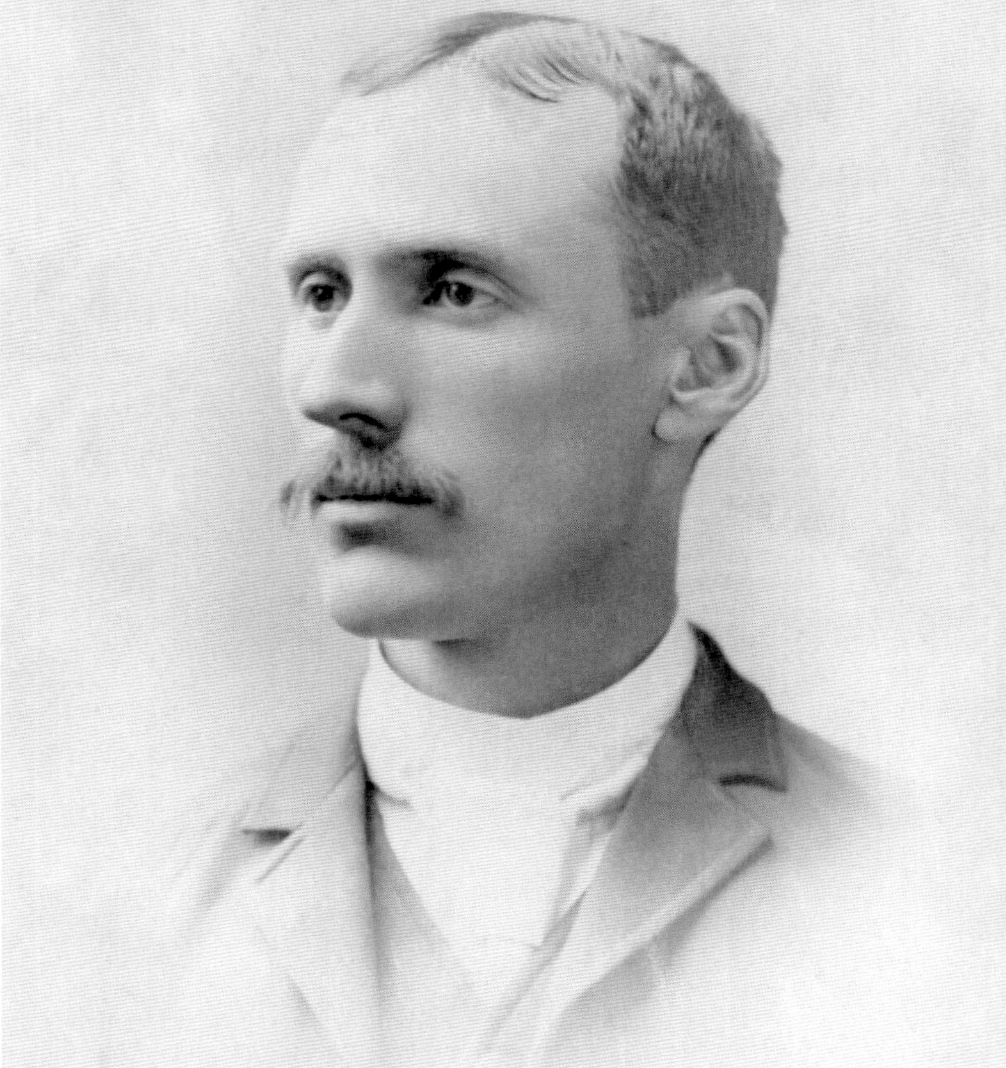

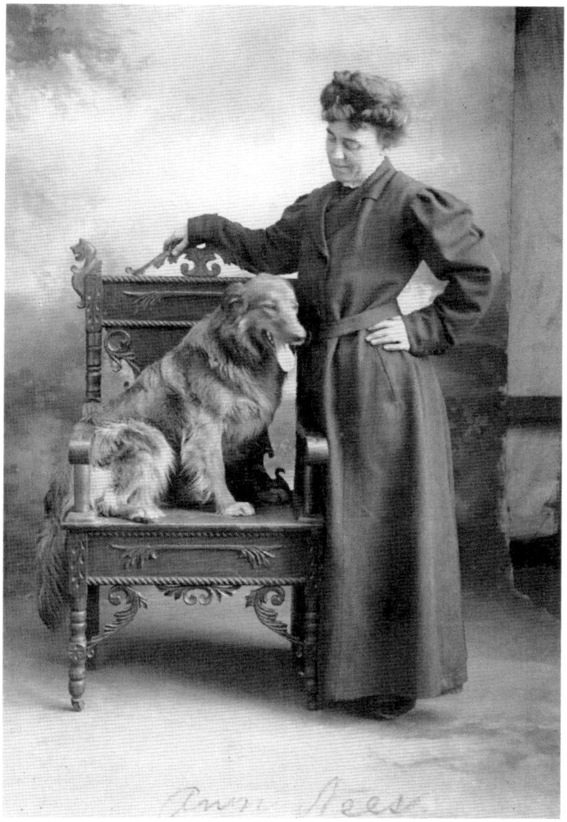

Ann Nees

Ann sent this postcard in 1909 as an Easter greeting. The Nees family owned the Union Hotel on the corner of Third Street and State Highway 56. With its livery stable connected, it was considered the best in the city. The Union Hotel building is currently occupied by the Chase Heating and Air Conditioning company. (Coutesy of DCHS.)

Adam Hill & Sons

The wharf boat seen in the foreground of this photograph was managed by Adam Hill. A farmer and wharf boatman, Hill lived on a farm outside of Aurora. In 1874, he took charge of the wharf boat on the Aurora shore and business grew so quickly that, in 1877, he had to move to town. Stockholders declared an 85-percent dividend on their investments. Steamboats were able to load and unload from the boat, and he bought and sold hay and grain and ran a delivery service. The 1918 ice gorge destroyed the wharf boat by pushing it up to the end of Second Street. (Courtesy of DCHS.)

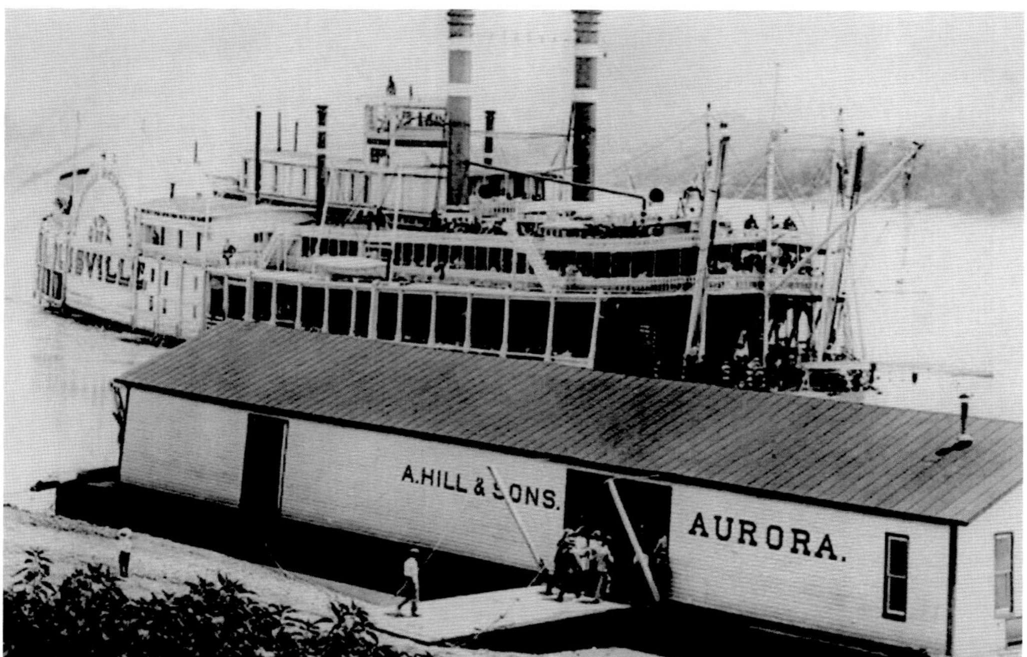

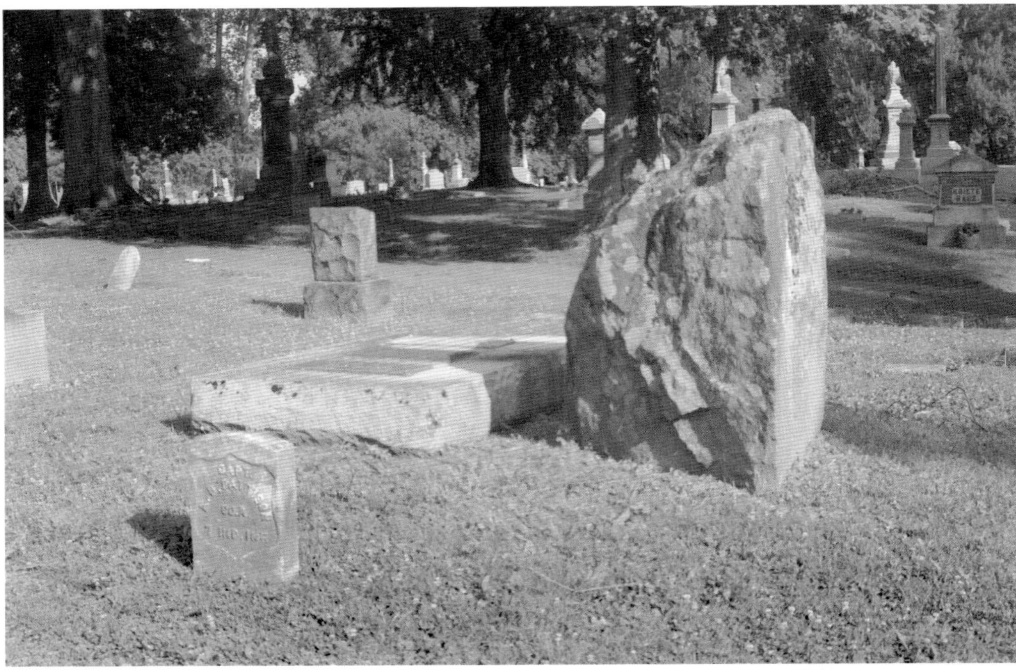

Capt. Alexander B. Pattison
Pattison was commander of Company I of the 7th Indiana Infantry during the Civil War. He credits this stone with saving his life in the battle of Culp's Hill at Gettysburg. The boulder was moved from Gettysburg to his grave at Riverview Cemetery after he died. Musket ball holes are still visible in the stone. In 1883, Pattison organized the Aurora National Bank, where he worked as a cashier. (Courtesy of McKenna Murray.)

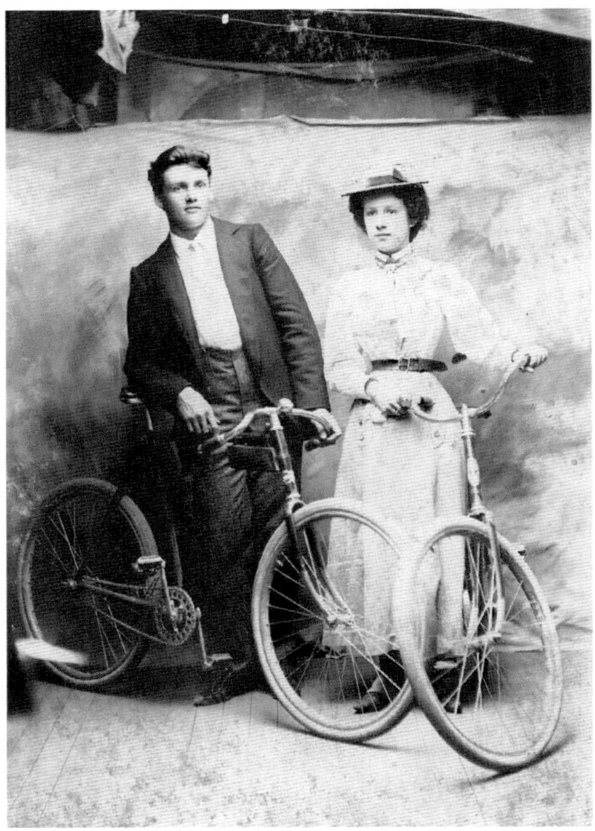

Charles and Lulu Schumacher
Charles and his wife, Lulu, lived on Sunnyside. Charles worked at the chair factory. Note Lulu's fashionable ankle-length skirt. The bicycle craze fed into a movement for so-called rational dress, which contributed to women's liberation. Before long, young women began wearing bloomer-type pants, creating a scandal. (Courtesy of the Schumacher family.)

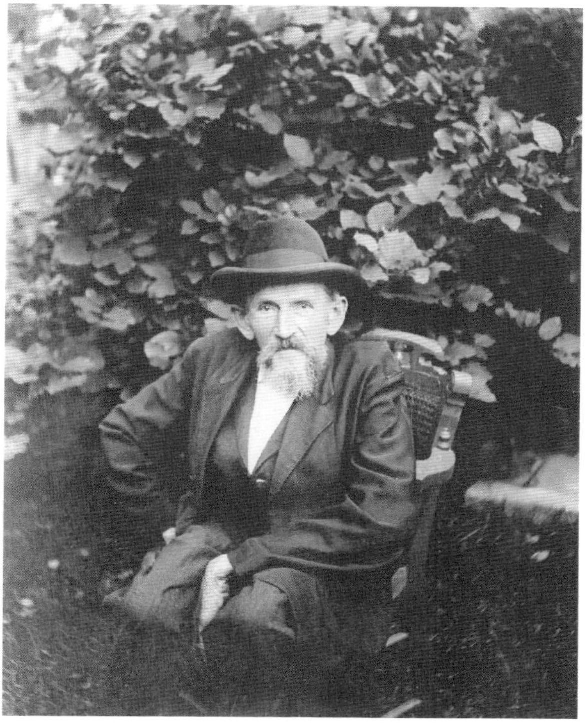

William Lieve
Lieve, a native of Hanover, Germany, grew to manhood in Aurora and learned the trade of watchmaker. In 1861, he established a watch business in what was the old opera house building and continued in the trade until his death in 1910. (Courtesy of DCHS.)

Scharf's Meat Market
Adam Scharf ran a grocery and butcher shop on Main Street. He and his wife, Emma, lived on Fourth Street with their son William and daughter Aleen. In this photograph, Adam Scharf is on the left, and William is on the truck. The man in the center is unidentified. (Courtesy of Ullrich Studios.)

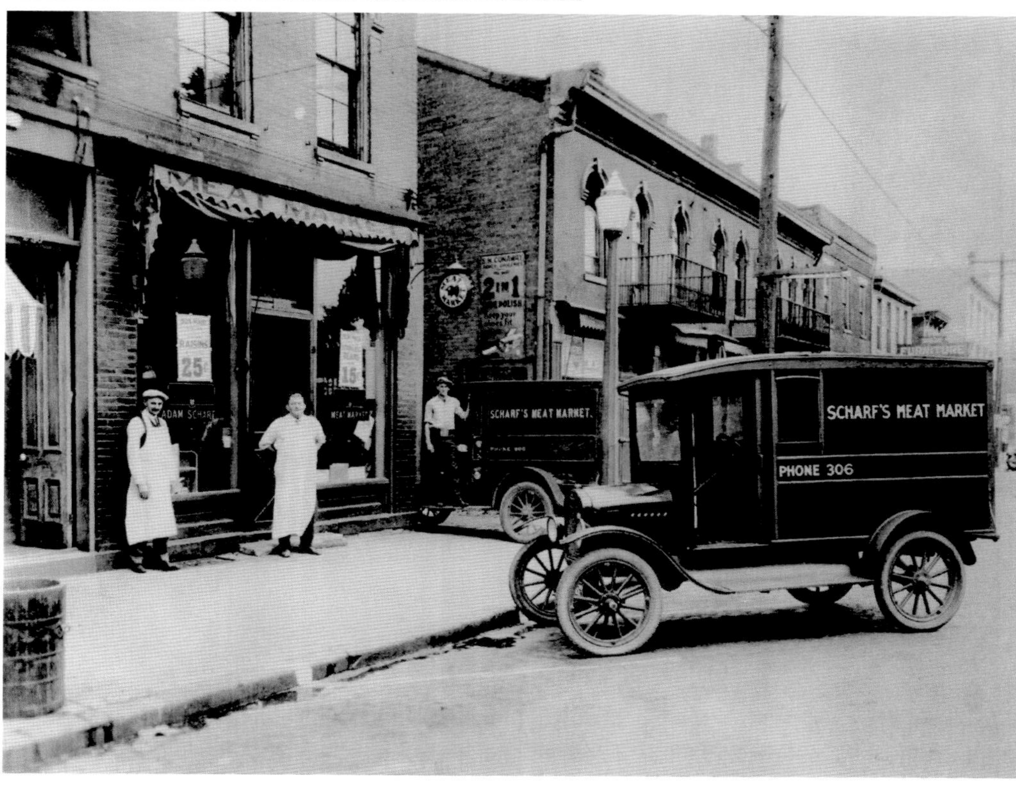

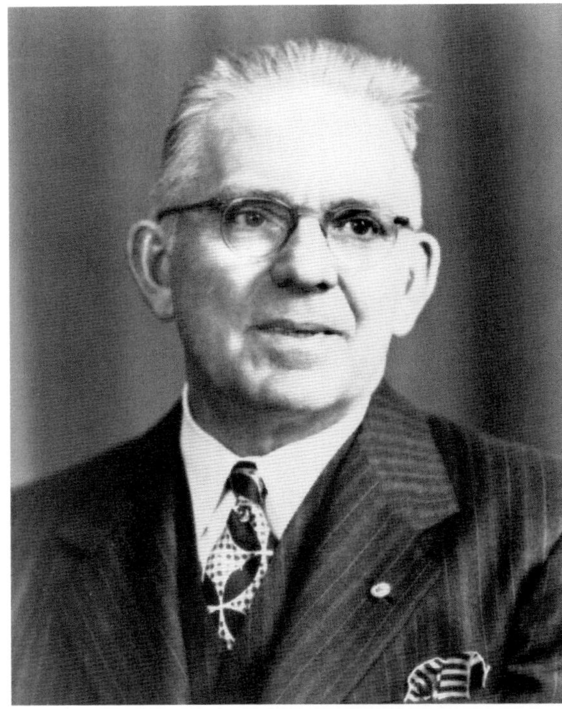

William Ullrich

Ullrich (1883–1956) was the son of John and Helena (Nees) Ullrich. He became a druggist at his father's store after completing college. William was married to Irene Schipper, and the first of their four children was Wilfrid. (Courtesy of the Ullrich Family.)

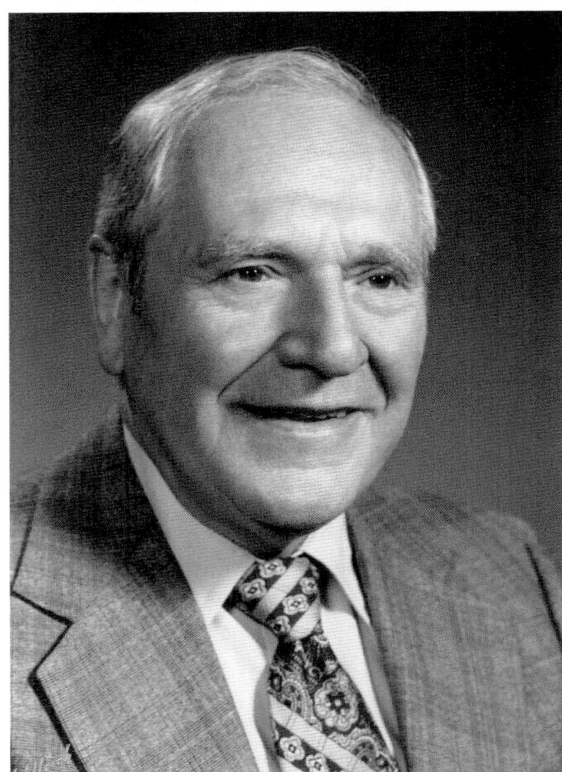

Wilfrid "Werb" Ullrich

When asked his name as a toddler, Wilfrid's pronunciation came out sounding like "Werb," and this became his nickname for the rest of his life. Werb (1908–1977) graduated from Notre Dame College of Pharmacy and married Eleanor Klimek. He worked at the drugstore and was active all of his life with the Boy Scouts. He was also a bank director, first president of Aurora Utilities, and, in 1963, was elected to the Indiana Senate. His parents were William and Irene Ullrich. (Courtesy of the Ullrich family.)

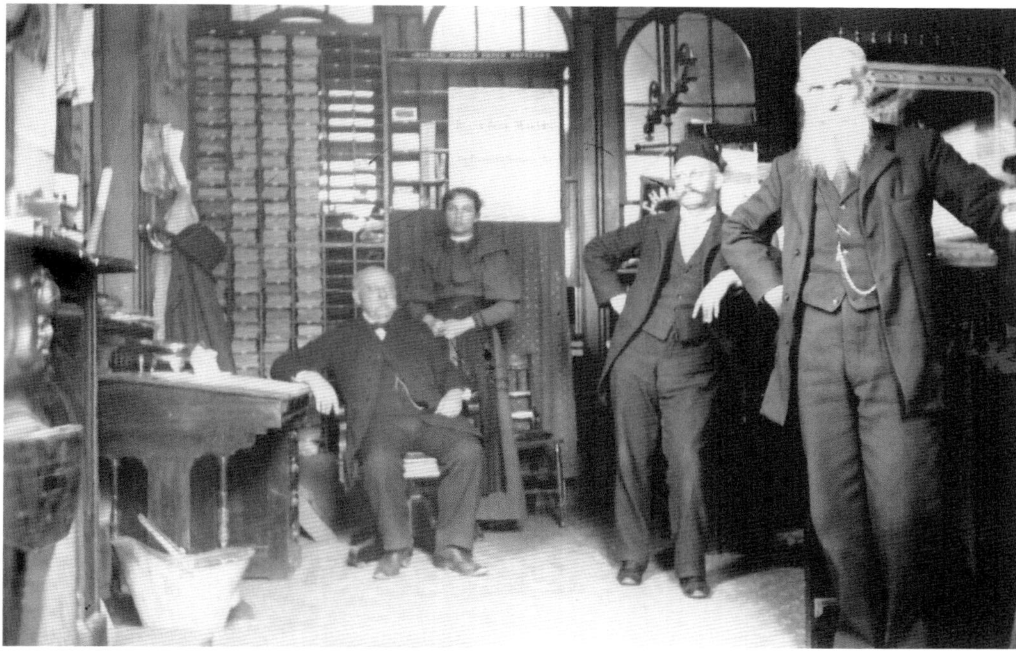

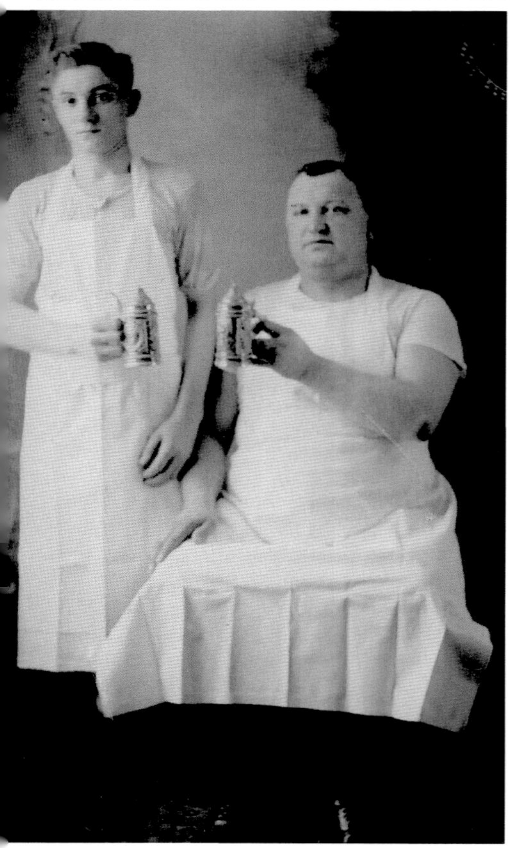

Chambers & Stevens Company
The Chambers & Stevens Company, established in 1840, was located on the northeast corner of Second and Main Streets. The family-owned business carried a wide range of dry goods, clothing, and groceries. It was operated by several generations before closing in the early 1920s. From left to right are William Frank Stevens, secretary Bess Bleasdal, owner Charles Carroll Stevens, and Mr. Miller, the bookkeeper. (Courtesy of DCHS.)

William and Joe Karsh
Holding beer steins and posing in clean, starched, and ironed aprons are William (left) and Joe Karsh (right). These gentlemen were the bakers at the Vienna Bakery in 1911. Herman Loew and his wife, Mary, operated the bakery on Third Street. Their son Bretzel delivered bread in a wagon drawn by a horse named Grover. (Courtesy of the Herman Loew family.)

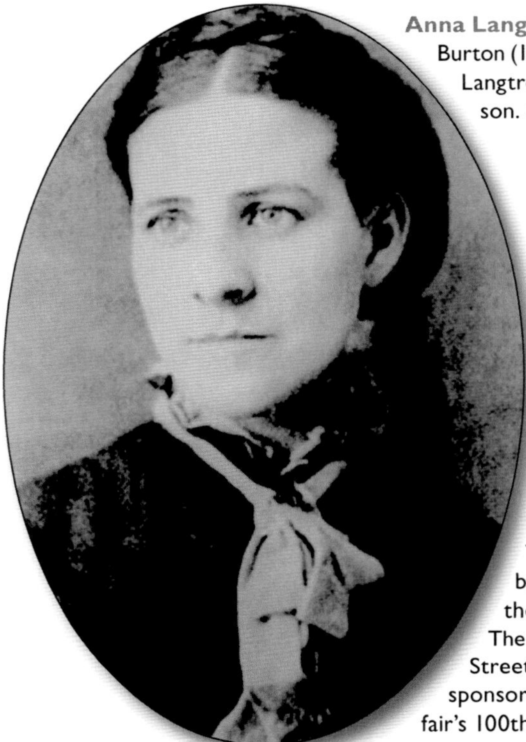

Anna Langtree Burton

Burton (1847–1909), a seamstress, was the daughter of Joshua Langtree. She married William Riley Burton and had one son. (Courtesy of Steven Lawsongatch.)

We Pay on Demand!

This early Aurora Farmers' Fair float was sponsored by the Aurora State Bank. There was a parade led by the Aurora Civic Band, directed by Frank Hubbard. There were horse-and-rig–driving competitions on Third Street for both ladies and gentlemen. The fair today is sponsored by the Aurora Lions Club, which celebrated the fair's 100th anniversary in 2008. (Courtesy of DCHS.)

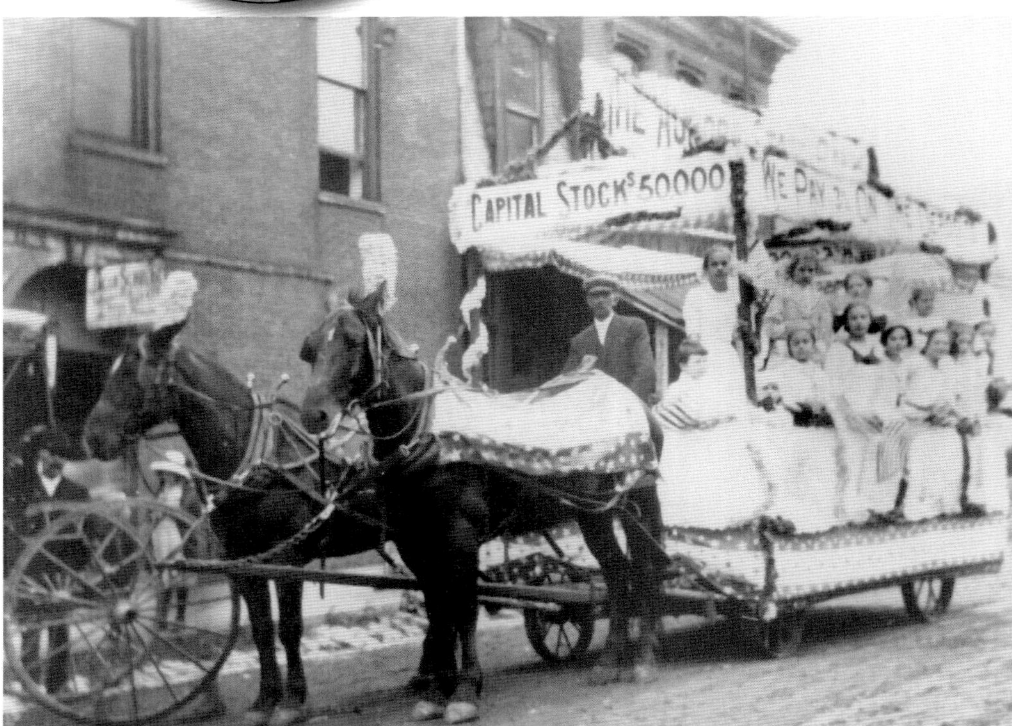

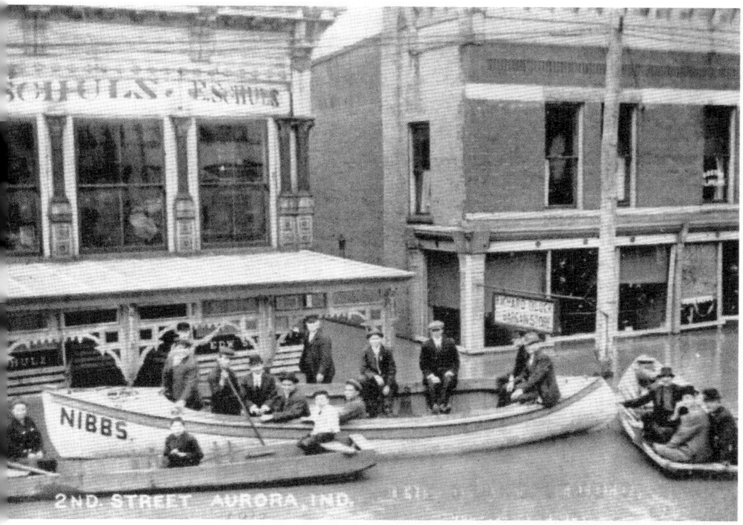

Frank Schipper
The 1913 flood was one of the worst in Aurora's history. When the town flooded, people would remain in the upstairs floors of their flooded businesses until the water receded. Stranded residents would rely on various sightseers to bring them supplies. Shown in the boat *Nibbs* are its owner, Frank Schipper (holding the oar), and his family. (Courtesy of DCHS.)

Mike Honan
Honan is shown clowning around as he hangs off what may well be his home on George Street. Honan's parents were Irish immigrants, and he worked as a laborer at the chair factory. (Courtesy of DCHS.)

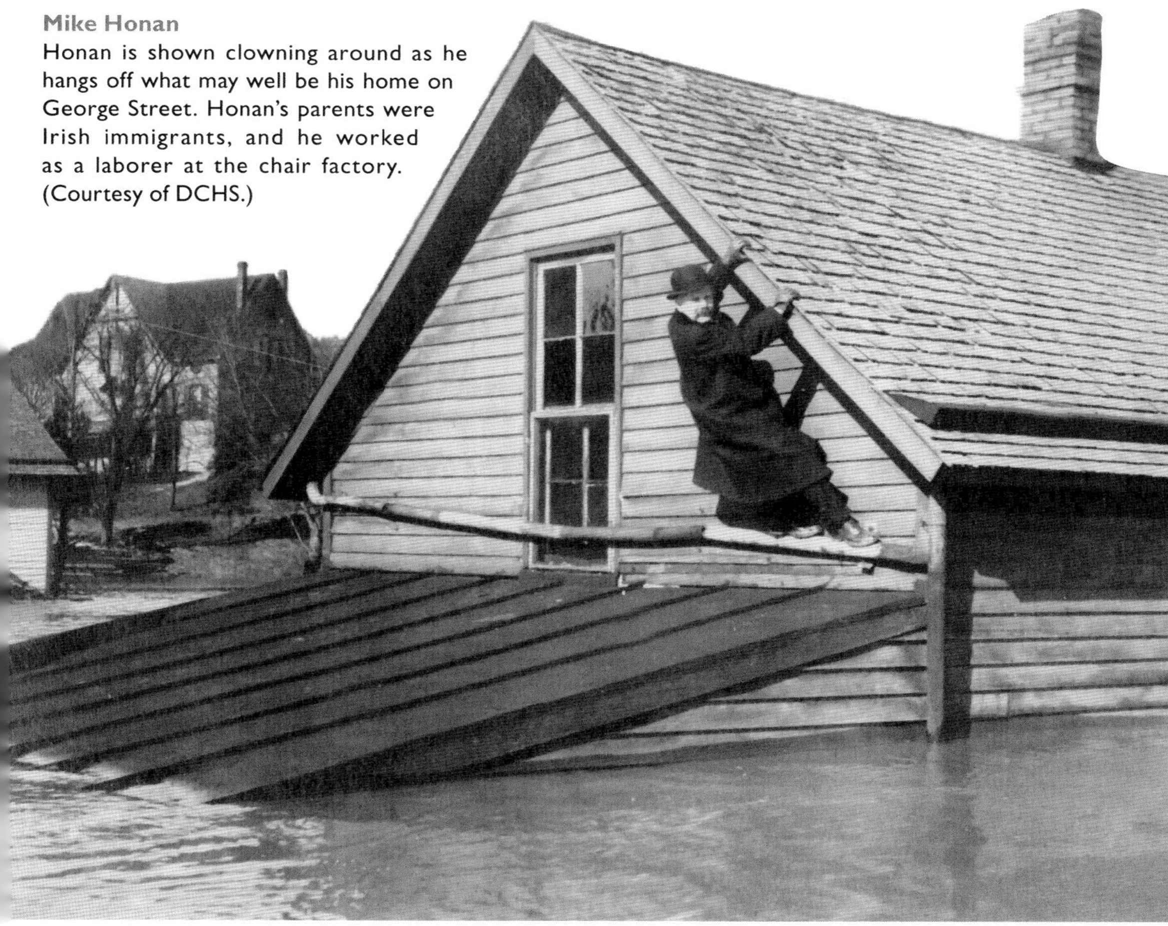

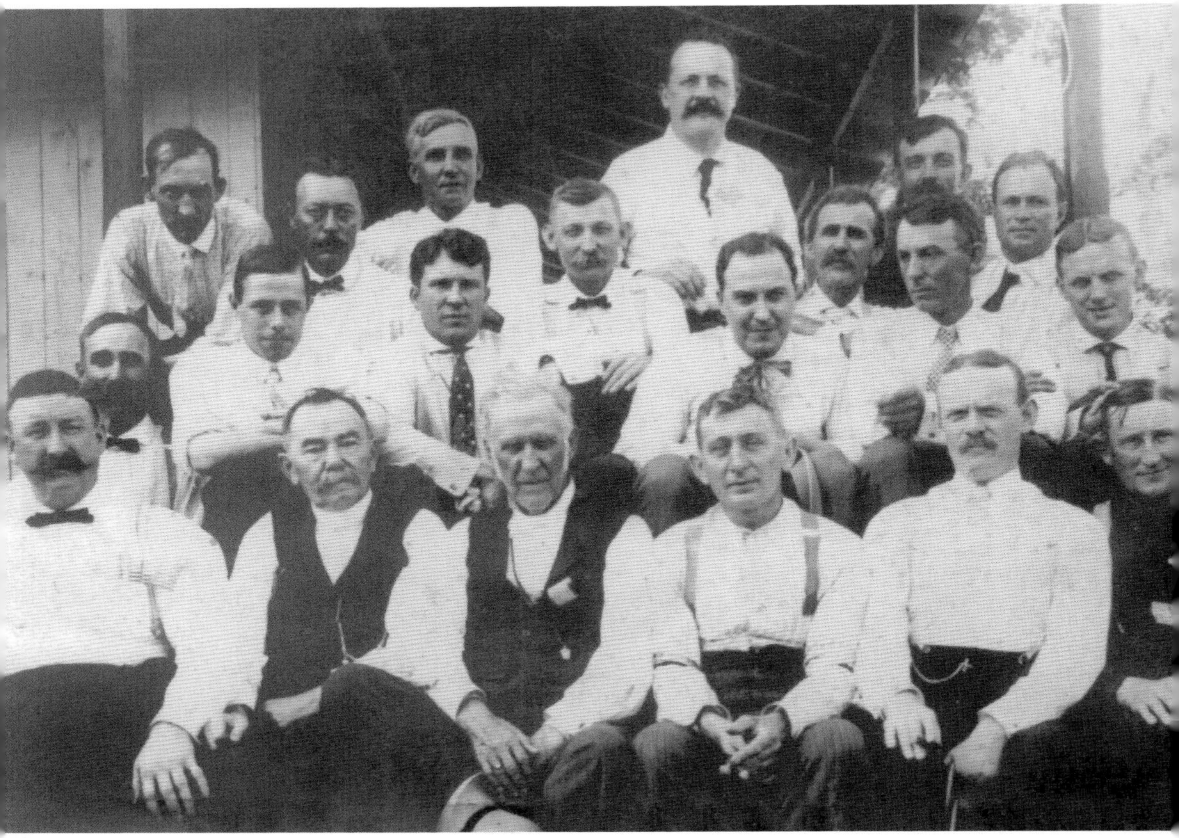

North Hogan Country Club

This group jokingly called themselves the North Hogan Country Club. It basically was a place where the men could enjoy each other's company, have some fun, and talk business. This photograph identifies many of the town's early business owners. Some of these men fought in the Civil War together. Shown here are, from left to right, (first row) John Ullrich, Capt. H.P. Spaeth, William McMullen, August Stoll, Louis Foulk, and Charles Heive; (second row) Charles Cole, Willard Stier, Carroll Stevens, M. Lowe, Vanden Canfield, Louis Paul, George Stedman, and Robert Cass; (third row) Wood Heath, William Hoskins, Alex Squibb, Ed Schulz Sr., Ed Swarthout, and John Stier. (Courtesy of DCHS.)

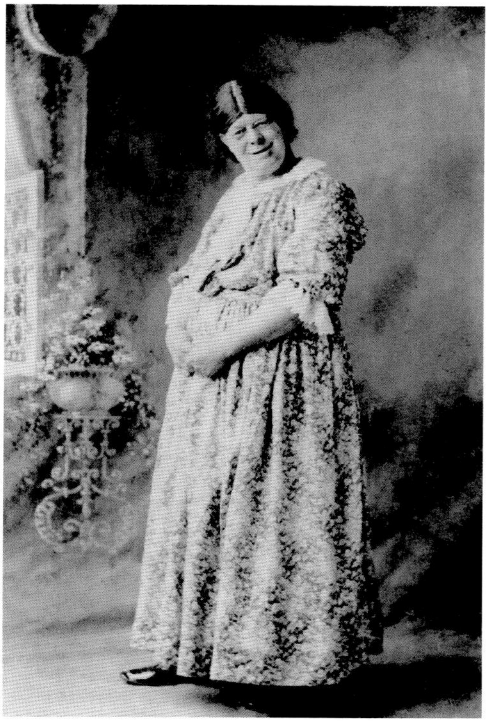

Charles McIntyre
McIntyre was a minstrel, owner of the Grand Theater, and proprietor of a bar on Third and Main Streets. He loved to entertain the crowd dressed as an old Irish washwoman. He could also sing and play music. (Courtesy of Aurora Lions Club.)

Women After Prohibition
When Prohibition began, Charles McIntyre stated, "Mark my words, the time will come when Americans will drink again, and women will drink as much as men." McIntyre is shown sitting on the railing of the "McIntyre Bungalow" on south Hogan Creek, where he liked to host parties. Everyone liked him, and the bungalow was a place where men in town would enjoy camping, card playing, and fishing while drinking cold beer. (Courtesy of DCHS.)

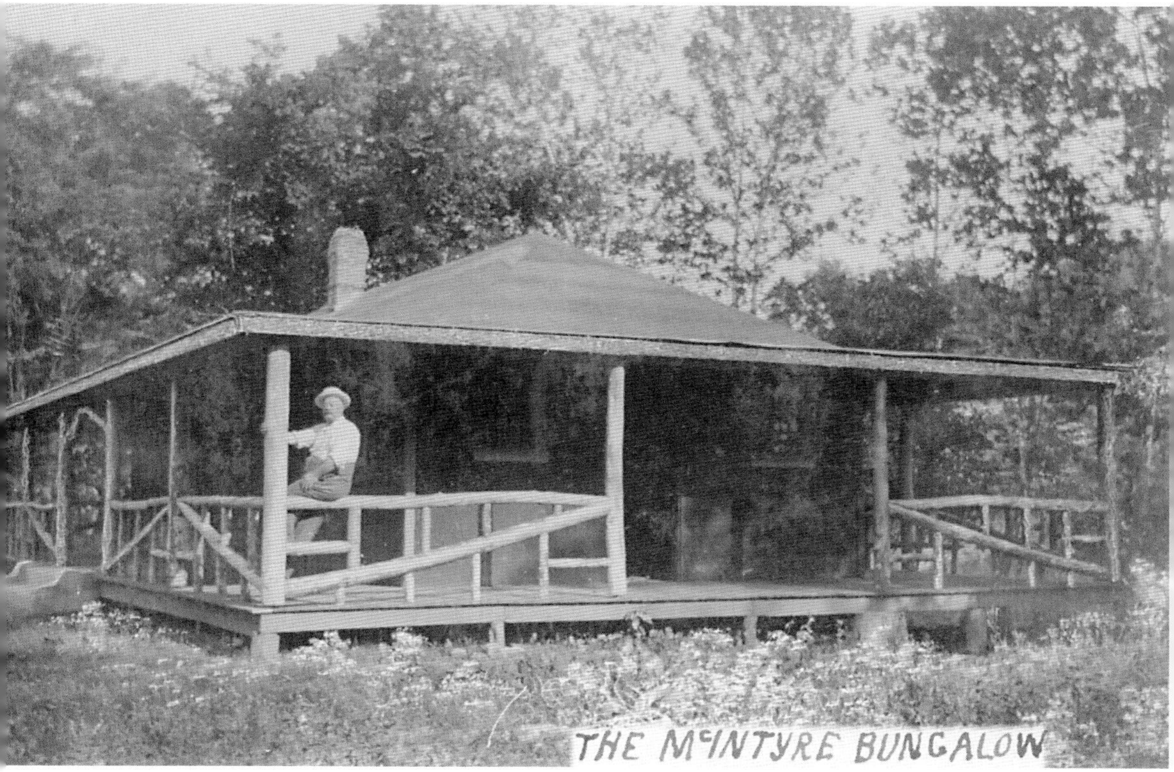

H.F. Wunderlich Agency, Inc.
Henry F. Wunderlich opened this insurance agency in 1907. After 105 years, his great-grandson David Wunderlich proudly maintains the family business as an agent. Also working as agents are his wife, Jana, his father, John, and Mary Ann Teaney. (Author's collection.)

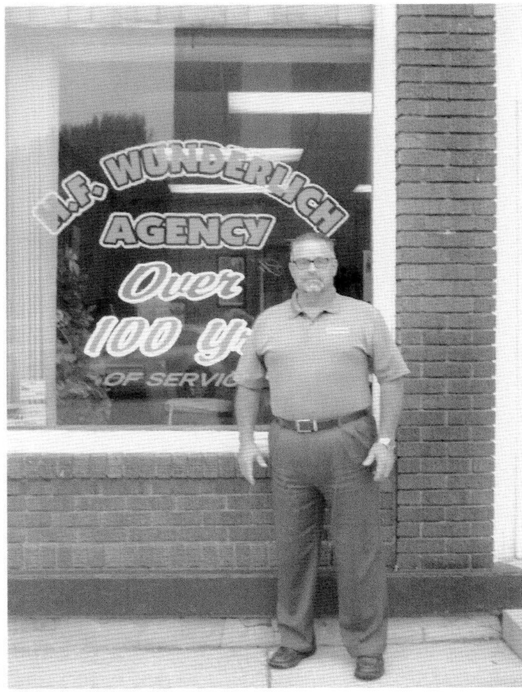

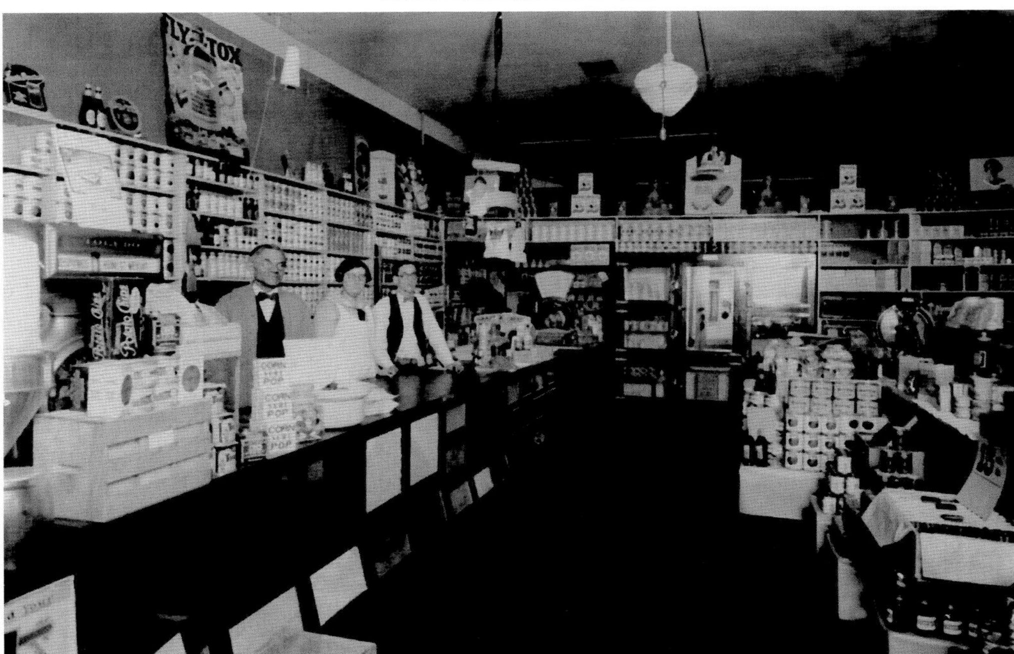

Kern's Grocery Store
Shown from left to right, Harry Kern, Tillie Cofield, and Russel Zeh ran Kern's Grocery Store. In its time, it was said to be a better grocery store than Kroger. Located at 427 Second Street, it later became Russel Zeh's Grocery Store. (Courtesy of DCHS.)

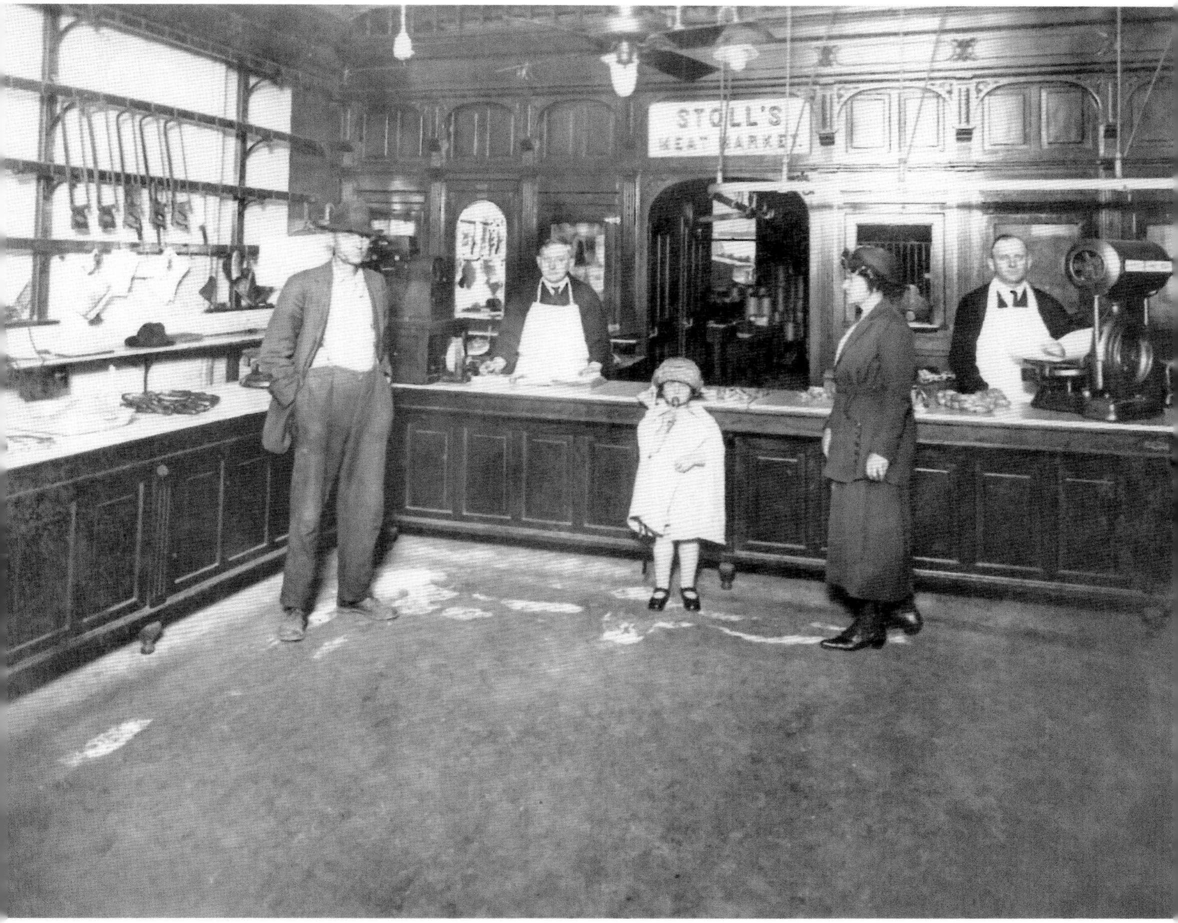

Stoll's Meat Market
Stoll's Meat Market was established in 1878 by Leonard Stoll and his son Louis. In 1915, sons August (left, behind counter) and William (right, behind counter) headed the business. The customers in front are Mr. Johnson, young Phyllis Funck, and her mother, Elda Funck. (Courtesy of Telford Walker.)

Keeping the Peace

There being, at one time, over 30 saloons in Aurora, these men kept the peace in the late 1800s. "Loony" Sassaman (left), Chief Frank Doerr (center), and Patrolman William "Field" Teaney are shown standing in front of the "escape-proof" jail. The vertical slits in the limestone were the jail's windows. When these men walked the night beat, residents could hear their nightsticks clicking against the iron fences as they passed. Although the jail is no longer used, it is still on display in the city building. (Courtesy of DCHS.)

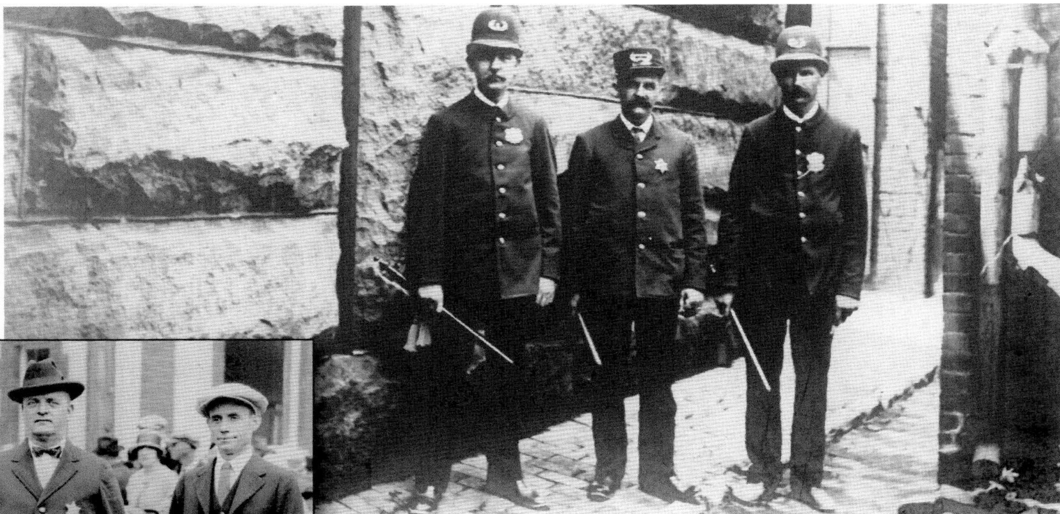

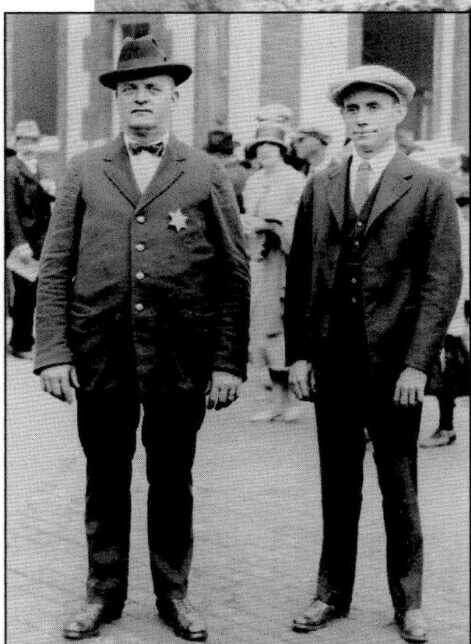

Patrolmen

Patrolmen Tom Owens (left) and Earl Huffman (right) stand ready to direct traffic and crowds, as thousands of people arrive in town to watch the 1916 Aurora Farmers' Fair parade. (Courtesy of Ullrich Studios.)

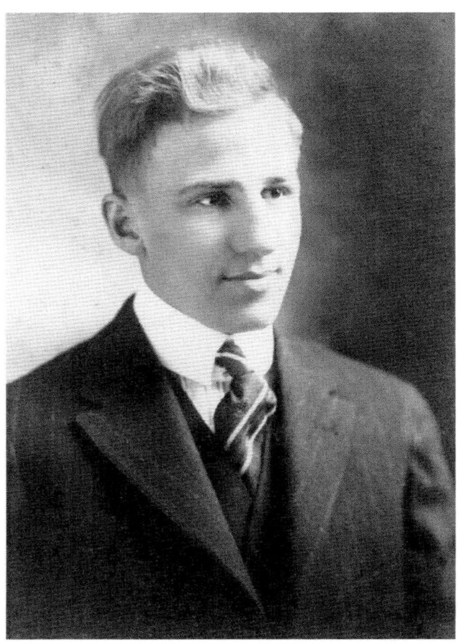

Gervaise Braunagel

When Braunagel (1901–1977) was 30, he worked at the Aurora Coffin factory as a trimmer. His parents were tavern owners Mike and Margaret Braunagel. After moving from home, he lived in Cochran, in a boardinghouse on Railroad Avenue. (Courtesy of DCHS.)

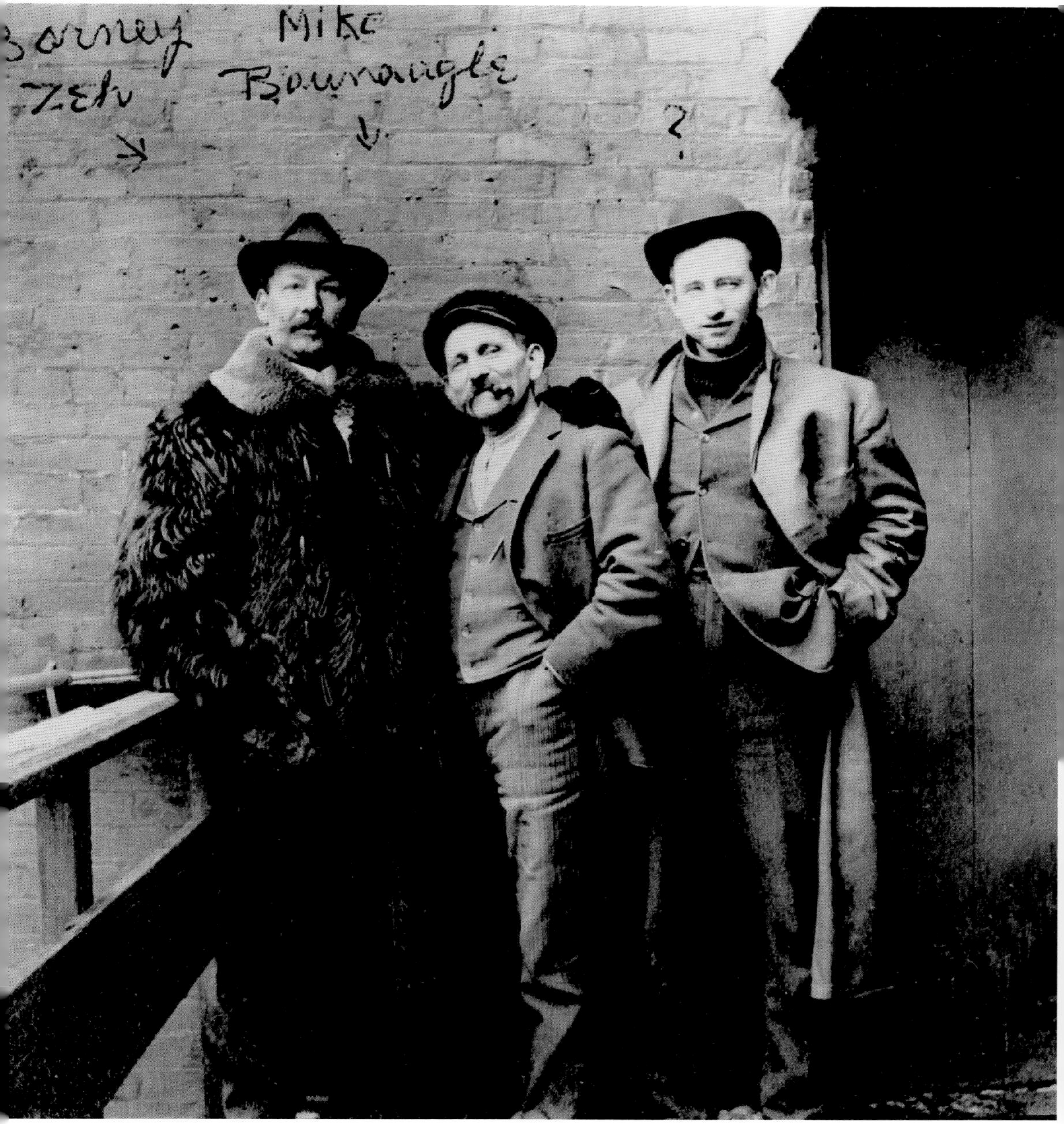

Mike Braunagel

Mike Braunagel and his wife, Margaret, owned and operated Barney's Café. It was a bar on one side and a café on the other. When Mike was in his sixties, he worked at a furniture factory. Shown here are Barney Zeh (left), Mike Braunagel (center), and an unidentified man. (Courtesy of DCHS.)

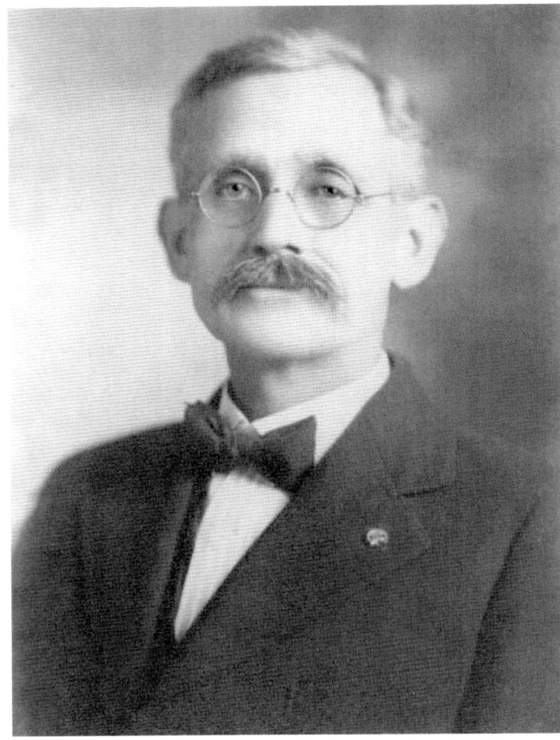

Samuel Sommerfield

Sommerfield owned a dry goods store on Second Street. His parents, Louis and Mary Sommerfield, were Polish immigrants. Samuel, like the rest of his brothers and sisters, worked in the store. His father was a tailor. (Courtesy of Steven Lawsongatch.)

Second and Main

This early photograph is looking up Second Street. John Ullrich's Drug Store was on the corner, and Sommerfield's was next door. When the Sommerfield family closed their business, the Ullriches removed the connecting wall to make room for a sandwich bar and a popular soda fountain. (Courtesy of DCHS.)

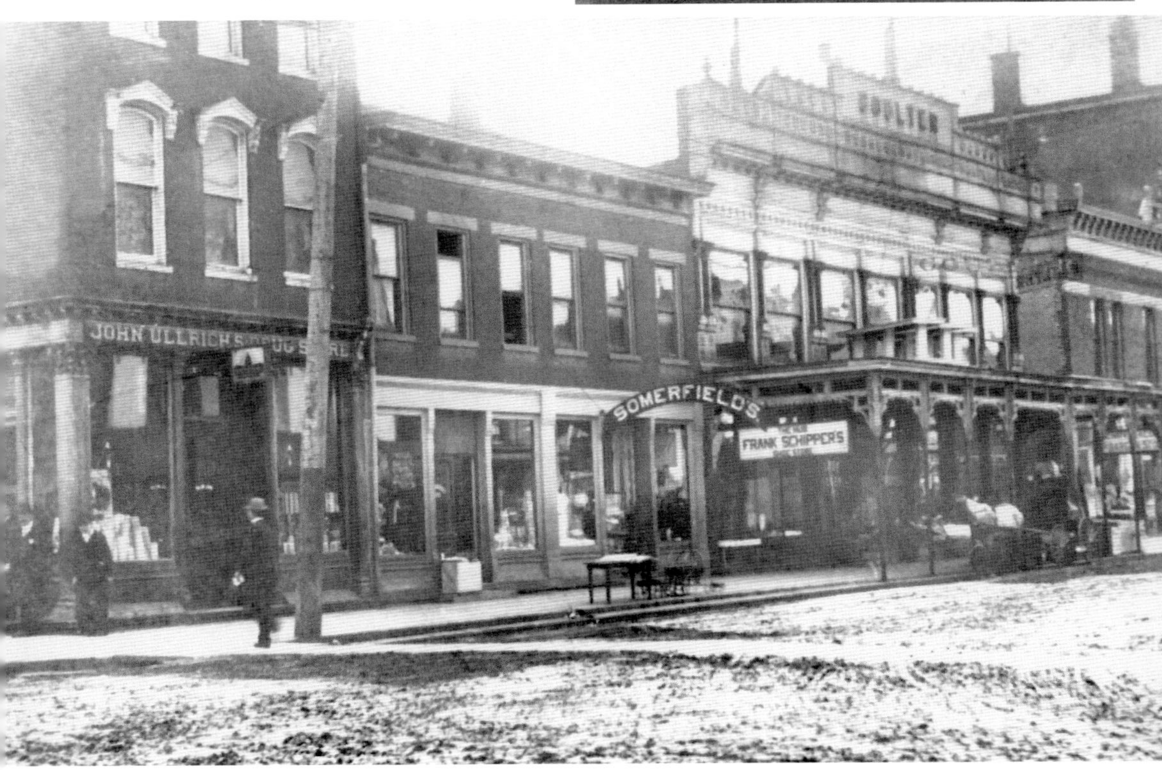

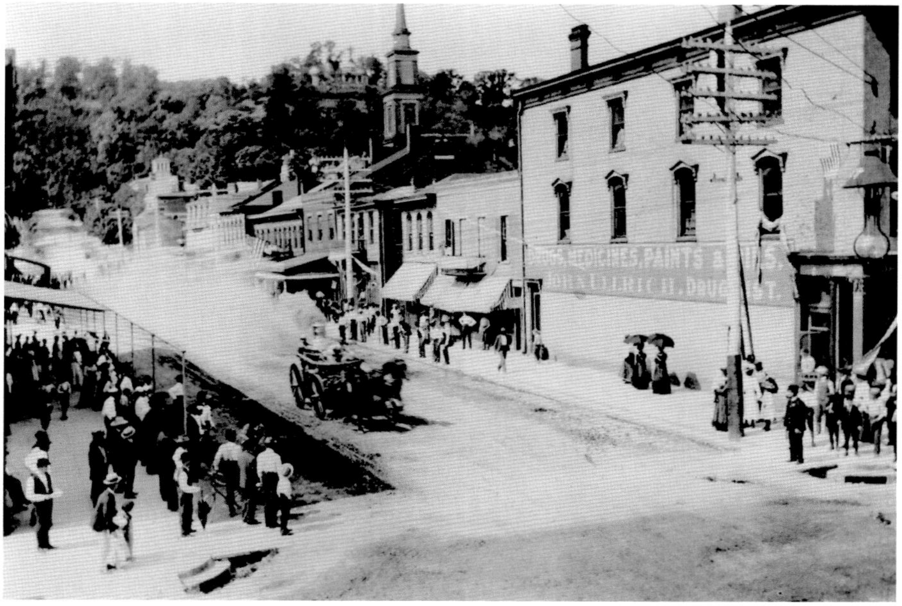

John and Charlie

July Fourth has always been a celebrated event in Aurora. About one hour before the parade was scheduled to start, Frank Huffman, with his team of black horses, John and Charlie, made a thrilling run down Main Street. Crowds watched as the horses pulled the steam fire engine *Aurora* at breakneck speed. The steamer is now on display in the Cincinnati Fire Department Museum. (Courtesy of DCHS.)

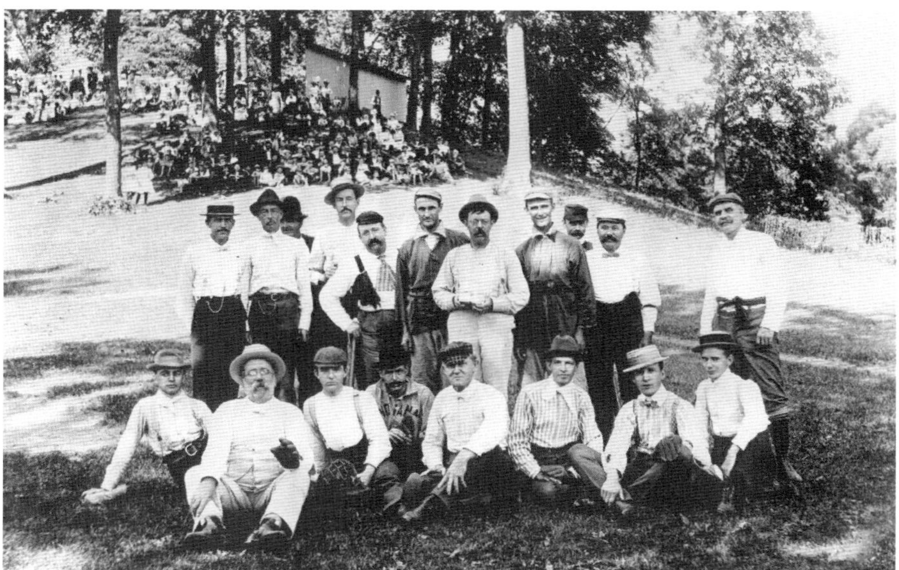

Picnic in the Shade

After the July Fourth parade, there would be a picnic and games in the park. Women, in their long dresses, would sit on the hill among the trees to try and keep cool, sharing a picnic basket while cheering on their favorite ball team. (Courtesy of DCHS.)

George Neaman

George Neaman (shown at center) operated a horse-drawn taxi service between the B&O Railroad depot and Rising Sun. He also owned the Neaman Hotel, seen on the right. The wooden depot building was replaced by a brick structure after a flood. The train no longer stops at the building; after several changes of ownership, the Aurora Public Library now owns it and maintains its genealogy department there. (Courtesy of Telford Walker.)

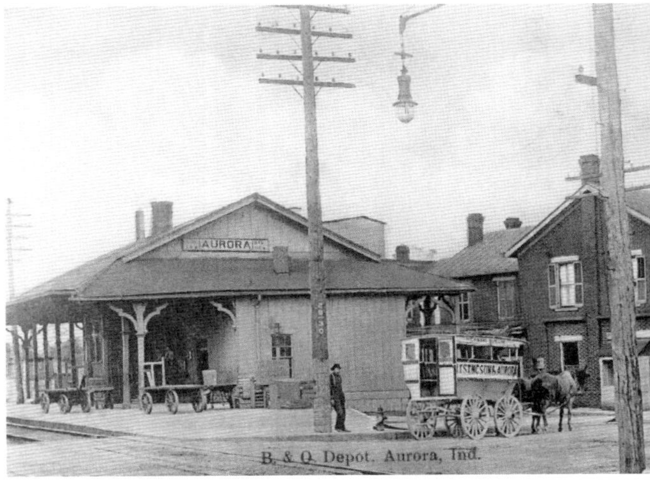

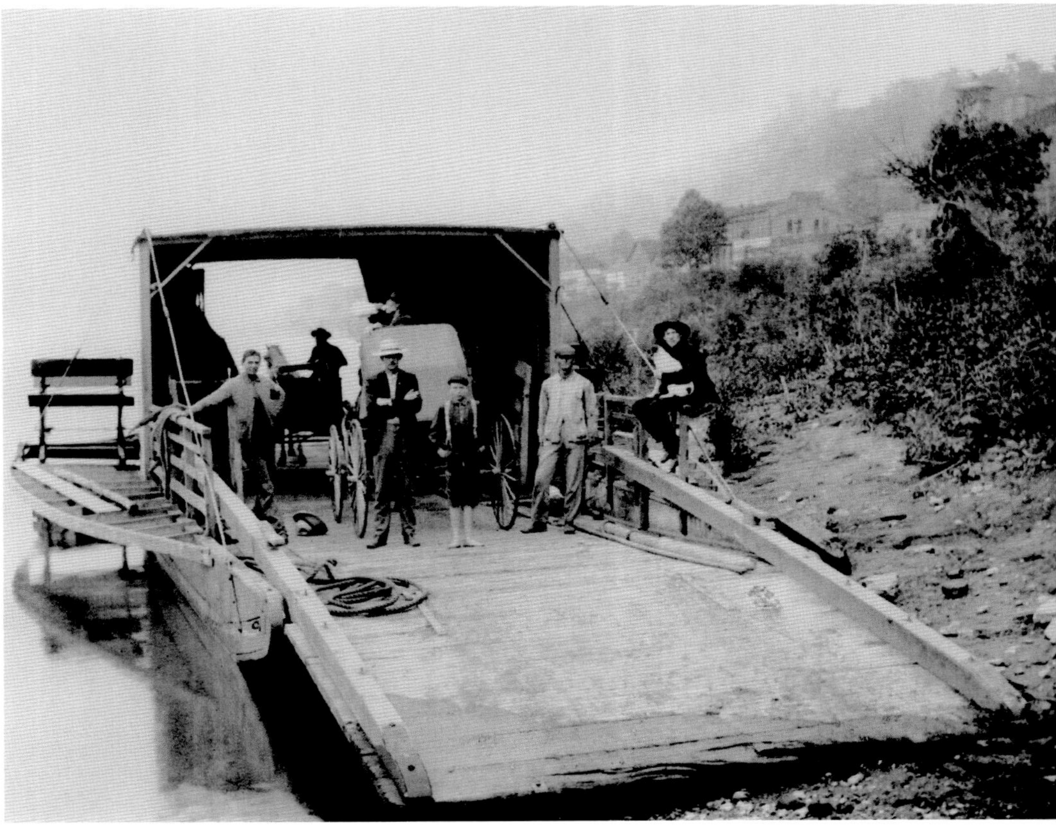

Aurora Ferry Operators

The original ferry was operated by Capt. Marcus Colling in 1819. The Aurora Ferry was driven by two blind horses walking a treadmill on each side of the boat. John D. Klopp operated the ferry for seven and a half years. Weighted beams from the aprons permitted a single man to raise and lower them at the shore. It was a slow but sure way to travel to Petersburg, Kentucky. The ferry service was discontinued after the I-275 bridge was built. (Courtesy of DCHS.)

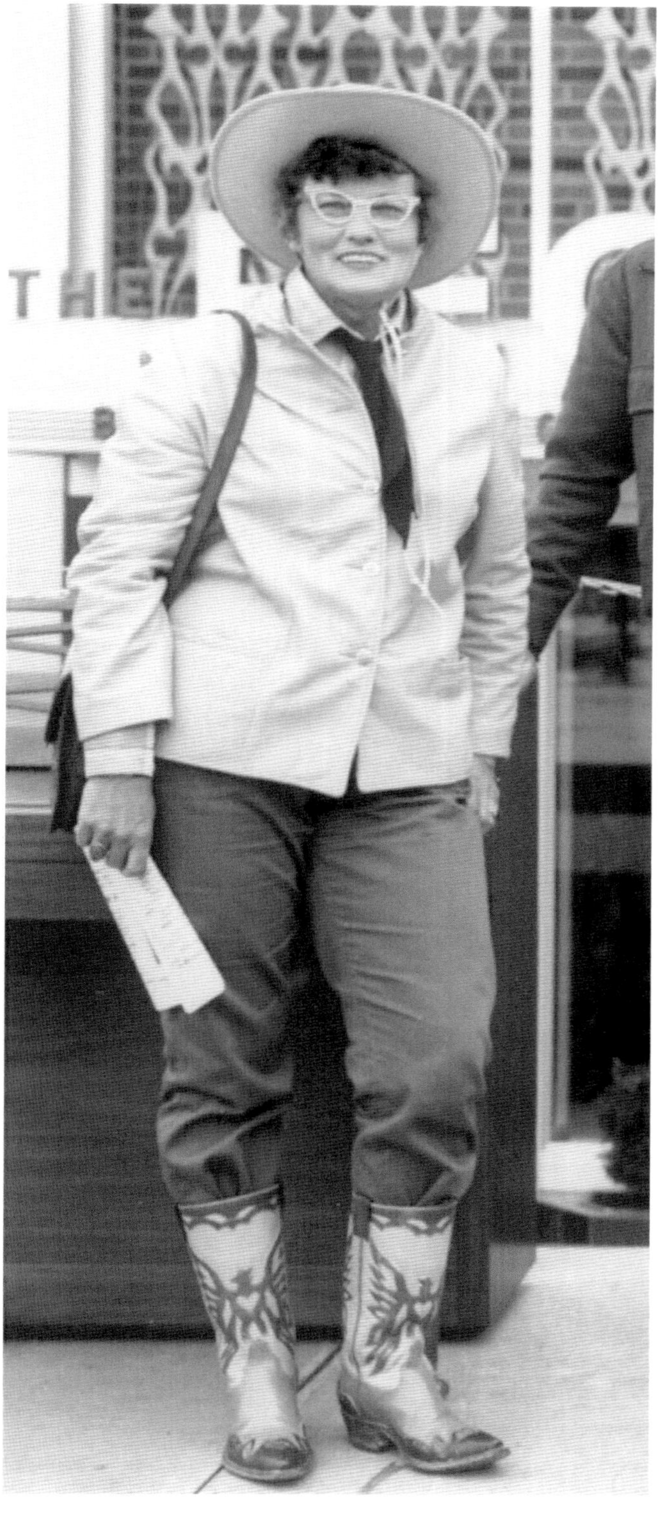

Pricilla "Podie" Lowe

"Podie" (1915–1995) was a character. She wore cowboy boots and pants like a man, and she reminded people of Annie Oakley. Her parents were Herman and Mabel Lowe, owners of the Vienna Bakery. Stories about her family were handed down by her mother and her aunts. Her ancestor John Gillis came west to look for land and to settle down. When he reached the area, he saw opportunity and only four cabins. Once settled, he cut down large trees on the hills, an area now called Langley Heights. Gillis dragged the logs down the trail to his building site, about where the Aurora depot now stands. There, he built a cabin and trading post near the creek.

A stream of springwater ran off the hill between Sutton Hill and Langley Heights, where it emptied into Hogan Creek. Second Street was a deep rock gulch and the first point to be filled in a flood. It was said that Hogan Creek received its name from all of the Indian huts, called "hogans," that were located on the west side of the creek. Gillis had red hair and blue eyes, and very white skin. Indians would stare in awe at him as he built his cabin.

Since much historical documentation was almost lost in a courthouse fire in 1863, it was important for Podie Lowe to make sure the next generations had the information she retained. She wanted future residents to enjoy reading about the progress and the changes undergone by the citizens and Aurora itself, from its beginning as a small settlement to its development into a city, built by sturdy folks of different origins. (Courtesy of DCHS.)

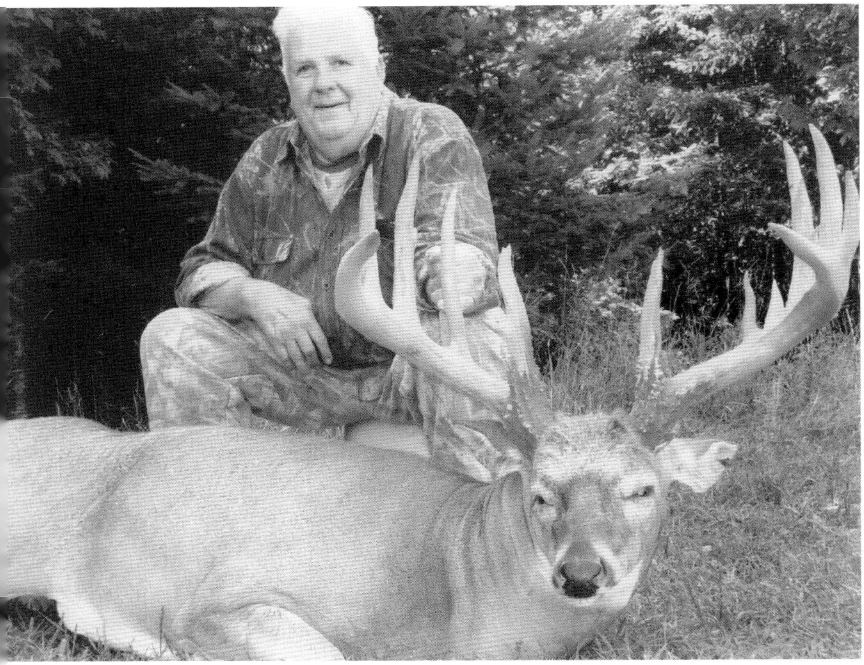

William Backman Jr.
Before retiring, William Backman Jr. was president and chief executive officer of Aurora Casket Co., Inc. He has hunted all over the world and is known for his collection of trophies and love of nature. William and his wife, Catherine, along with their children, continue to live in the area. (Courtesy of William Backman.)

Aurora Casket Co., Inc.
The Aurora Coffin Co. was founded in 1890 by Col. John J. Backman. The company started with 25 employees on Conwell Street. As a result of smart business sense, it grew into a 400,000-square-foot manufacturing and marketing support facility on US Highway 50. The Backman and Barrott families sold the company to outside interests after 122 years in business. (Courtesy of DCHS.)

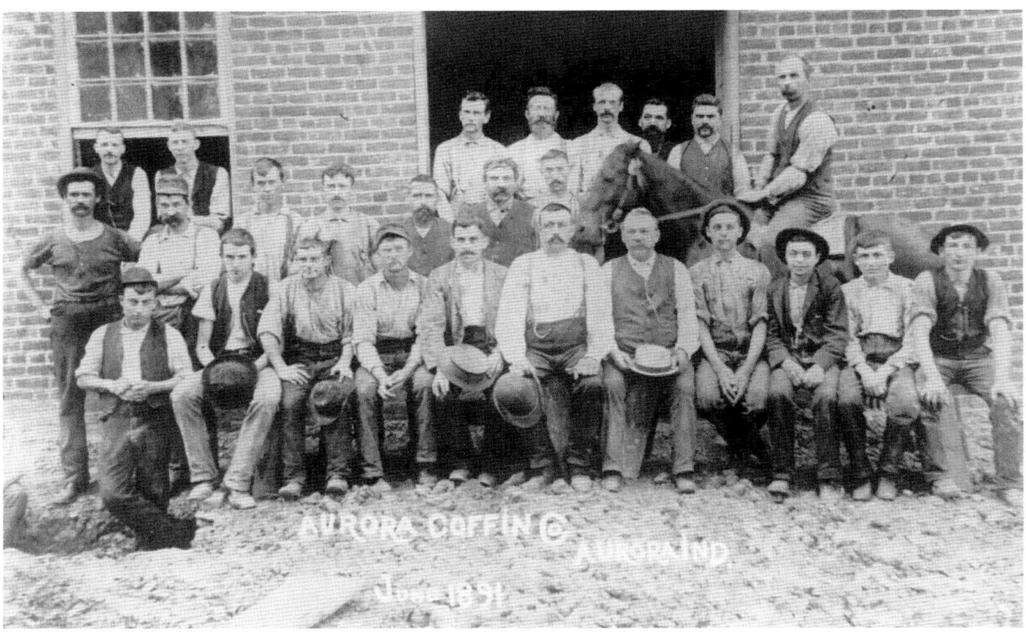

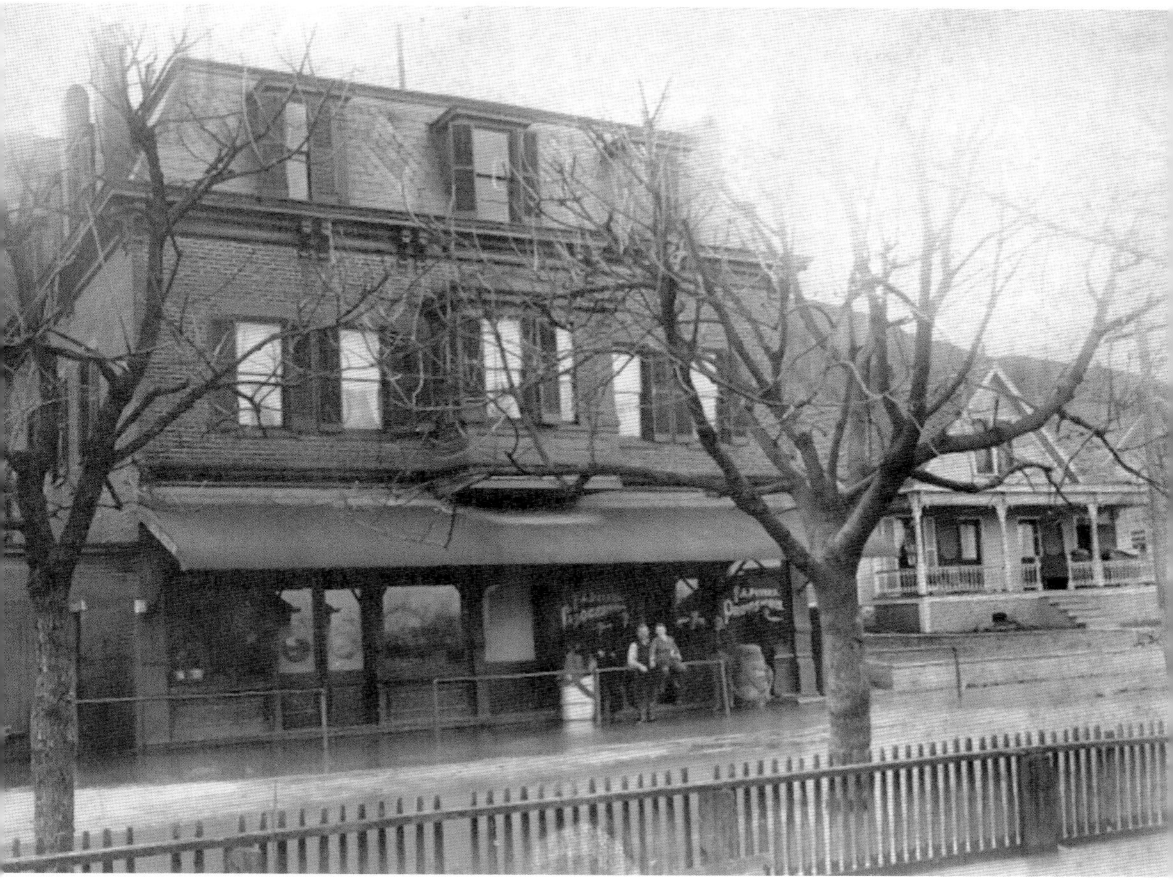

The First and Last Chance Saloon
Three businesses were housed in the Peters building on Decatur Street. On the right side of the main floor was the Peters Provisions grocery store. The First and Last Chance Saloon occupied the left side of the building. The tavern offered a first or last chance to drink, depending on which way one was going. Frederick and Ida May Peters lived on the second floor, and a large dance hall was on the top floor. There was a raised platform for the band, accessed by climbing a ladder and entering through a hole. Neighbors were invited to hang wash in the room during bad weather. It was said that John L. Sullivan once gave an exhibition boxing match here. Crawford "Happy" Peters, future attorney and civic leader, was born and raised here. (Courtesy of the Peters family.)

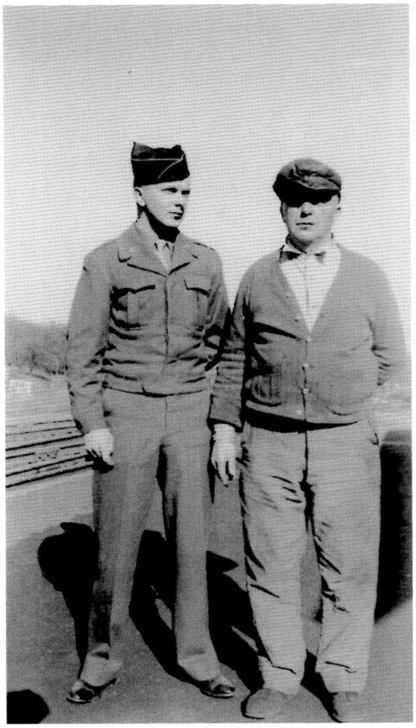

Charles and Edward Dierking

Home on leave from the Army, Edward Dierking (left) stands next to his father, Charles Dierking. Charles started the family-owned business, Dierking Coal and Ice Delivery Company, in 1921. Charles and his Aurora friends would play football for money "thrown in a pot." No one wanted to lose, so most games were settled with a fistfight. During one such fight, a Lawrenceburg opponent bit off part of Charles's ear. (Courtesy of the Dierking family.)

Ray Baer

Charles (left) and William Fehrman stand behind the printing press as Ray Baer operates the old Whitlock press, one sheet at a time. William Fehrman began his newspaper career working at the *Dearborn Independent* for L.W. Cobb. Fehrman, and his family purchased it in 1927 and renamed it the *Aurora Journal*. Baer played Santa Claus each year for the city. Children brought him their Christmas lists, and Baer kept them all. (Courtesy of DCHS.)

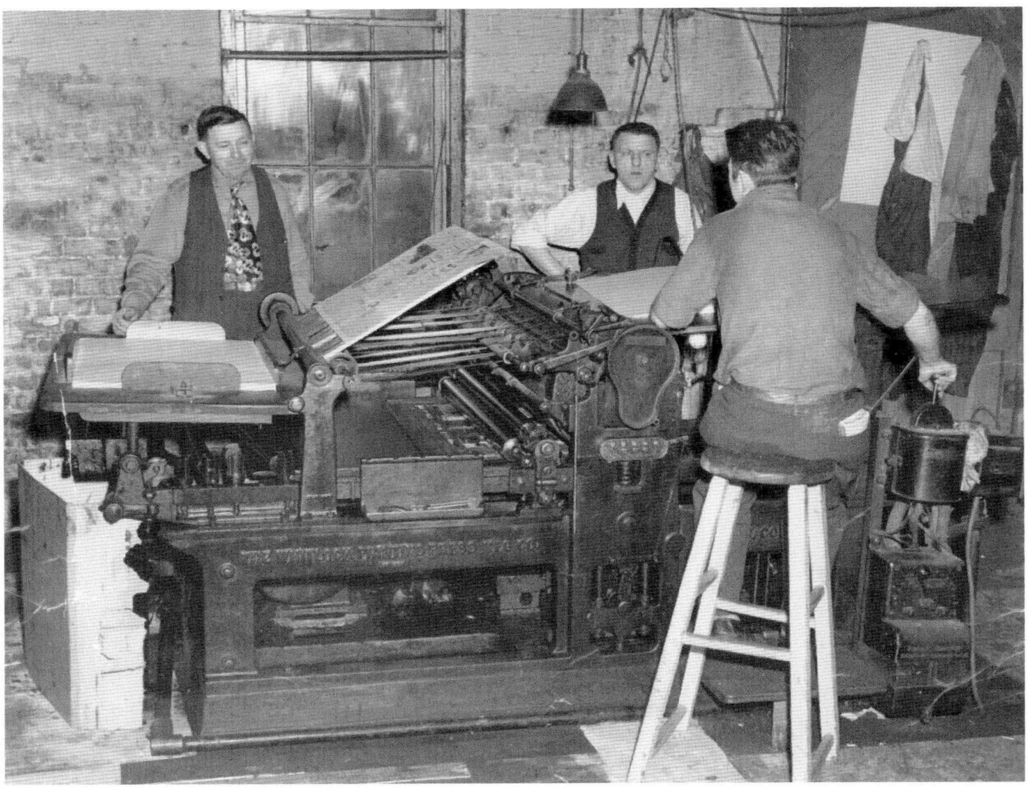

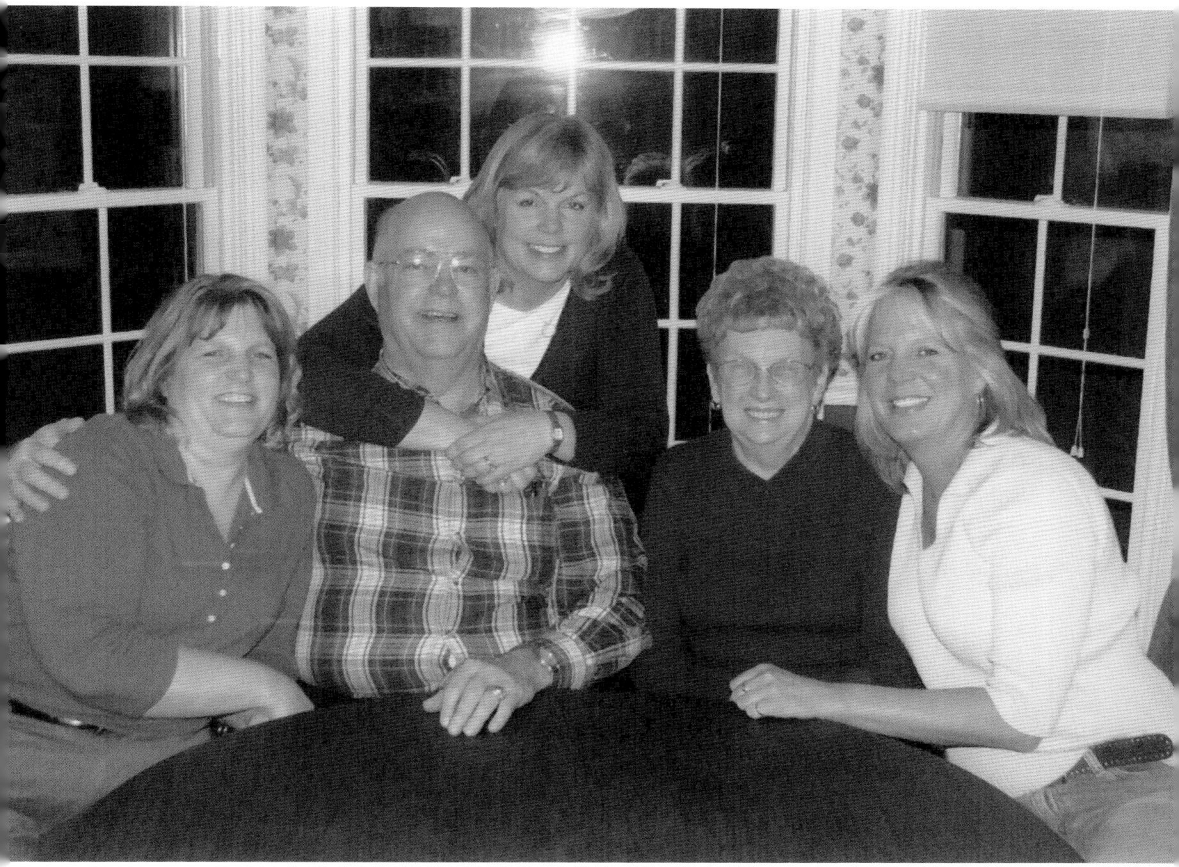

Jack, Dolores, and the Girls

Jack and Dolores (Fillenwarth) Tandy were high school sweethearts and married in 1952. In 1954, at the age of 22, they opened their first business, Tandy's Fashion Bar, on Second Street. They worked hard and at one time owned two stores in Aurora, one in Dillsboro and one in Brookville. In 2006, they closed the doors to their clothing store business. In 1961, Jack, his brothers Joe and Pete Tandy, and Robert Laker and Bobby Lischkge became partners under the name Valley Enterprise, Inc. In 1987, the group purchased the Cochran Chair property and built storage lockers. In 1990, they purchased the old Ullrich's Drug Store building. Jack and Dolores have three daughters, Cindy (left), Terry (standing), and Kathy (right). (Courtesy of the Tandy family.)

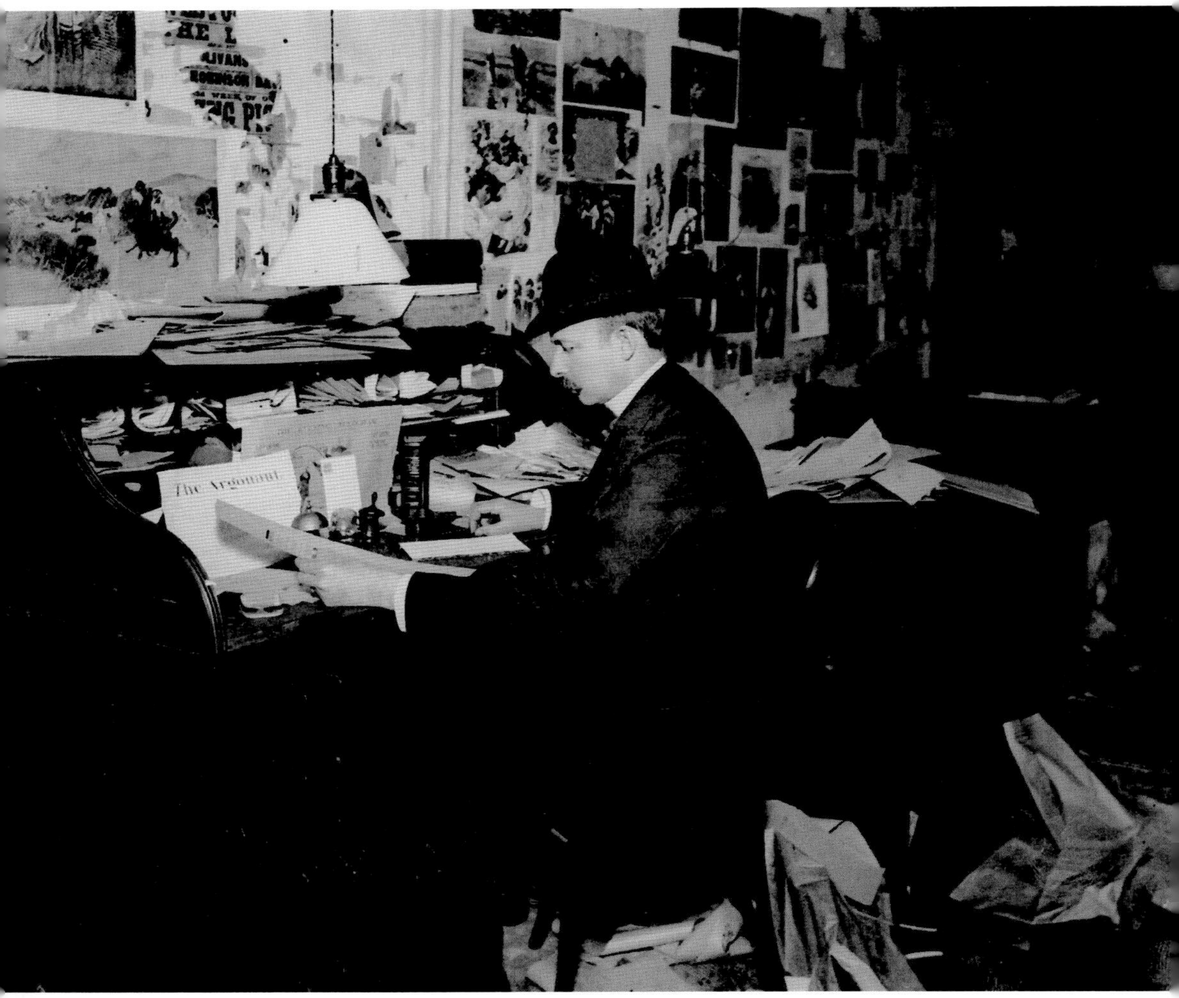

Robert W. Criswell

Criswell was born and raised in Aurora. He became the editor of the *New Yorker,* a society-based weekly. In 1905, Criswell was arrested on a charge of criminal libel brought against him by Congressman Joseph L. Rhinock of Covington, Kentucky. The charge was based on an article in the *New Yorker* that criticized the rebellious life of Alice Roosevelt, daughter of the president, while on a visit to Cincinnati. It was thought he was running a scam with Robert A. Irving by running a column known as "The Social Editors Society," containing gossip about famous families. The price to read it varied between $100 and $250. Before an article was even written, Criswell and Irving had collected $6,500. Fearing jail time, Criswell either jumped or fell in front of a subway express train at the Seventy-second Street station and was instantly killed. (Courtesy of DCHS.)

CHAPTER THREE

Community Service Legends

Aurora is known for its willing volunteers, neighbors helping neighbors. Aurora has lost brave volunteer firemen in the line of duty. In times of flooding, volunteers turn out to fill sandbags or move merchandise to avoid floodwaters. Since the early 1800s, volunteers have worked on restoration efforts, reclaiming unsightly areas and beautifying places such as Mary Stratton and Lesko Parks. While looking at these photographs, note how often the same last names seen, spanning more than 200 years. It is said that the more a person volunteers for their community, the more he or she becomes a part of it. This chapter begins with 102-year-old volunteer Luella Roppers. Volumes of books could be filled with community service legends like her.

Luella Roppers

Luella Roppers, shown in an early photograph wearing her Sunday clothes, is a model of how to live life at 102. She is a hard one to keep up with. Each Friday, she calls the "Catch A Ride" bus to take her to Dearborn County Hospital, where she has volunteered for the last 27 years, accumulating over 4,200 volunteer hours. She writes a monthly newsletter for her church, plays cards with friends, and matches Retired Senior Volunteer Program volunteers with students from six schools as pen pals. Roppers credits the Lord for her long life. "He's given me health and I haven't had any bad days, I've always had what I need," she said. (Courtesy of Louella Roppers.)

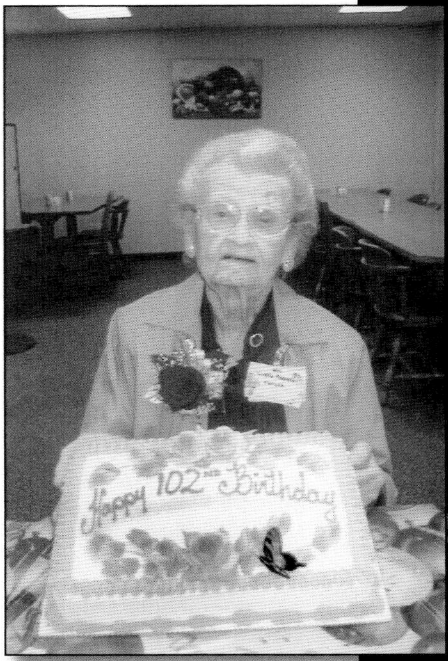

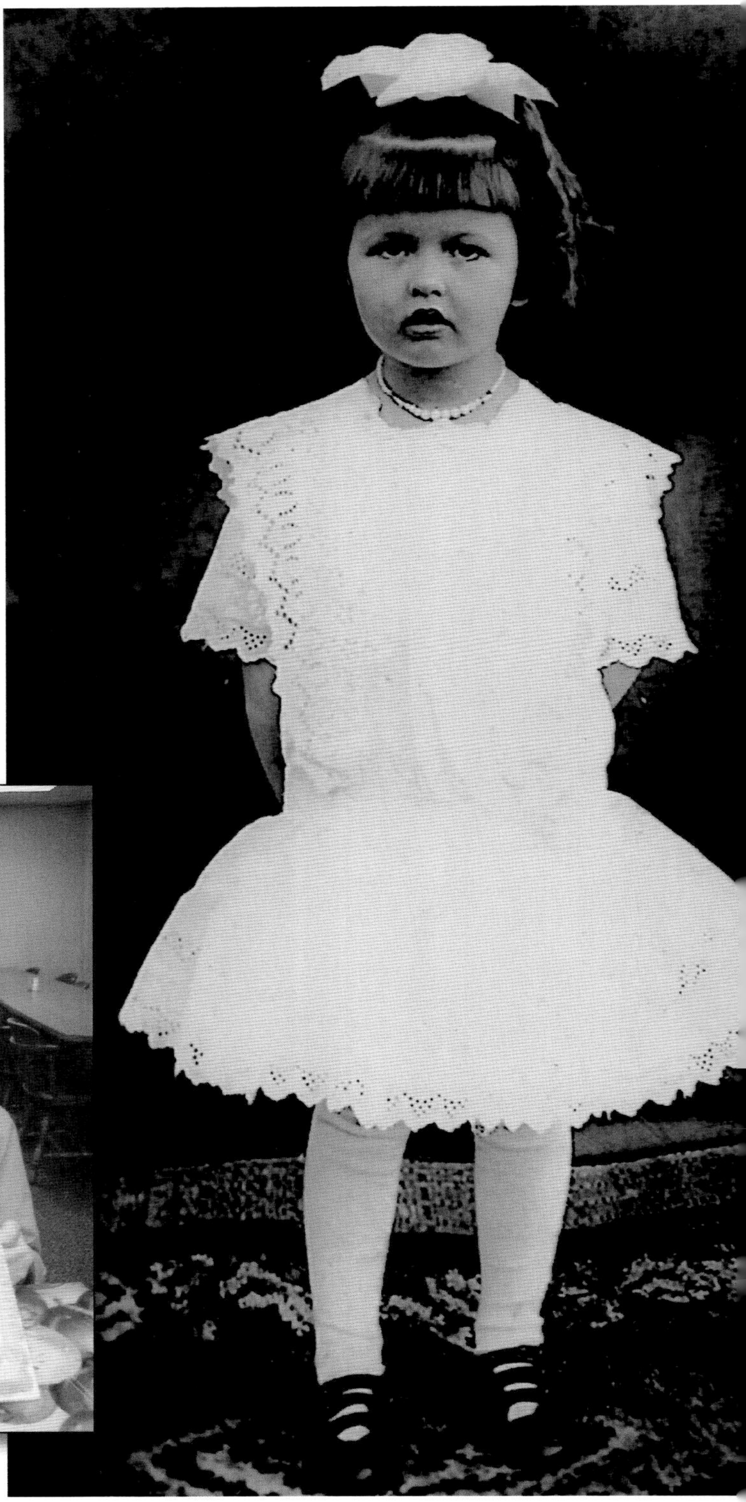

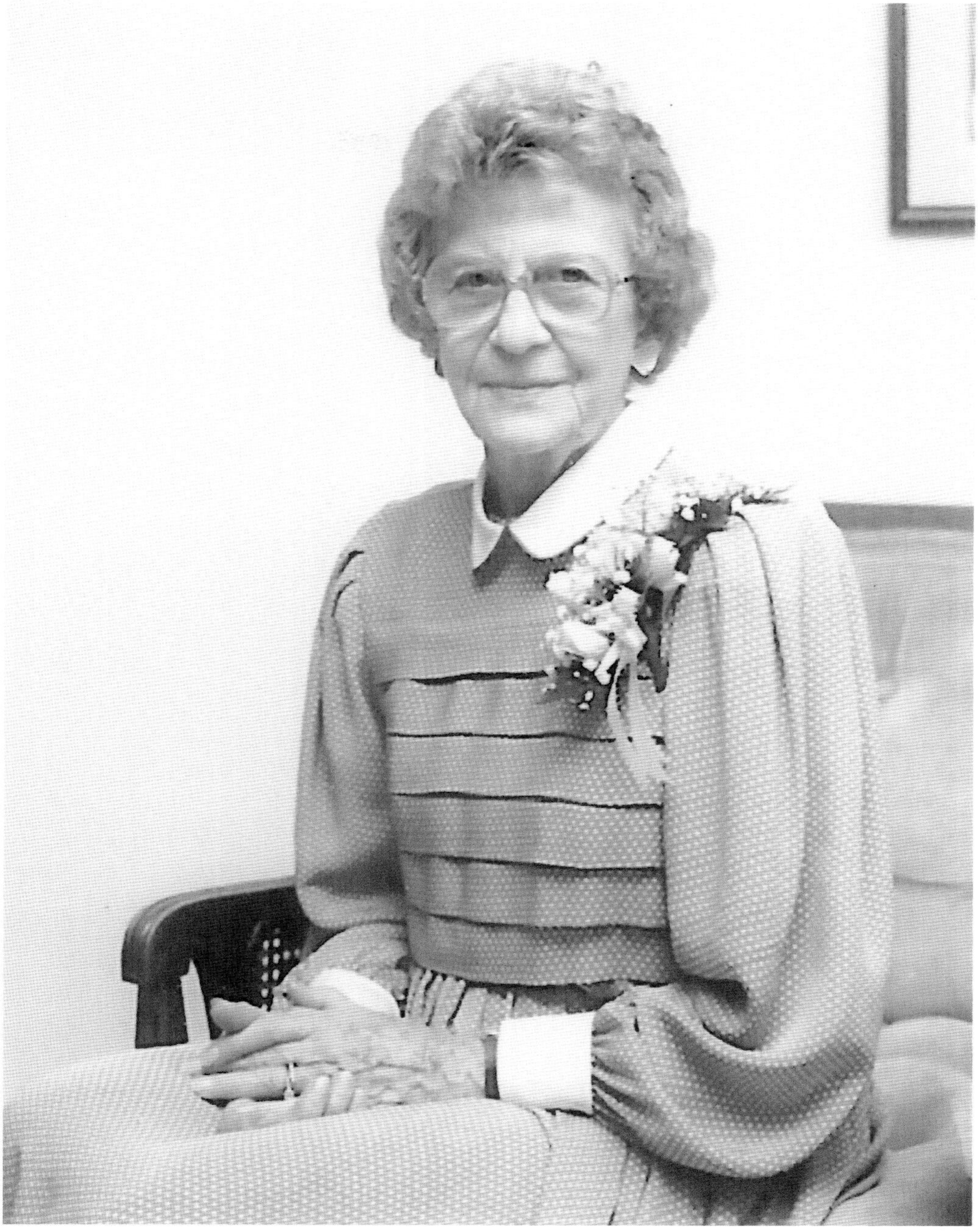

Helen Petscher, a "Gift Of God"
Petscher was able to live alone and drive well into her nineties. When she passed away at the age of 104, she was the oldest member of the Aurora First Presbyterian Church. She was a founder of the Ohio Valley Choral Festival. In 1926, she started as a music supervisor at Aurora schools and was responsible for the West Aurora and Southside grade schools and for all 12 grades at Northside School. She also started the first Aurora High School band. (Courtesy of Phee Ellinghausen.)

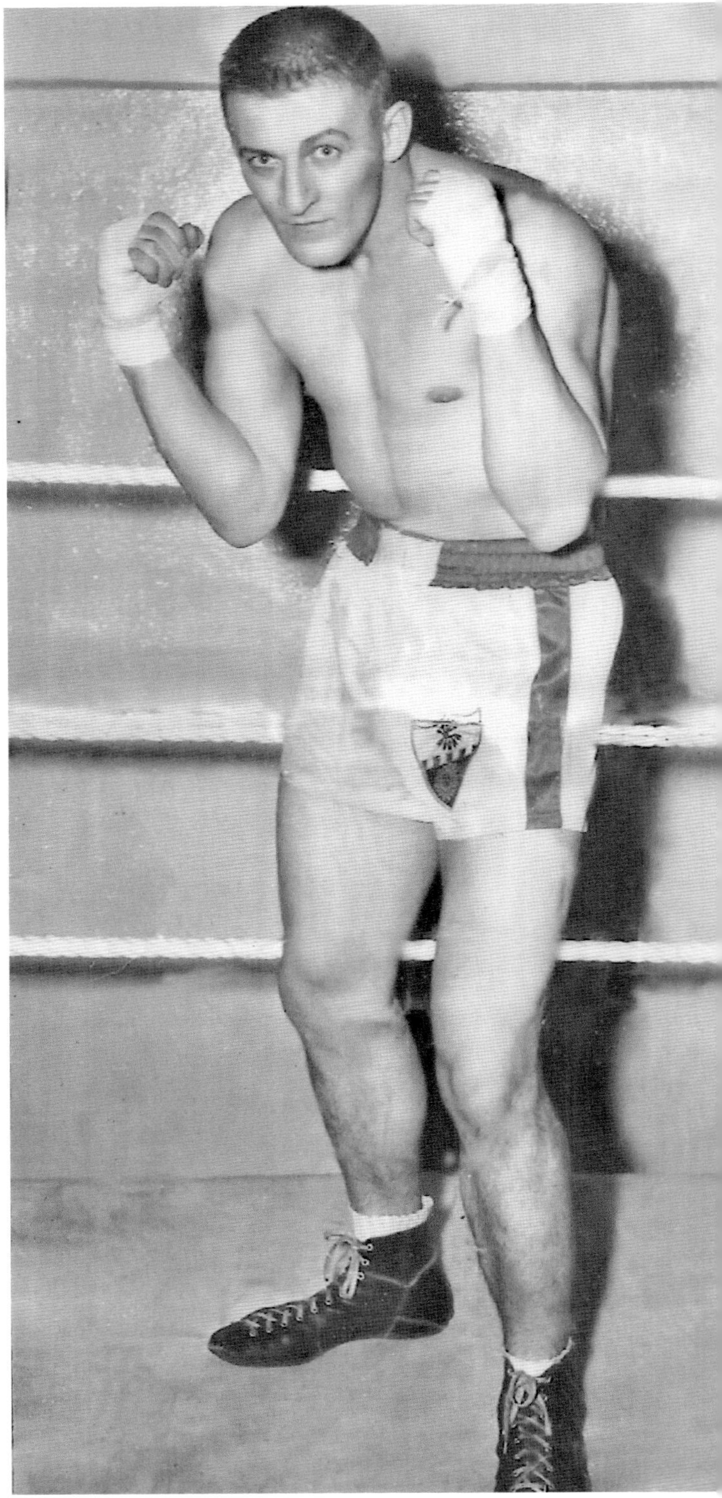

Charles "Charlie" Thayer
Thayer served 40 years on the Aurora City Council, making him the longest-serving Hoosier city council member. He held the office from 1969 to 2008. On his first day in office, he was on the back of a truck shoveling salt on the streets. The city had no salt spreader, and the snow was about two feet deep. He served his country from 1952 to 1955. While at Fort Knox, Kentucky, he received extra training due to his ability on the softball field. Thayer and his team won the European championship in softball in 1954, playing in France, Austria, and all over Germany. He was also a championship boxer. When he came back home, he married Sandy McPherson and continued to play softball. At age 60, he started working with the girls' softball teams at South Dearborn High School. In 2008, he was diagnosed with multiple myeloma. After months of radiation and chemotherapy, he received a bone marrow transplant and now is "doing good and feeling fine," he says. Now 79, Thayer continues to work with the girls' softball teams and chops wood. In his spare time, he and Sandy love to sing karaoke at local restaurants. (Courtesy of Charles Thayer.)

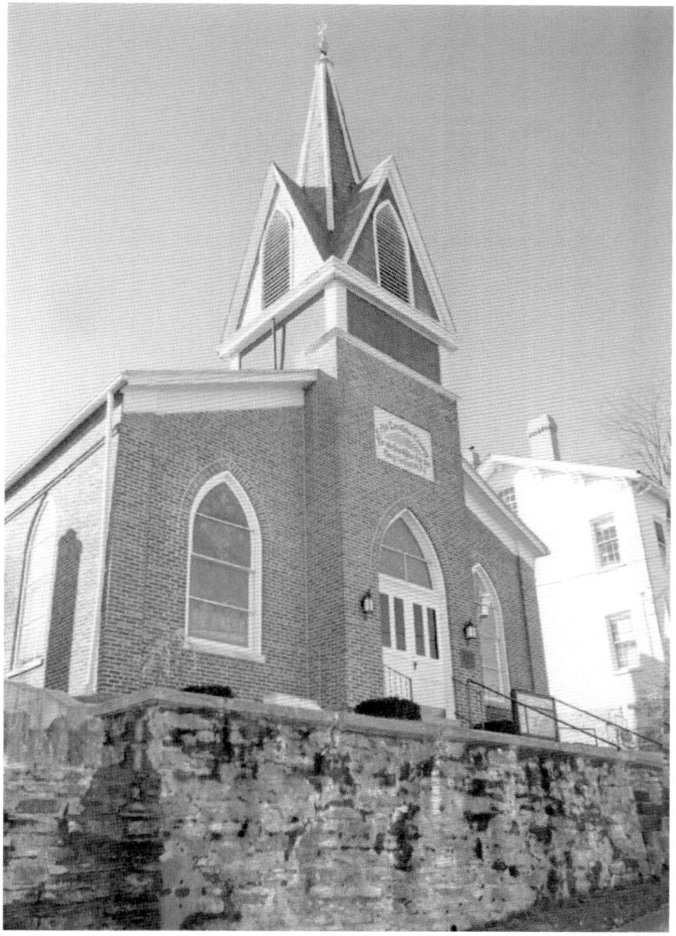

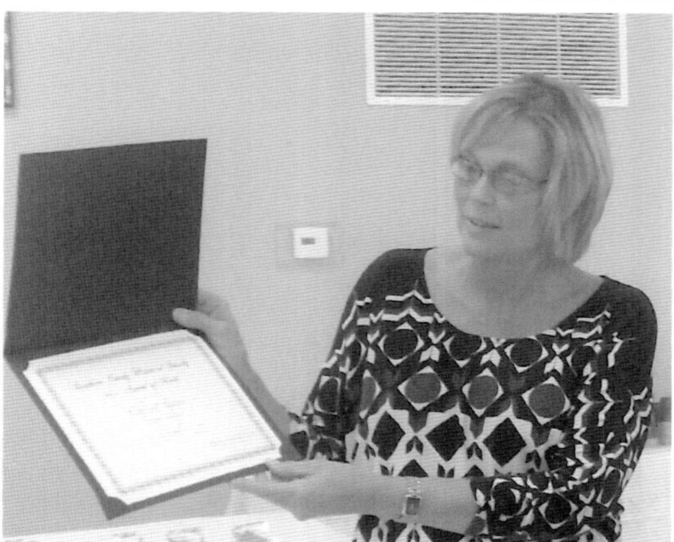

City of Spires Museum
The First Evangelical United Church of Christ was first built by the Baptists in 1848. After a dwindling membership, the oldest Aurora church had to close its doors to weekly worship. In 2010, the remaining congregation, and Aurora Main Street, gave new life to the historic building. The 1848 sanctuary and social hall is still an ideal setting for gatherings. Now called the City of Spires, it is a local museum available for weddings and other events. Operated by volunteers, the museum features displays of local interest. At bottom, Debbie Fehling, a lifetime member of the church, recently accepted a Historic Preservation Award from the Dearborn County Historical Society. (Author's collection.)

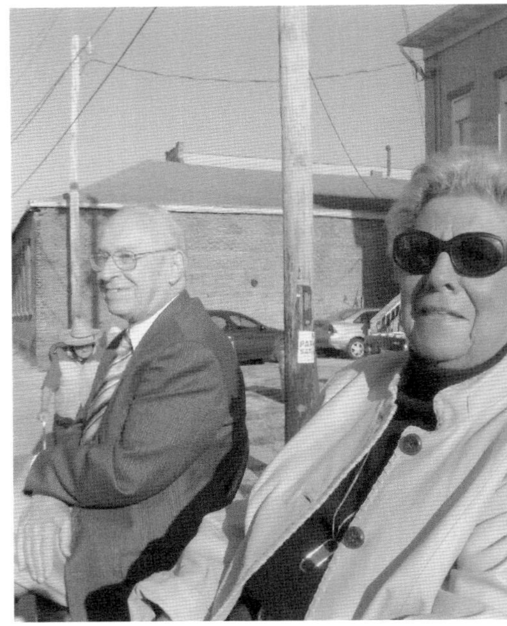

Shirley and the Judge

Whenever people would see this couple, they would often say, "There's Shirley and the judge." The Meyers lived and raised their family in downtown Aurora. Shirley Meyer has a humorous quick wit and a deep love for her town. She is famous for her history tours of Riverview Cemetery and colorful stories of the past. Shirley went to Marion College in Indianapolis. One of three girls, she was born on July 28, 1936, to local city attorney Crawford "Hap" and Celestine M. Peters. Shirley has four children, ten grandchildren, and one great-grandson.

Anthony "Tony" Meyer (1933–2012) was committed to public service. He was admitted to practice before the US Supreme Court, was the prosecutor for Dearborn and Ohio Counties for eight years, the Aurora city attorney for many years, and senior partner at Ewbank & Meyer. He liked to laugh about the time his father-in-law ran against him as Dearborn County prosecutor, but lost. (Courtesy of the Meyer family.)

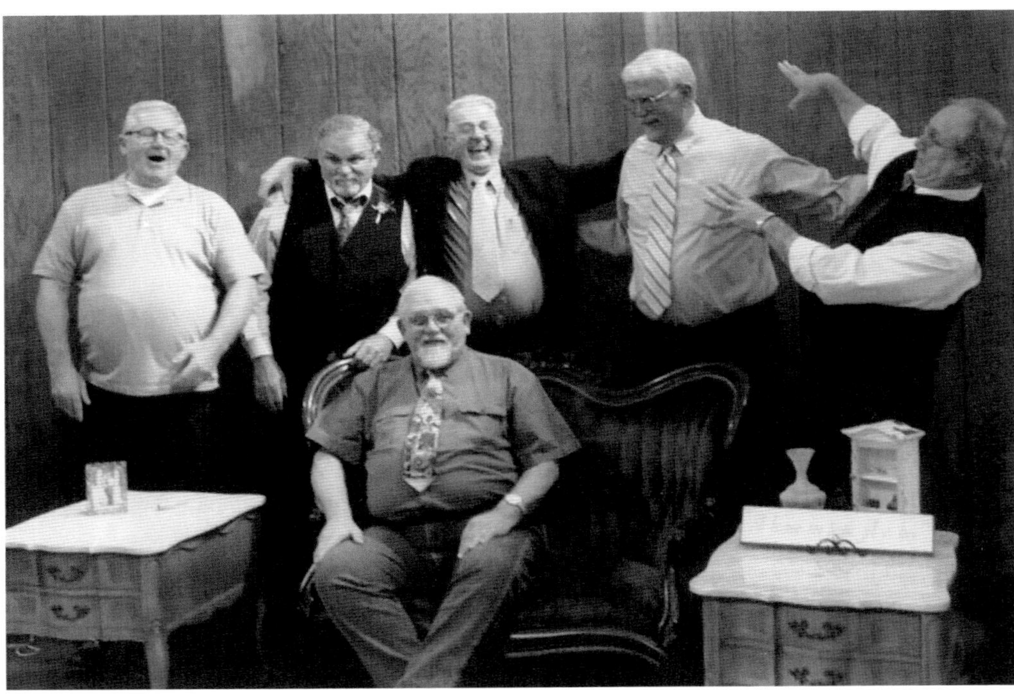

The Turner Boys

Ben L. Turner Sr. and his wife, Lucy Kidwell Turner, raised seven gentle, fun-loving boys. Although they grew to be tall in stature, she gave them pet names. Seated in front is Michael "Tulip;" standing, from left to right, are Stephen "Pan Head," Benjamin, Dennis, Randolph "Rose," and Kenneth. Not shown is Lucian, now deceased. (Courtesy of the Turner family.)

Even Bing Does His Part

During World War II, children collected scrap to help with the war effort. This 1944 photograph of a neighborhood scrap drive was taken near the Chrisman home at 266 Decatur Street. Kneeling in front is Charlie Peasely, and standing from left to right are Larry Giffin, Bing the dog, Joyce Chrisman (partially hidden), Charlie Kinzer, and Jerry Chrisman. (Courtesy of Kurt Cook.)

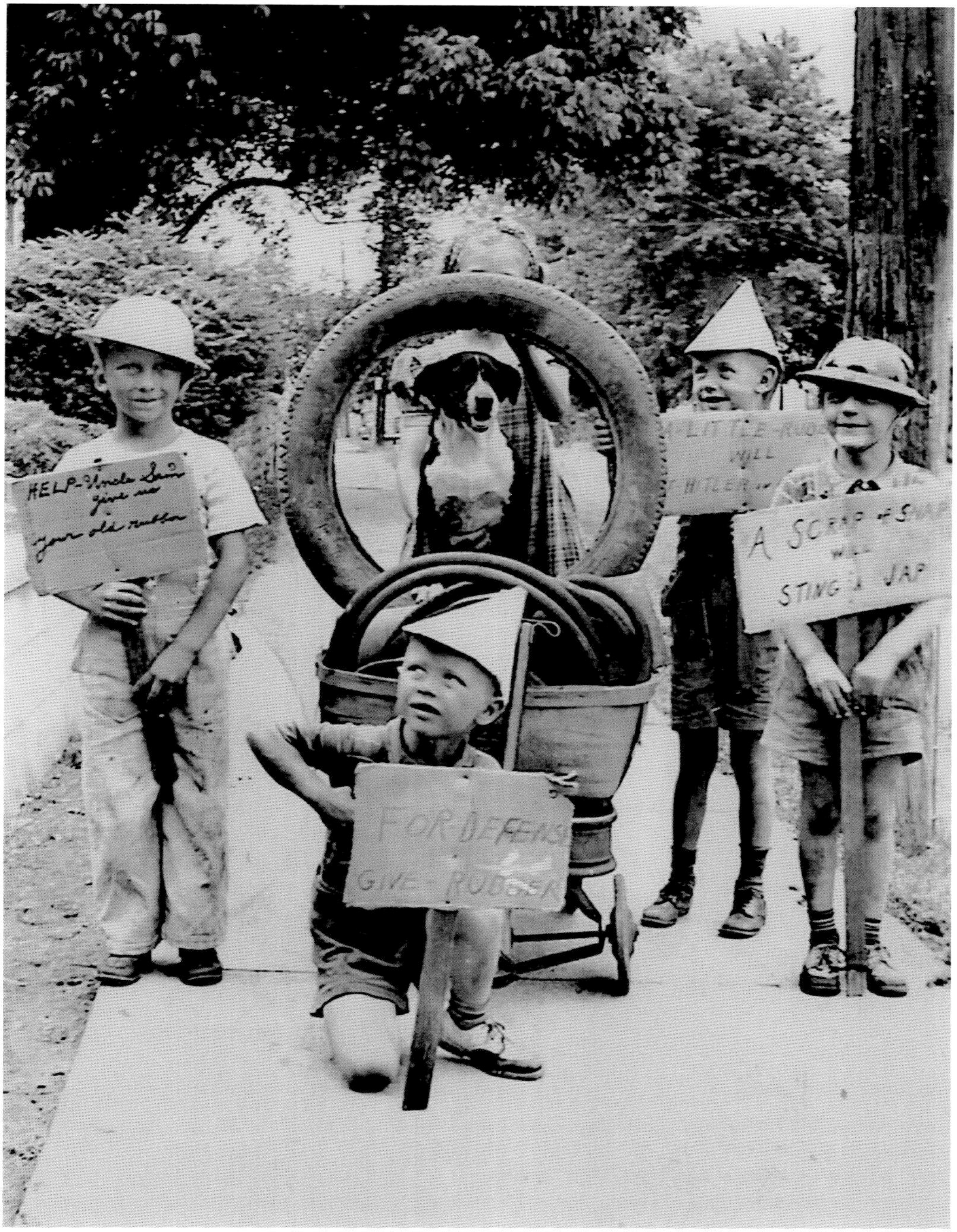

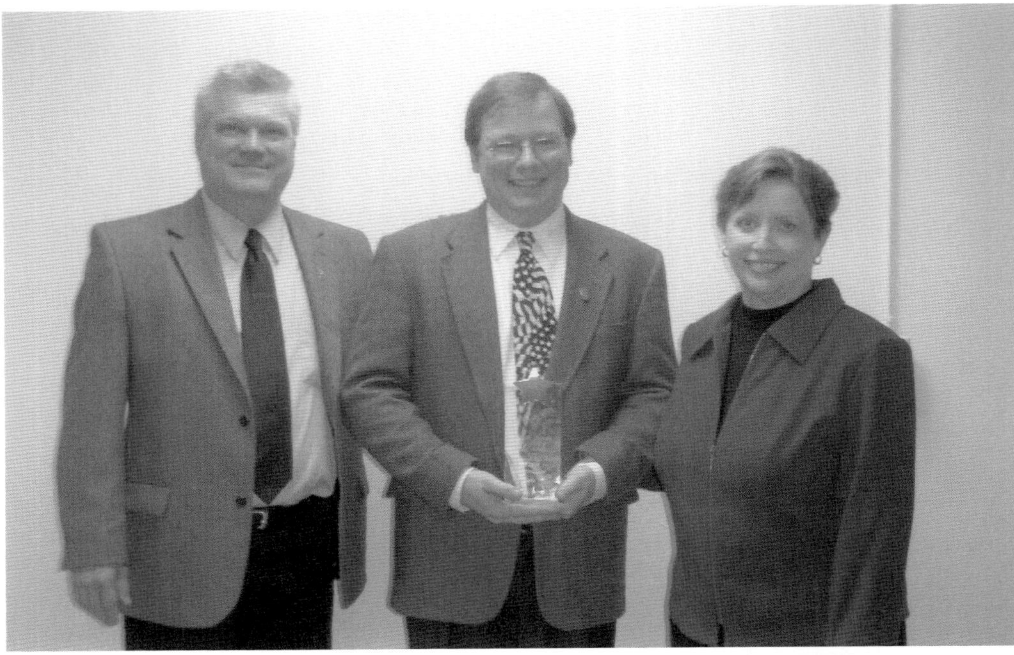

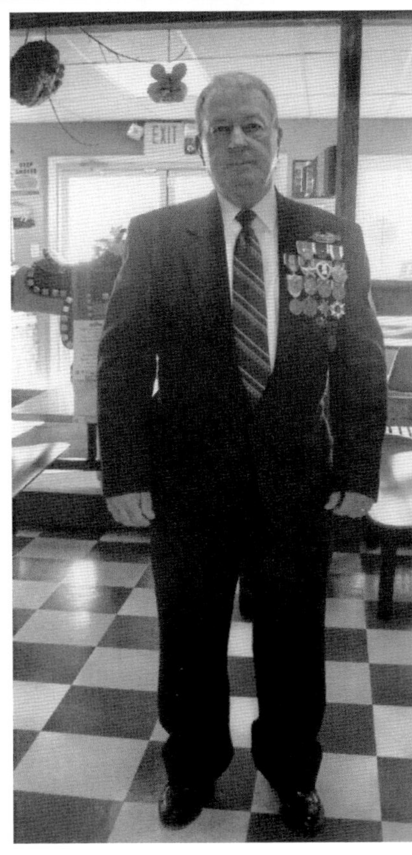

Main Street Aurora
The Aurora mayor works closely with the nonprofit Main Street, promoting businesses and events. Shown here are Donnie Hastings Jr. (left), the city's 44th mayor, Dr. Matthew B. Probst (center), president of Main Street Aurora and regional dean of Ivy Tech Community College, and Karla Fry Schmeltzer, executive director of Main Street Aurora. These individuals work hard to make sure that Aurora is putting its best foot forward. Mayor Hastings and Schmeltzer were raised in Aurora. Probst is the grandson of milkman Eddie Probst and the son of Rick. He attended high school in Hawaii while his dad was in the service, then moved back to Aurora. He received his bachelor's degree from Indiana University, his masters from Xavier University, and his doctor of philosophy degree from Capella University. (Courtesy of Main Street Aurora.)

Brave American
Do not let the quiet, demure bearing of Walter Bryant fool you. This brave American wears 15 medals on his chest and is one of the most decorated veterans in the area. Bryant served two tours in Vietnam, receiving three Bronze Stars for heroic deeds in action and two Purple Hearts. He tried to give one Purple Heart back; a mortar blew him into a foxhole and after a body check, he did not feel the injuries warranted a Purple Heart. (Courtesy of Jerry Bondurant.)

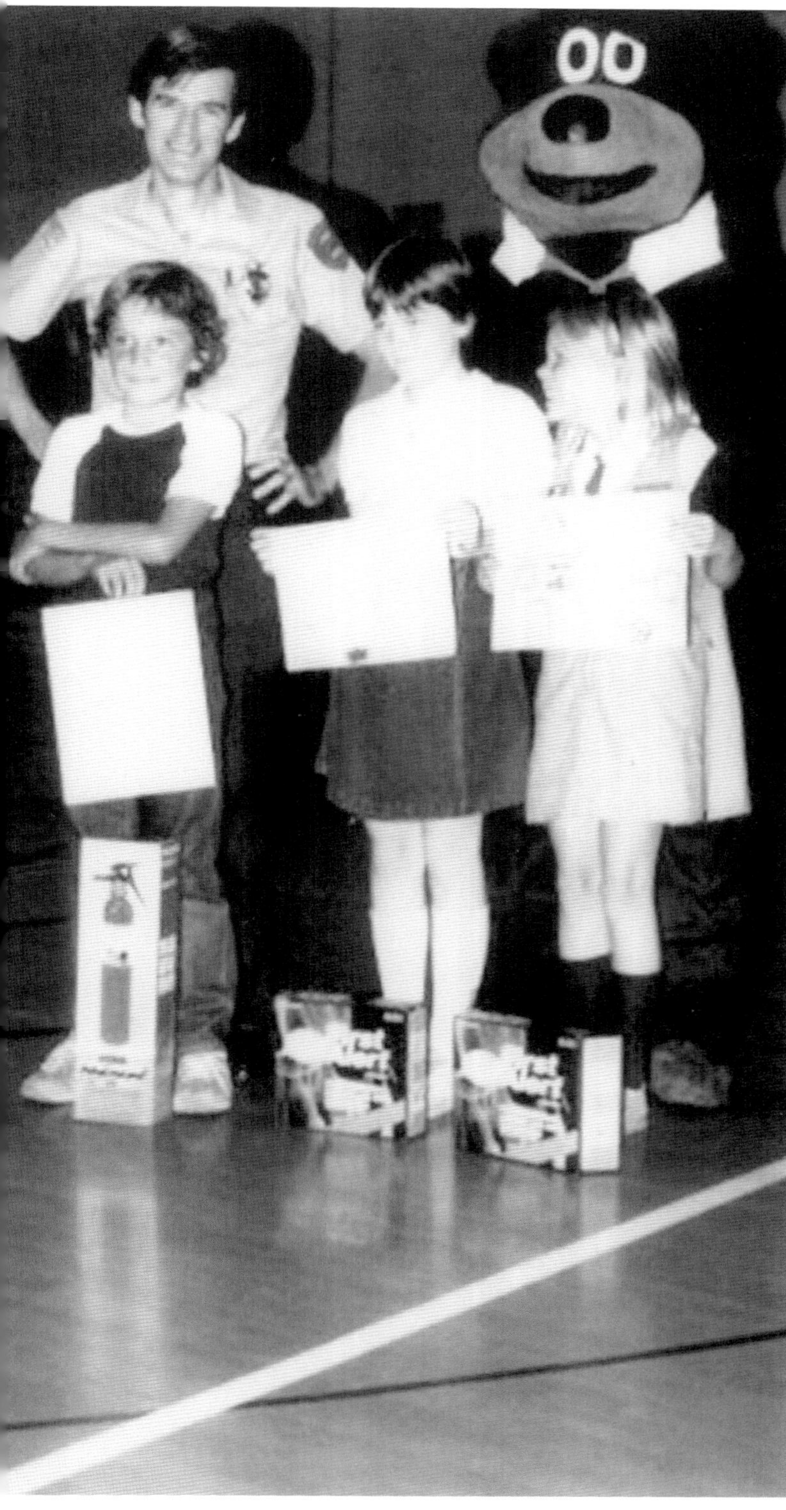

Fire Marshal Moses
Larry Moses was Aurora's first fire marshal. After the state made changes to civic titles, he became deputy chief. His primary responsibilities were fire prevention and fire investigation. He started a school fire-prevention program and sponsored poster contests in October during Fire Prevention Week. In addition to presenting school programs, he spoke to civic clubs, church groups, and anyone who would listen. (Courtesy of Larry Moses.)

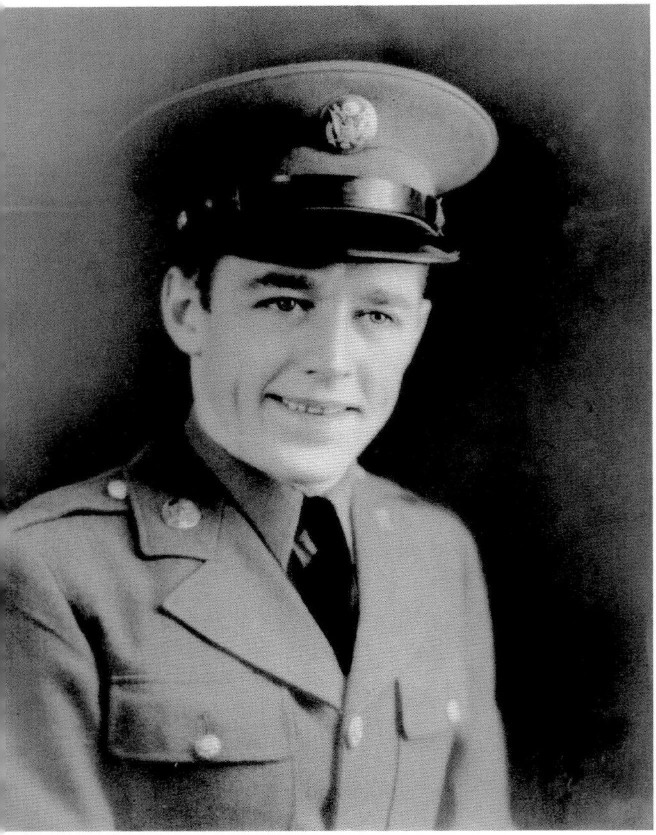

Lt. Harry "Gabby" McKain

McKain married Lucille Stierman in 1943. That September, McKain, a B-24 Liberator copilot, and his crew went missing when their plane went down. The plane was never recovered. His daughter Peggy was born just six months after his plane was lost. Lucille never remarried and would say, "We were married when he left, and we'll be married still when I'm gone." At Lucille's funeral, Peggy honored both parents' short time together on earth and celebrated their union in Heaven. (Courtesy of Peggy Lockwood.)

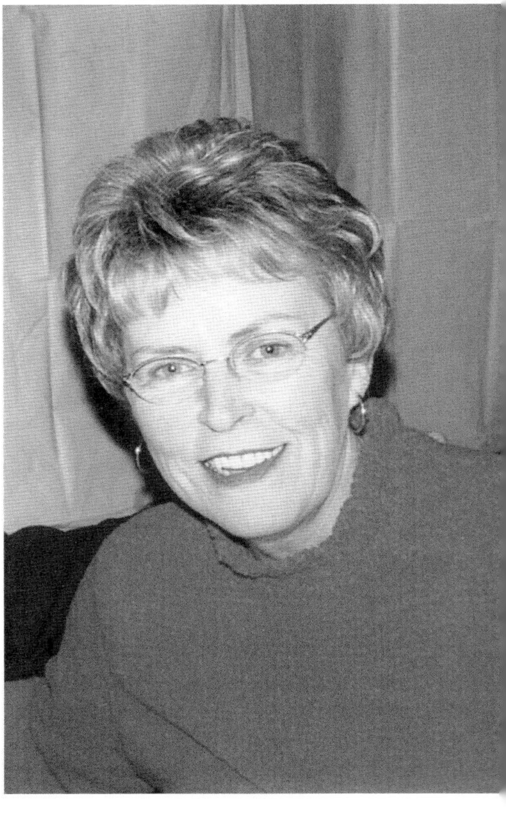

Peggy McKain Lockwood

Peggy, the daughter of Harry and Lucille McKain, was born after her father was killed in a World War II, B-24 plane crash. Because the plane was never recovered, Peggy has her DNA on file with the JPAC (Joint POW/MIA Accounting Command), which conducts global search, recovery, and laboratory operations that identify unaccounted-for Americans from past conflicts. Peggy is active in the AWON (American War Orphans Network) and prays for the day her father's plane will be found. (Courtesy of Peggy Lockwood.)

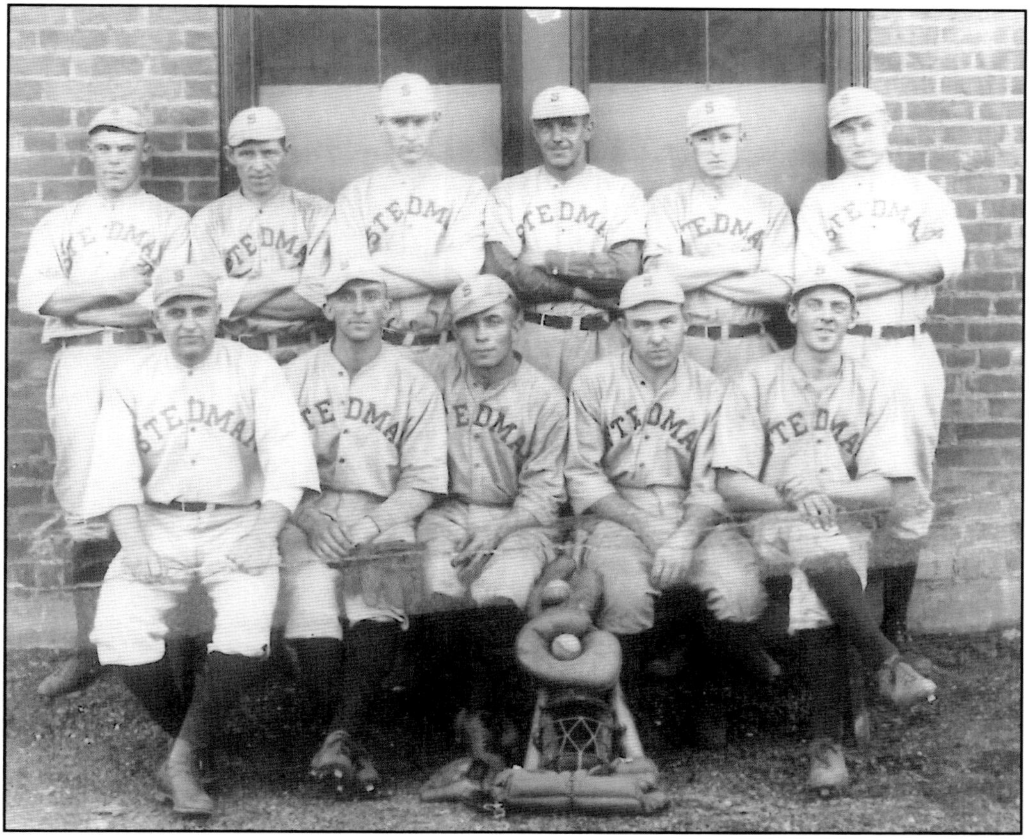

Stedman Baseball Team

Nathan Stedman (1814–1884) and Col. Pinkney James started Stedman Foundry in 1834. Shown in this 1920 photograph are, from left to right, (first row) Charles McClellan, Clayton Giffin, Earl Klingerhoffer, George Buffington, and Harry McKain; (second row) Louis Feustal, Louis Banschback, Clayton Meyers, Leonard Bauer, James Runyan, and Walter Rullman. (Courtesy of DCHS.)

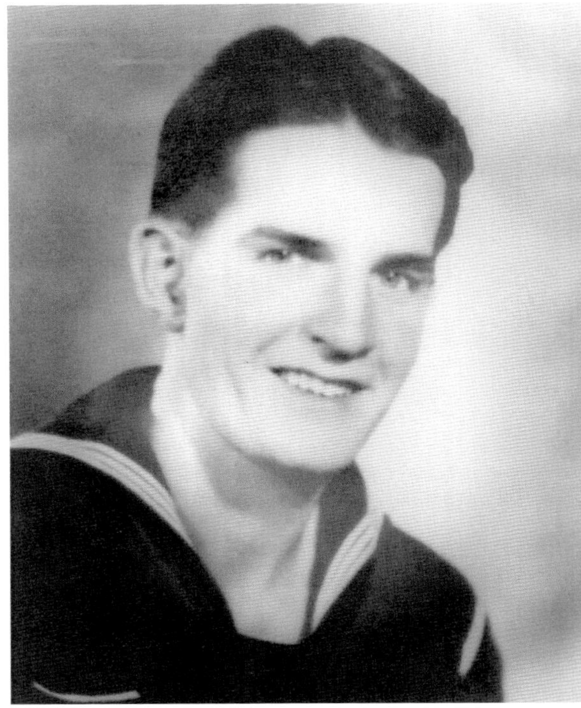

Emery Lee Nocks

Nocks (1922–1942) lived and attended high school in Aurora. He was killed onboard the Navy submarine USS *Bass* (SS-164) in World War II along with 24 others. The Emery Lee Nocks VFW Post 6582 honors him by bearing his name. (Courtesy of the Nocks family.)

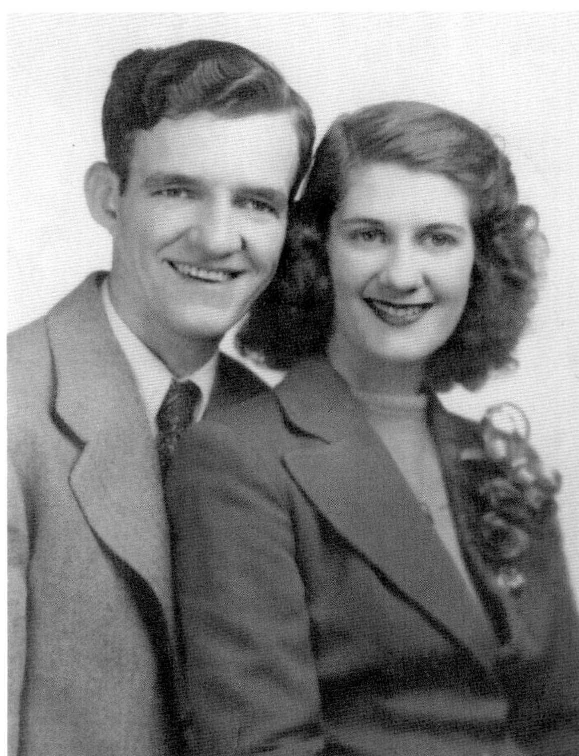

Jackie Nocks

Jackie Nocks (1926–1959) was a seaman, first class in the Navy, entering the service in November 1943. He served in the Pacific on LCT-1321 with amphibious forces operating in the Philippines. His son Peter Nocks is an active member and sits on the board of the Dearborn County Historical Society. Jackie is pictured here with his wife, Becky. (Courtesy of the Nocks family.)

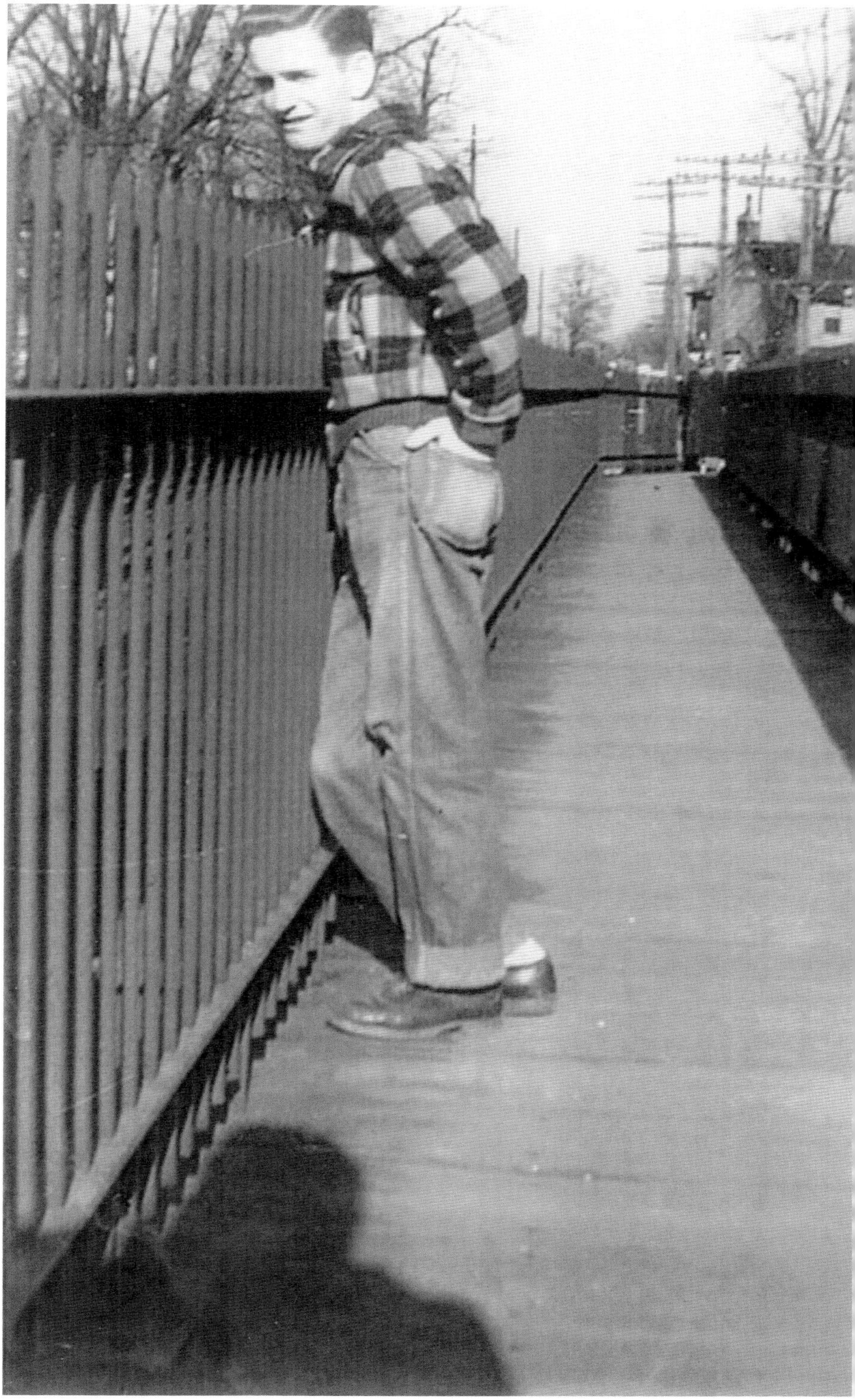

The Pig Chute
When Robert Nocks (pictured) stood on the "pig chute" in 1945, he was walking his sweetheart and future wife, Rose Wingate, home. The pig chute at one time ran along the railroad tracks that crossed Hogan Creek. At that time, there was no other way to cross to Green Boulevard. If one wanted to drive hogs to the railroad from Manchester, one had to get them across the creek. At one time, there were livestock holding pens at the north end of the chute. Imagine a first-grader's fear, making his or her first trip across the chute to get to school, with the creek 25 feet below. (Courtesy of the Nocks family.)

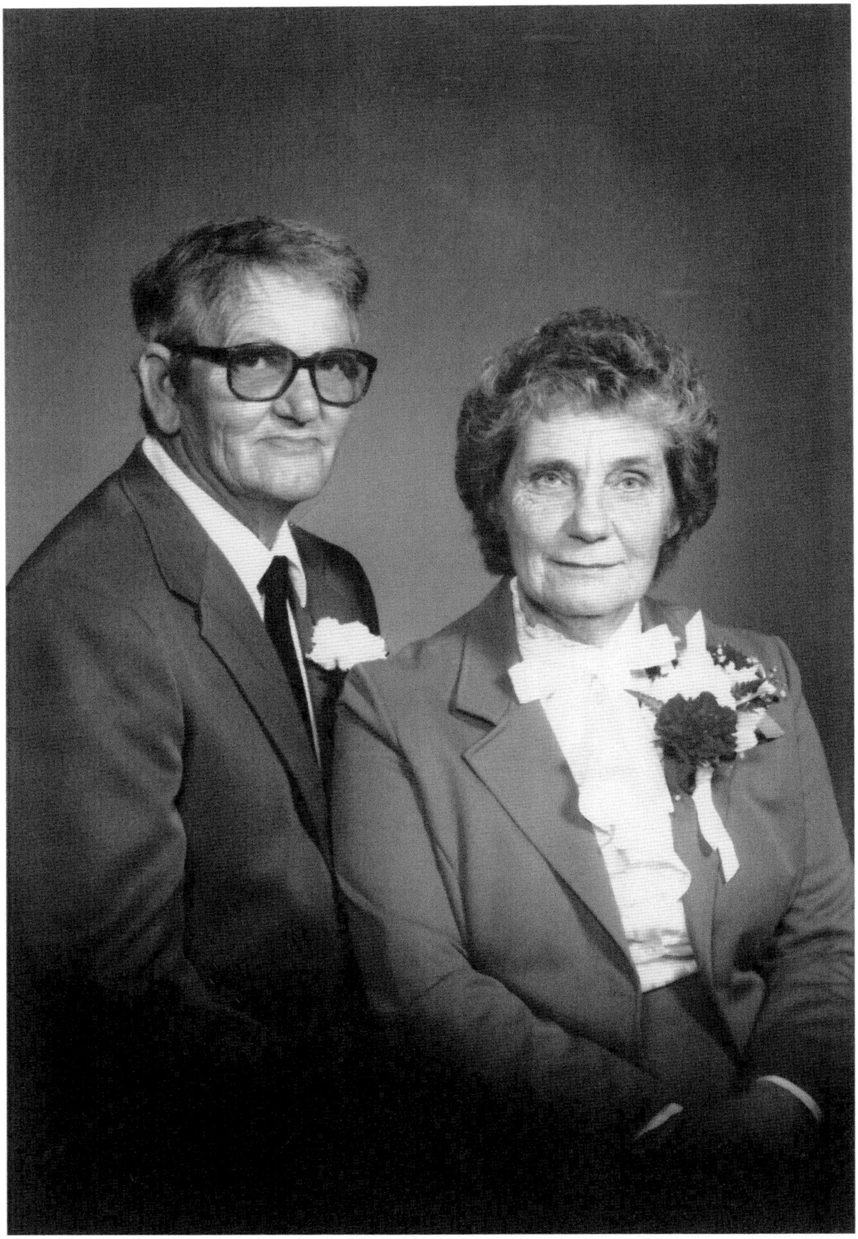

Ralph and Hazel Klueber

Ralph attended Aurora High School but never graduated. In 1972, he was the first city court judge in Aurora, handling approximately 400 cases each month. Hazel, his wife, worked at his side as court clerk. A court phone system was programmed to forward calls to his residence, and he would receive calls at all hours. He defeated candidates in three elections and was unopposed in his last two before his death in 1991. He was a volunteer firefighter for 32 years and served 10 years as Company No. 2 battalion chief. He was an auxiliary police officer for eight years and a member of the Knights of Columbus at St. Mary's Church. (Courtesy of Hazel Klueber.)

Clinton "Dutch" Ford

On March 21, 1967, fire raged through two frame buildings on George Street. Firefighter Clinton "Dutch" Ford, 63, suffered a heart attack while fighting the structure fire. At the time of his death, he had been a volunteer firefighter for 20 years. His wife was Marie, and he was a concrete contractor by trade. His granddaughter Connie (Carter) Lawless remembers him as an amazing man and followed him everywhere. He was her best friend and hero, and she thought he would be around to take care of her forever. He would stop by her house every morning and have breakfast with her, and he cried on Connie's first day of school. She was only six when her parents woke her up early one morning to tell her he had died that night fighting a fire. Lawless still talks to him every day in her prayers. Shown here in happier times are, from left to right, Ray Peters, Irene Peters, Patty (Peters) Carter, Dan Carter, Marie Ford, and Clinton "Dutch" Ford. (Courtesy of Dan Carter.)

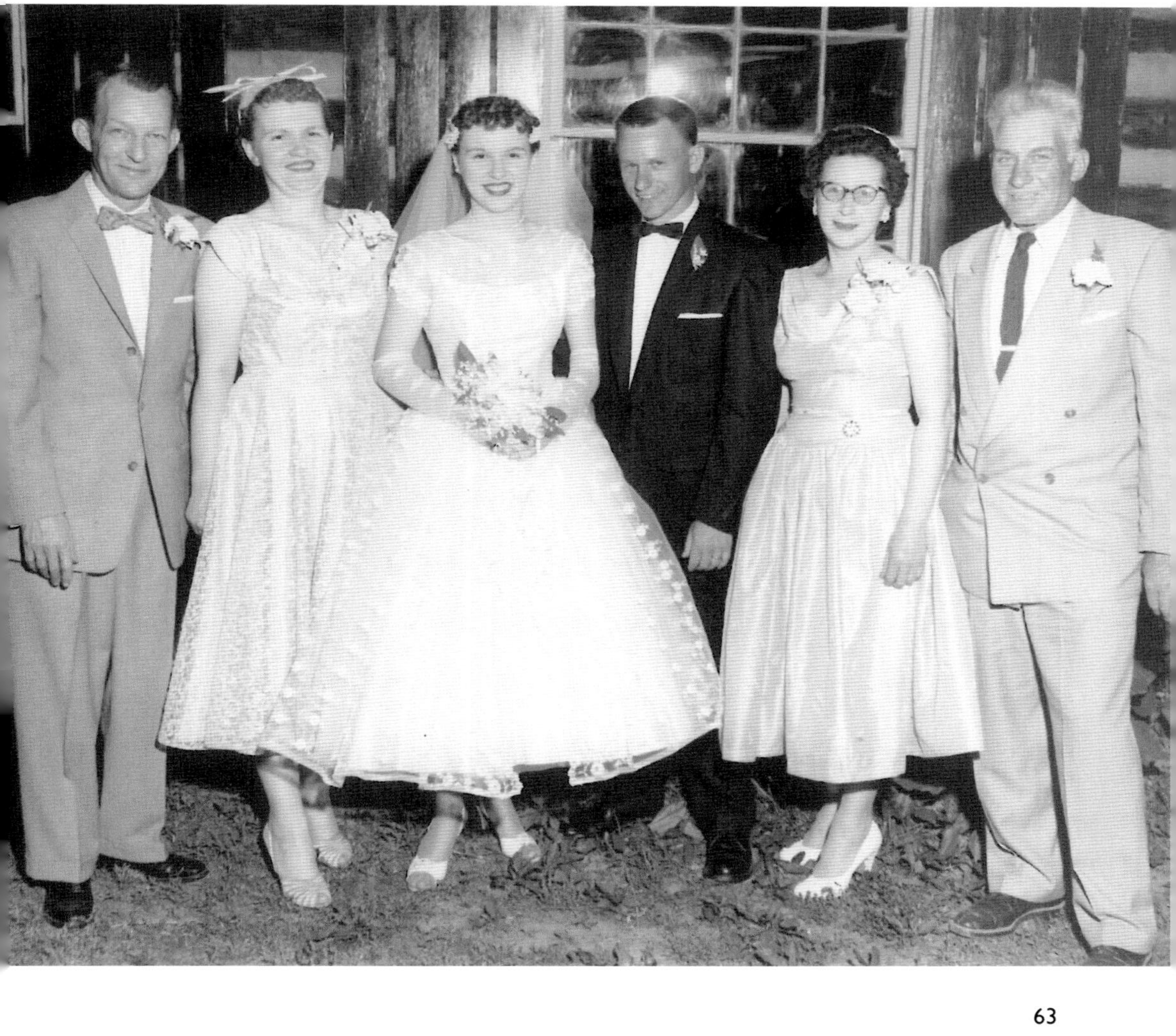

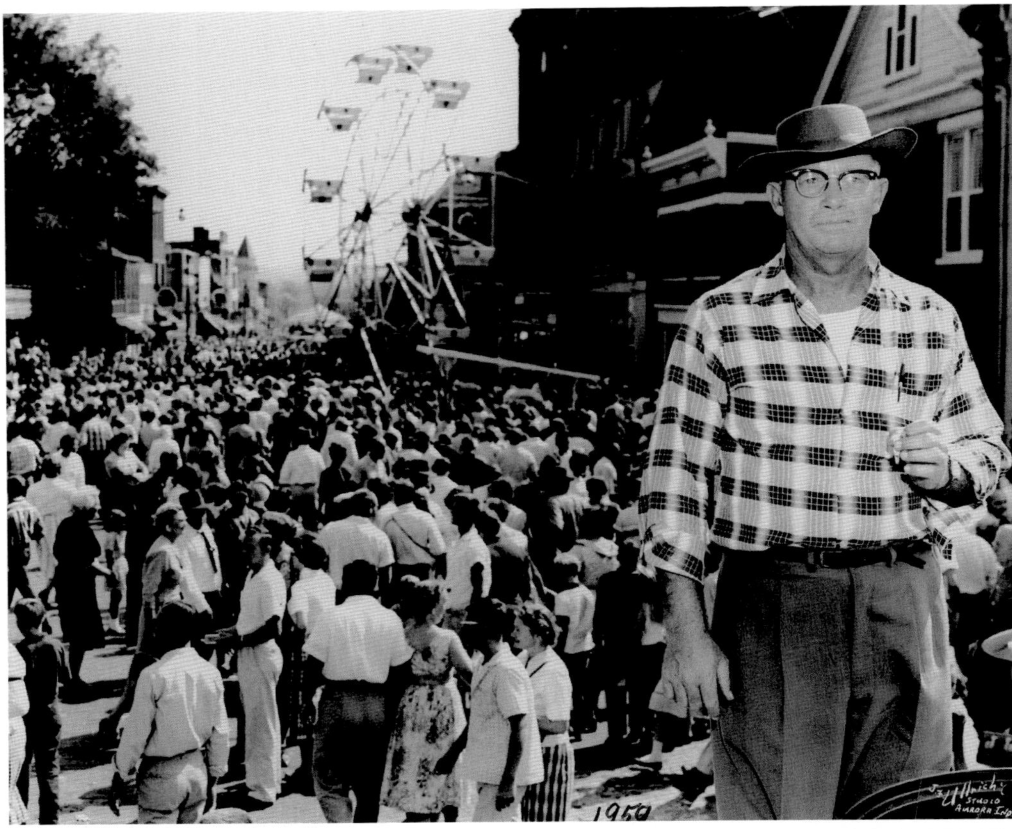

Harold "Pete" Stephenson

Stephenson (1915–1963) was battalion chief of Fire Company No. 1. He was fighting a house fire on Fourth Street when he was overcome with smoke. After being treated, he was taken home. The smoke aggravated a heart condition and Stephenson passed away several hours later. (Courtesy of the Ullrich family.)

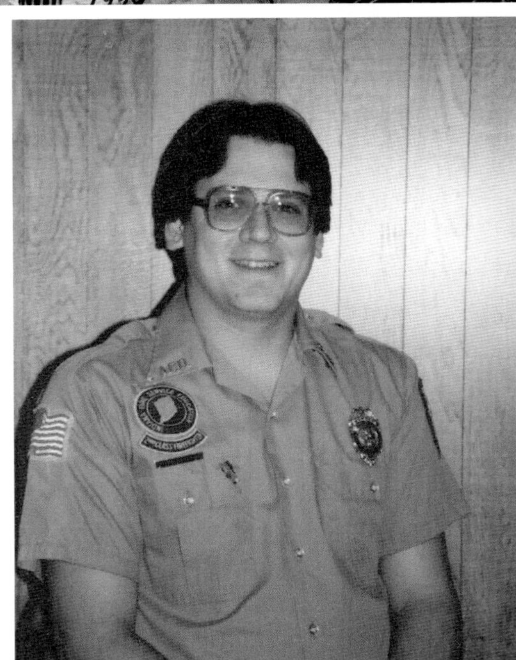

Jeff Reick

Safety Officer Jeff Reick was participating in a training session on April 1, 1998. He had been inside an abandoned house to start a small fire for training purposes. When he came out, he collapsed and went into cardiac arrest. He was immediately transported to University of Cincinnati Hospital, where he passed away the next day. He was a warehouse manager for the Aurora Casket Co. He is survived by his wife, Terry, and their two children, Ashley and Adam. (Courtesy of Larry Mason.)

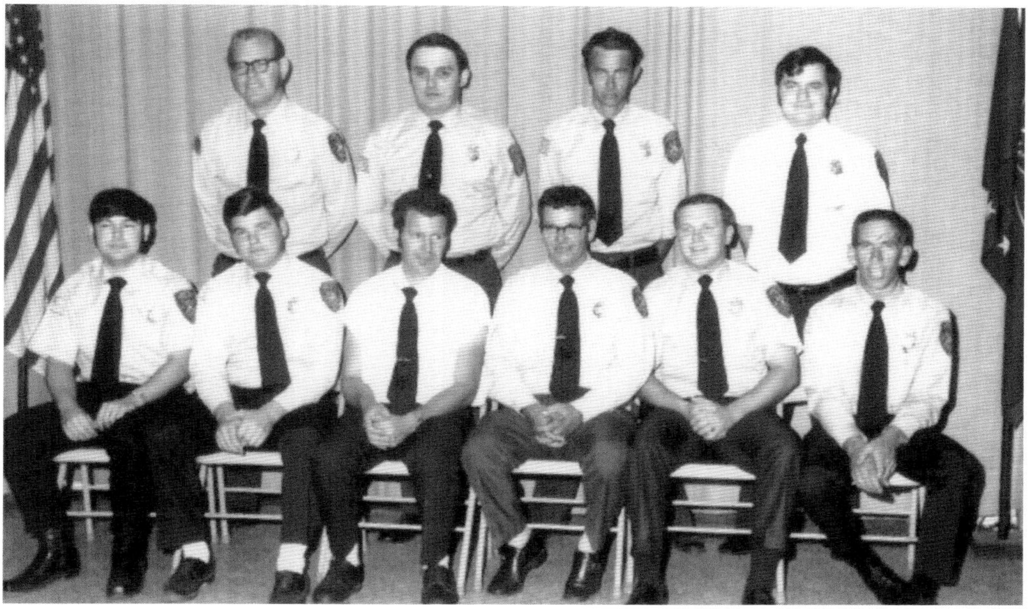

Aurora Fire Company No. 2

The brave volunteers of Fire Company No. 2 ran toward fires, not away from them. Shown here are, from left to right, (first row) William Doerr, James Sedler, Donald Bowling, Ralph Klueber, Basil Delay, and Fuzzy Meyer; (second row) Jerry Schmidt, Ken Turner, Donald Billingsly, and Snorky Harrell. This photograph was taken in the late 1960s. (Courtesy of Larry Moses.)

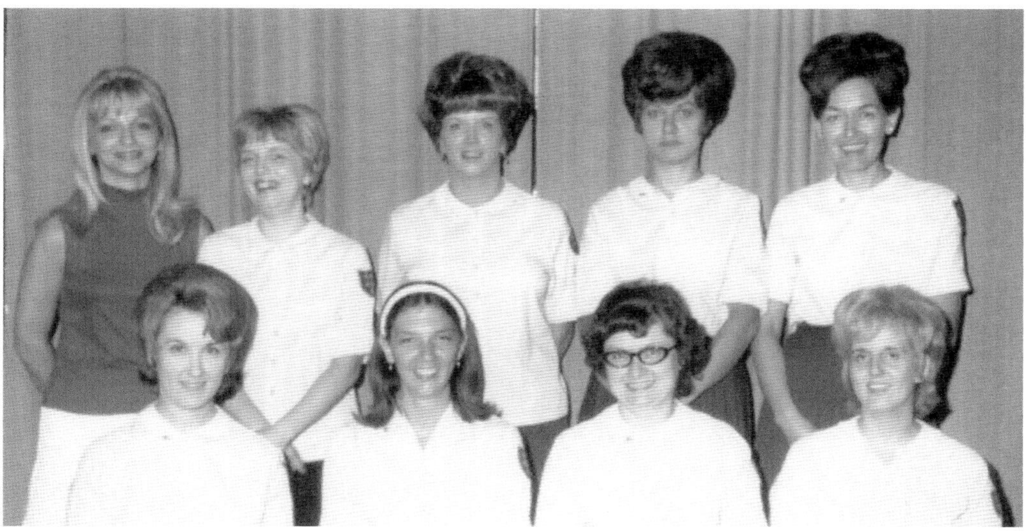

Ladies Auxiliary Company No. 2 Volunteers

The Ladies Auxiliary Company No. 2 volunteers were as brave as their husbands. Shown here are, from left to right, (first row) Karen Schmidt, Sue Turner, unidentified, and Glenda Harrel; (second row) Winnie Bowling, Geri Delay, Kay Meyer, Martha Sedler, and Betty Billingsley. This photograph was taken in the late 1960s. (Courtesy of Larry Moses.)

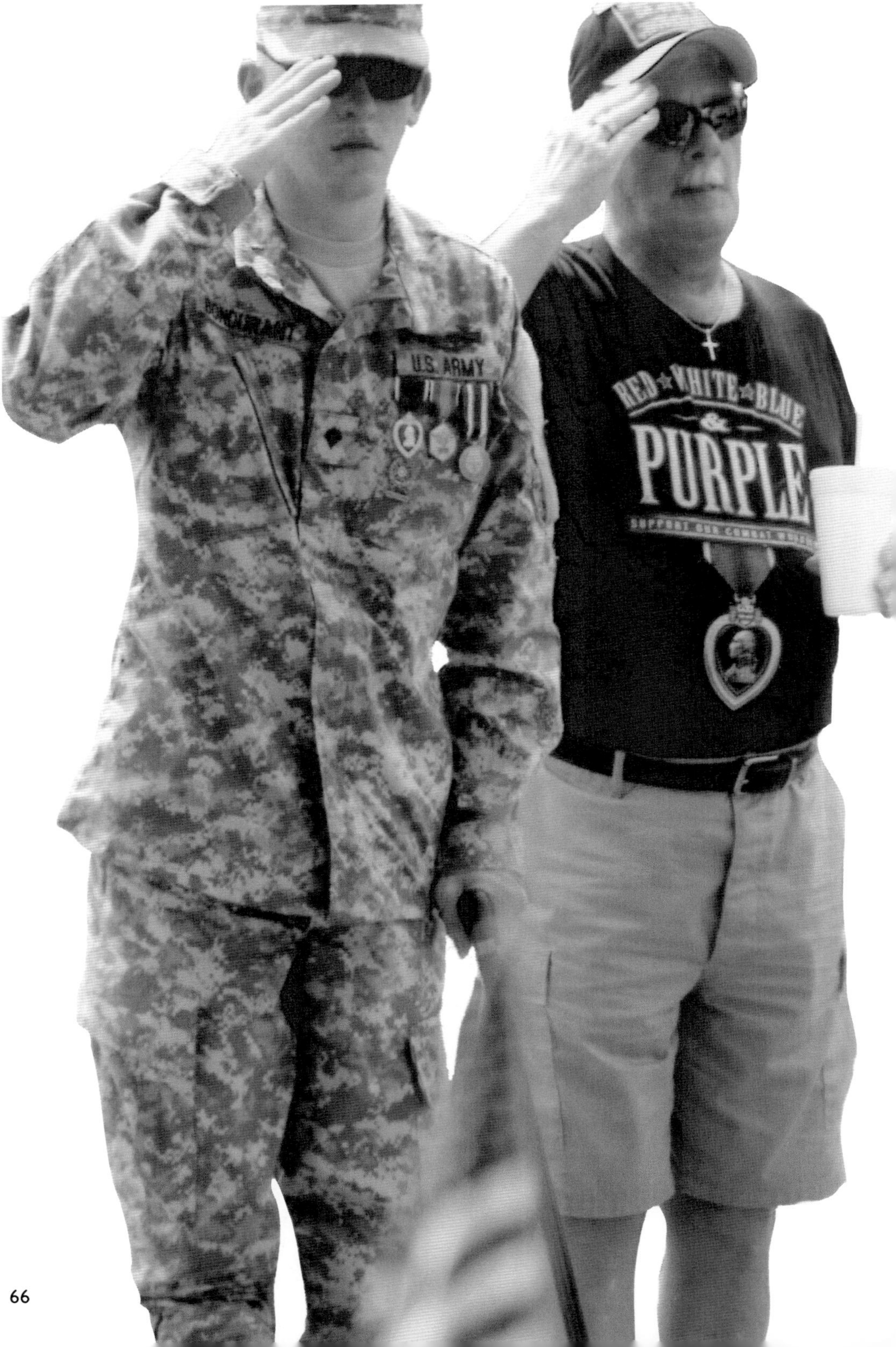
U.S. ARMY
RED WHITE BLUE
&
PURPLE

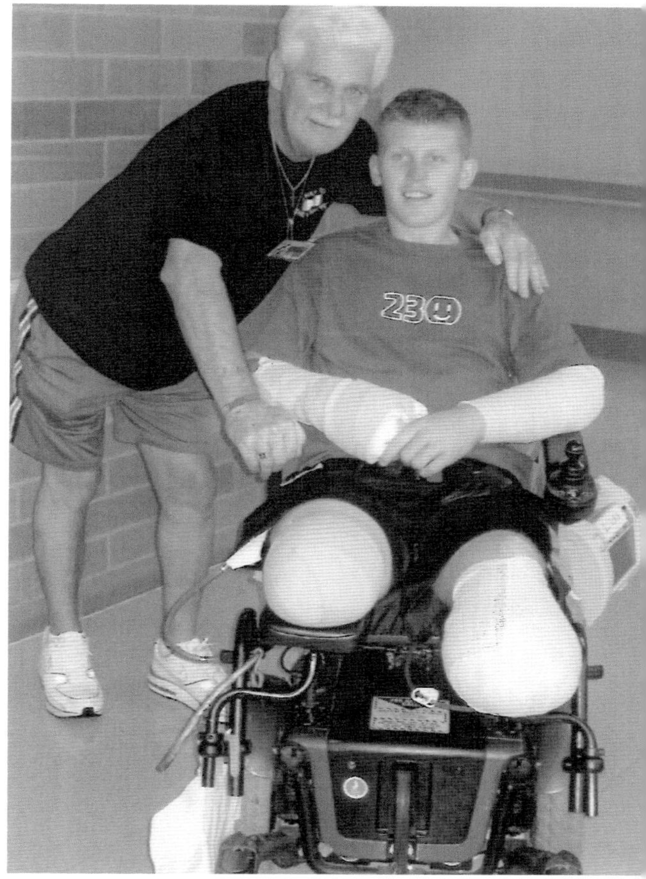

Pfc. Brett Bondurant

Pfc. Brett Bondurant (pictured opposite page and at right) has sacrificed much in his young life. On September 28, 2011, Bondurant was injured in an explosion of an improvised explosive device (IED) near the town of Mushan, east of Kandahar, Afghanistan. Bondurant survived but lost both legs and suffered burns. Bondurant continues to rehabilitate in the military and is involved in the Wounded Warrior Project. He also plays a mean game of wheelchair basketball. Proud grandfather Jerry Bondurant (pictured opposite page and at right) was there for Brett's first steps as a child and is once again helping him walk, now as a man. Together, they placed a wreath on the Tomb of the Unknown Soldier (below) and attend funerals in support of fallen comrades. Despite the cheers and applause he receives wherever he goes, Bondurant does not consider himself a hero. He calls his condition a "small injury." "Heroes are the ones that don't make it home," says Bondurant. (All courtesy of Jerry Bondurant.)

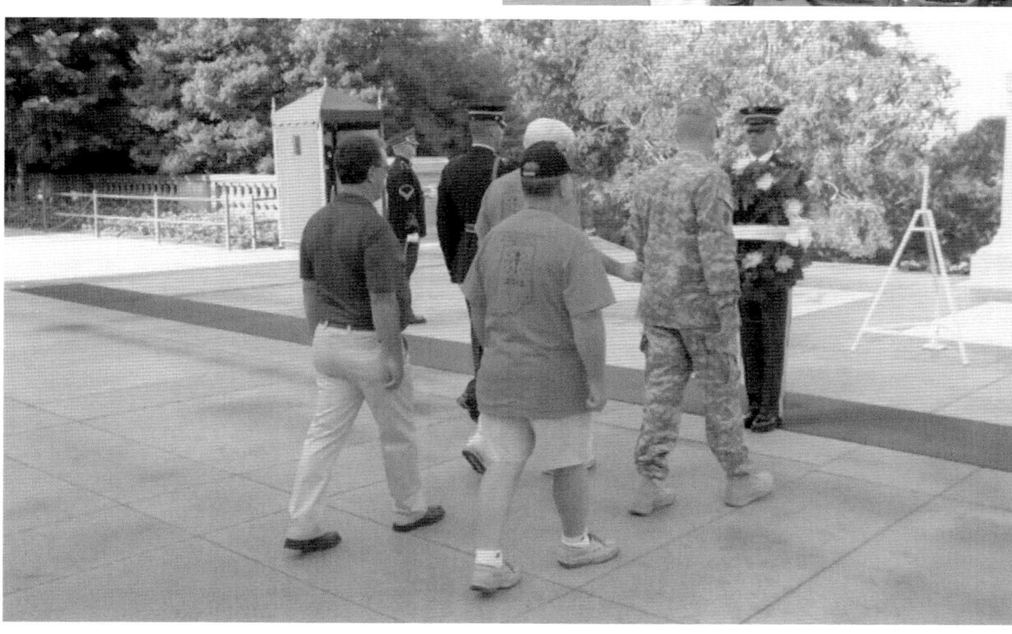

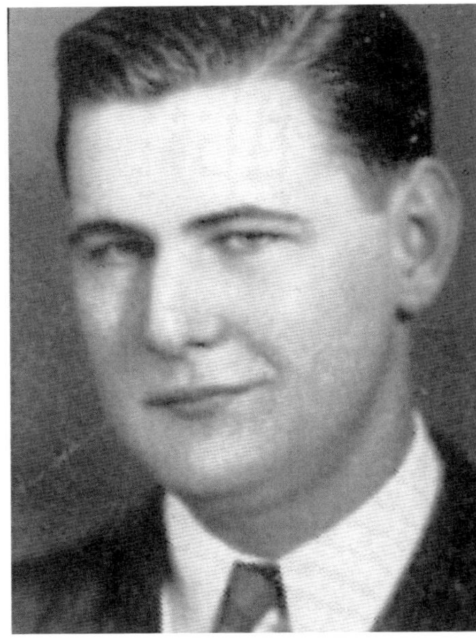

Frank Hill

Frank Hill graduated in 1938 and joined the Marines. On February 24, the Marines secured Mount Suribachi on Iwo Jima. One of the soldiers in the famous flag-raising photograph on Mount Suribachi is Ira Hayes, a Pima Indian from Arizona. The iconic image became a symbol of the battle and hope for Americans. In 1955, Hill received orders to be part of a detail at Hayes's funeral service. Hayes had never been comfortable with his newfound fame, and after his honorable discharge from the Marine Corps, he descended into alcoholism. When he died at the age of 32, he no longer had a uniform, and his family asked that he be buried in one. Without a second thought, Frank Hill gave the fellow Marine his uniform. Ira Hayes was buried with full military honors in Arlington National Cemetery. (Courtesy of Peggy Lockwood.)

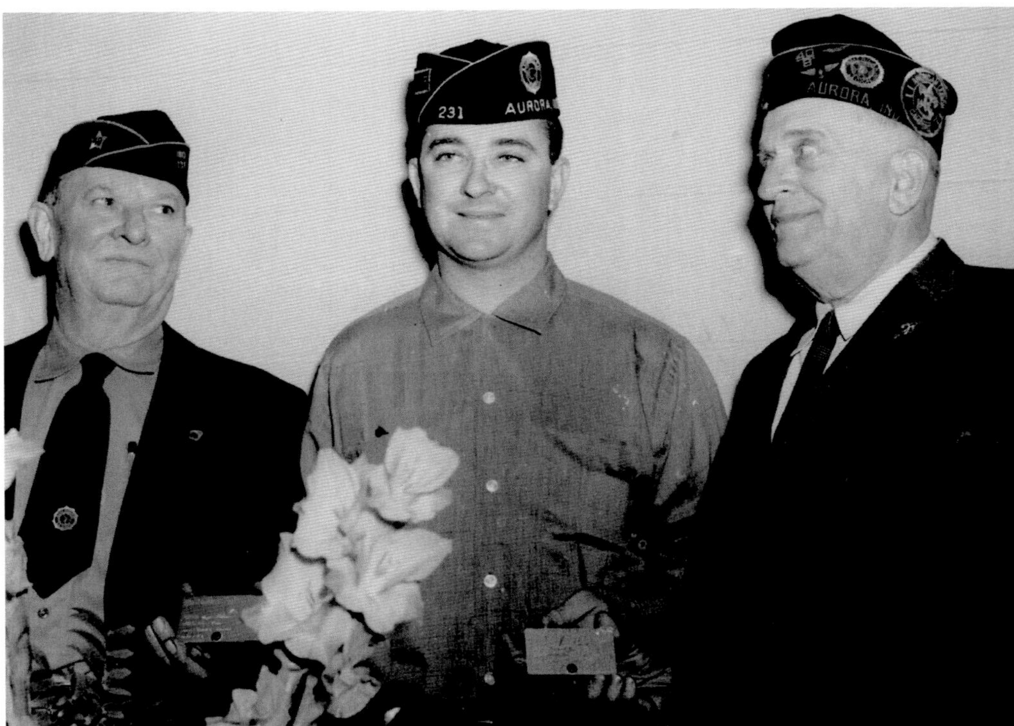

Denton Opp

In the early 1960s, Aurora Post 231 was active in World War I veterans' rights. Shown are, from left to right, Bryan Houston, Herschell Kent, and Denton Opp. Opp, represented Indiana World War I veterans in Washington, DC, asking Congress to increase pension pay to veterans to $102 a month. (Courtesy of DCHS.)

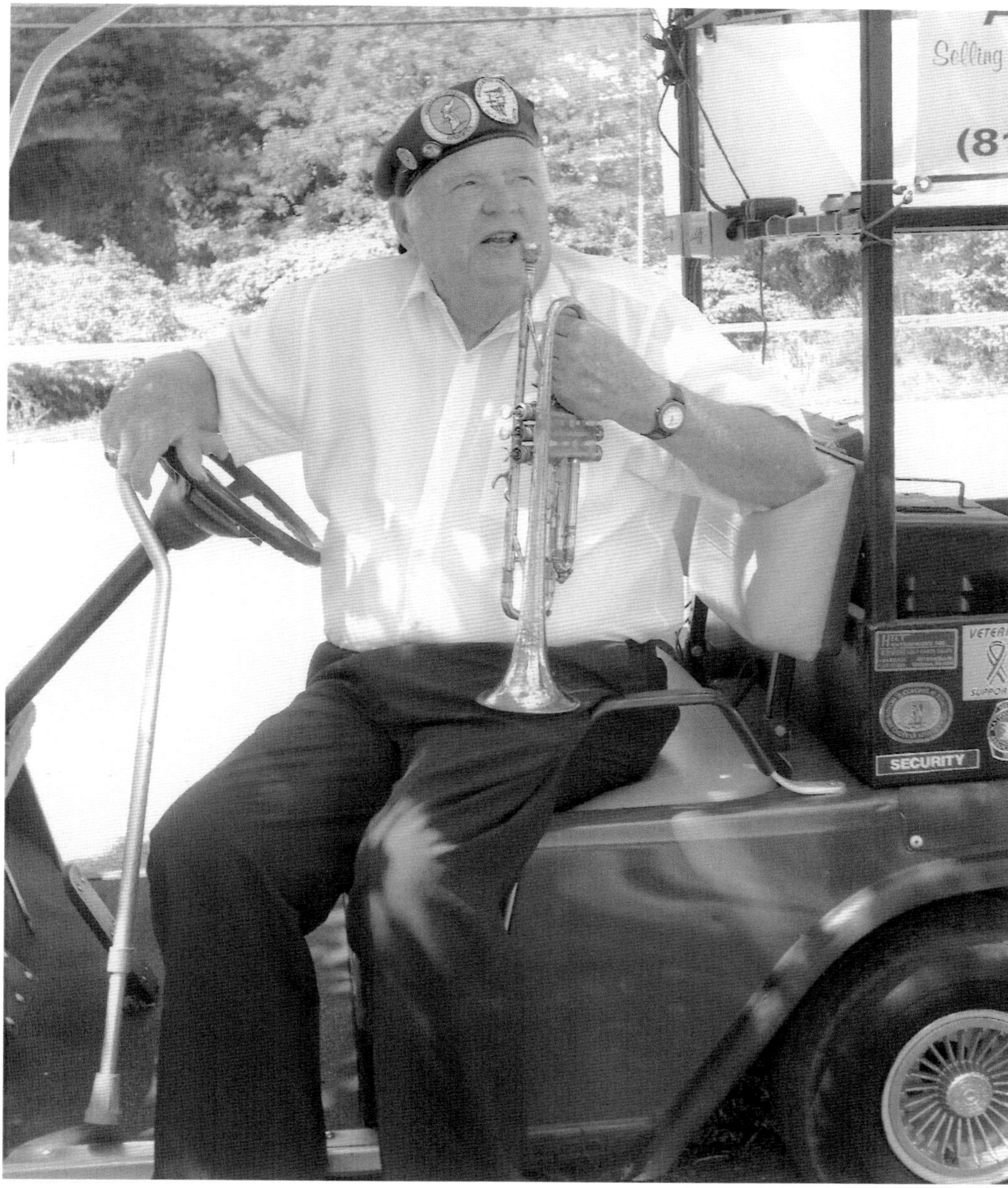

Nelson Elliott

Nelson Elliott still plays the trumpet his mother bought him. His son Paul Elliott recently asked him to write out his life resume, which came to over six pages. He was born on May 28, 1938, to Aaron and Miriam Elliott. After graduating from college, he began teaching music and playing trumpet in various big bands. He married Marcia Ann Ewing in 1960. His stage presence and booming voice makes him the perfect emcee for any event. He is a real-estate appraiser and auctioneer and has had his own talk show on a local television channel. Although he was never in the military, he has received special recognition from various military groups for his playing of "Taps" at military funerals beginning in 1955. In 2007, he received the "Citizen of the Year" award from the Dearborn County 4-H and Community Fair Board. His life resume's top honors are his wife, children, and grandchildren. (Author's collection.)

Esther Wilson Roache

Esther (1896–1982) is recognized for her efforts to save Hillforest in 1956. She worked tirelessly to authentically restore the house and to furnish it with appropriate artifacts. She graduated from Indiana University and followed the business path of her father, Clarence B. Wilson, by taking up banking at the Aurora State Bank. Esther and her husband, Frederick W. Roache, were also involved in numerous church and civic efforts. (Courtesy of Hillforest Foundation.)

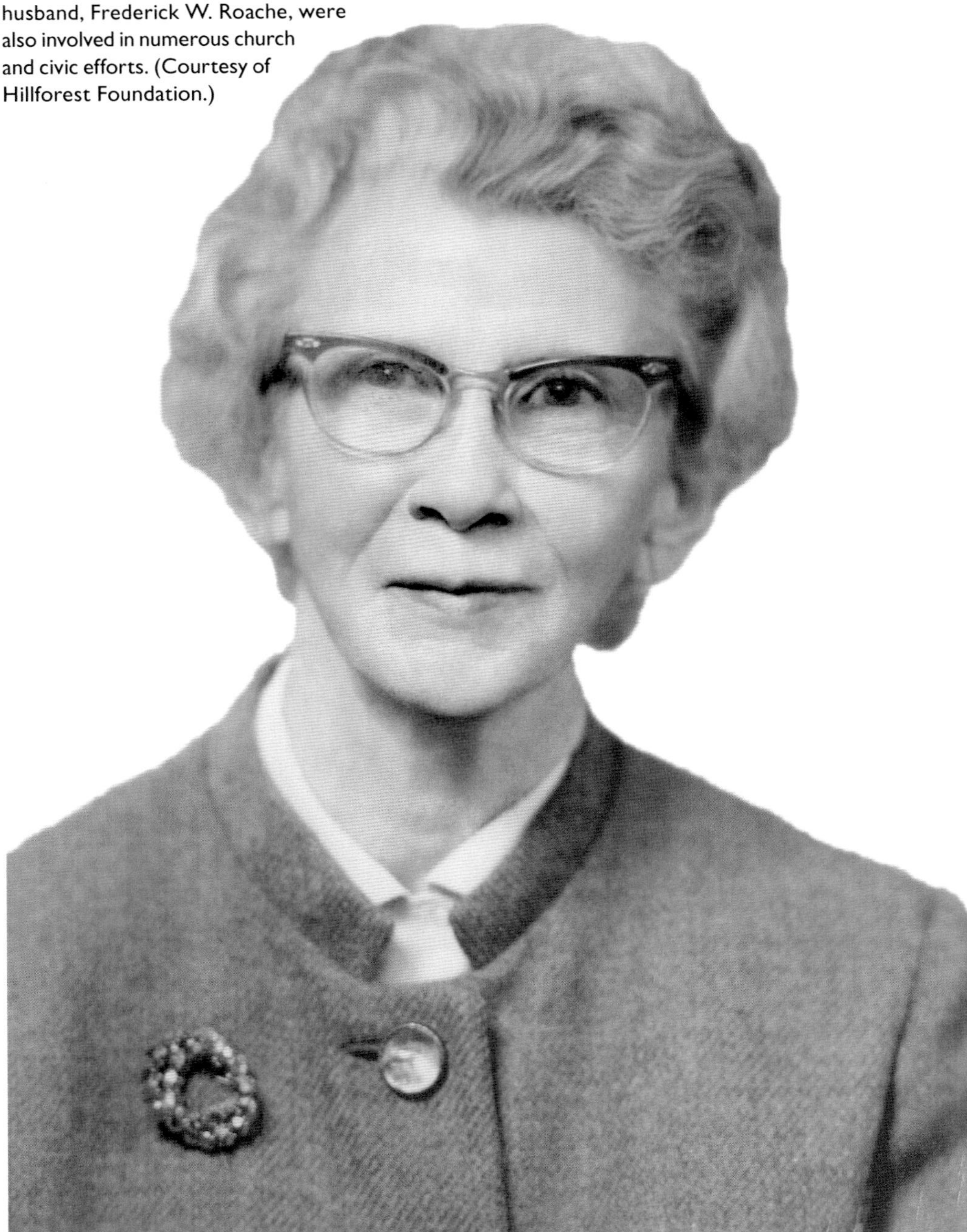

CHAPTER FOUR

Community Legends

A community legend may be someone of note, a local celebrity with larger-than-life accomplishments whose fame is well known. When living in a small town, however, a legend may be one's neighbor, and every neighbor has a story to tell. Today, the train no longer stops at the depot, and sometimes it is hard to remember the way things were.

Different groups, such as Aurora Historic Preservation, seek to preserve, conserve, and protect buildings, objects, landscapes, or other artifacts of historical significance in the Aurora historic district. The city's stone walls and limestone gutters are just a sample of pioneer ingenuity, attempts to control water coming off the hills. The city's stewardship of historic properties in their control allows future generations to experience its history.

To this day, people meet at coffee shops for breakfast, to swap stories and stretch the truth, just as they did more than 100 years ago at Ullrich's Drug Store. The next group of photographs tells a story of people who are part of the community—going to church, working every day, and enjoying living with other community legends.

Curtis Chipman Sr.

Chipman was 76-and-half years old and was still doing what he loved—welding and fixing things for people—up to within three months of his death. He was married to Geneva Walker for 53 years, and they had seven children. He was considered the area's "go to" man if one needed something welded. No job was too small or too large. Chipman is shown in the below photograph replacing the floor of the iron bridge over Hogan Creek. He worked at Seagrams for 40-and-a-half years, retiring at the age of 65. (Courtesy of Larry Moses.)

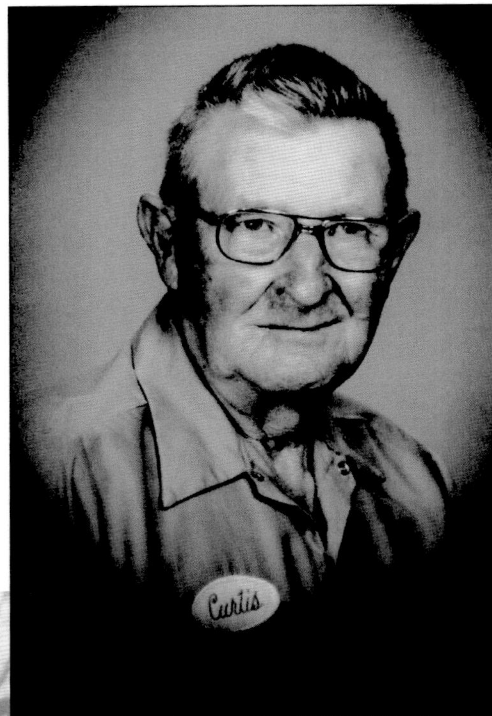

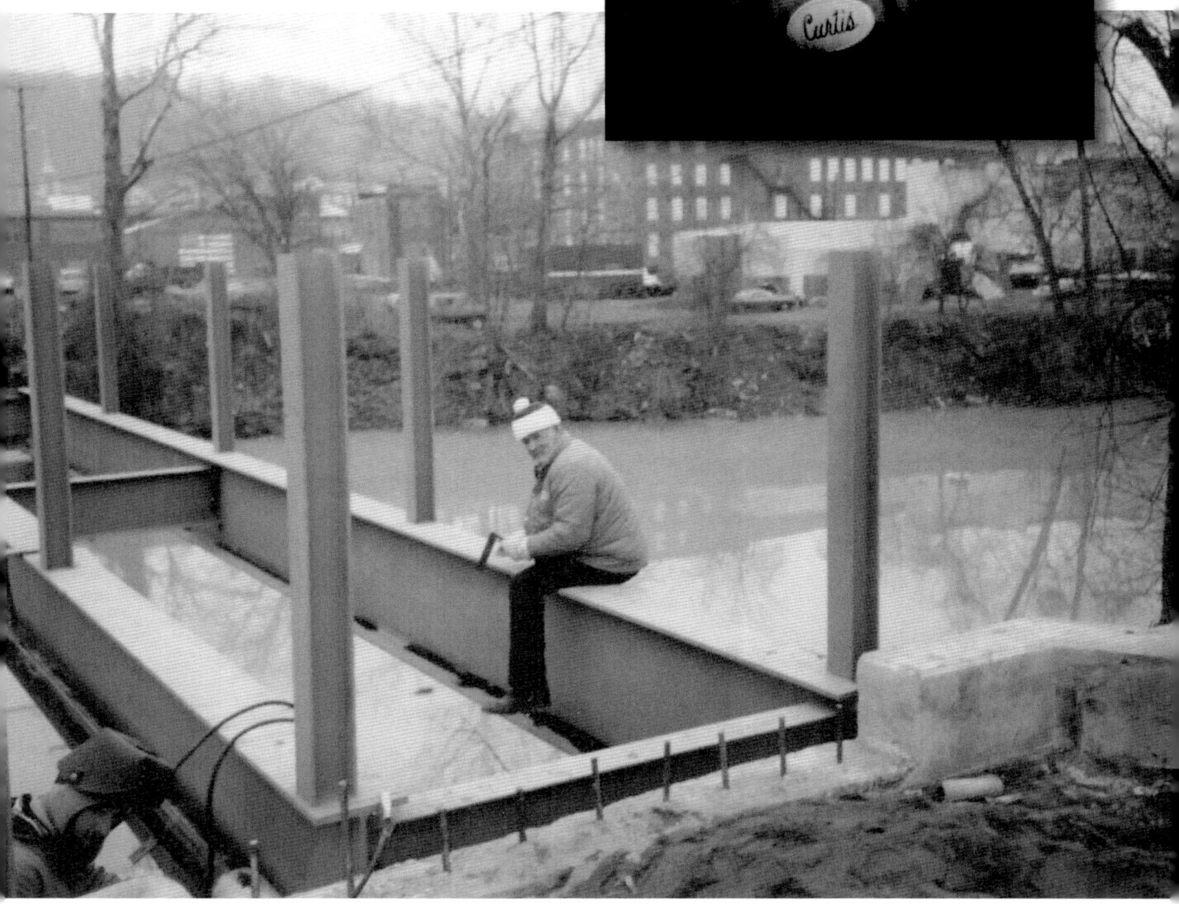

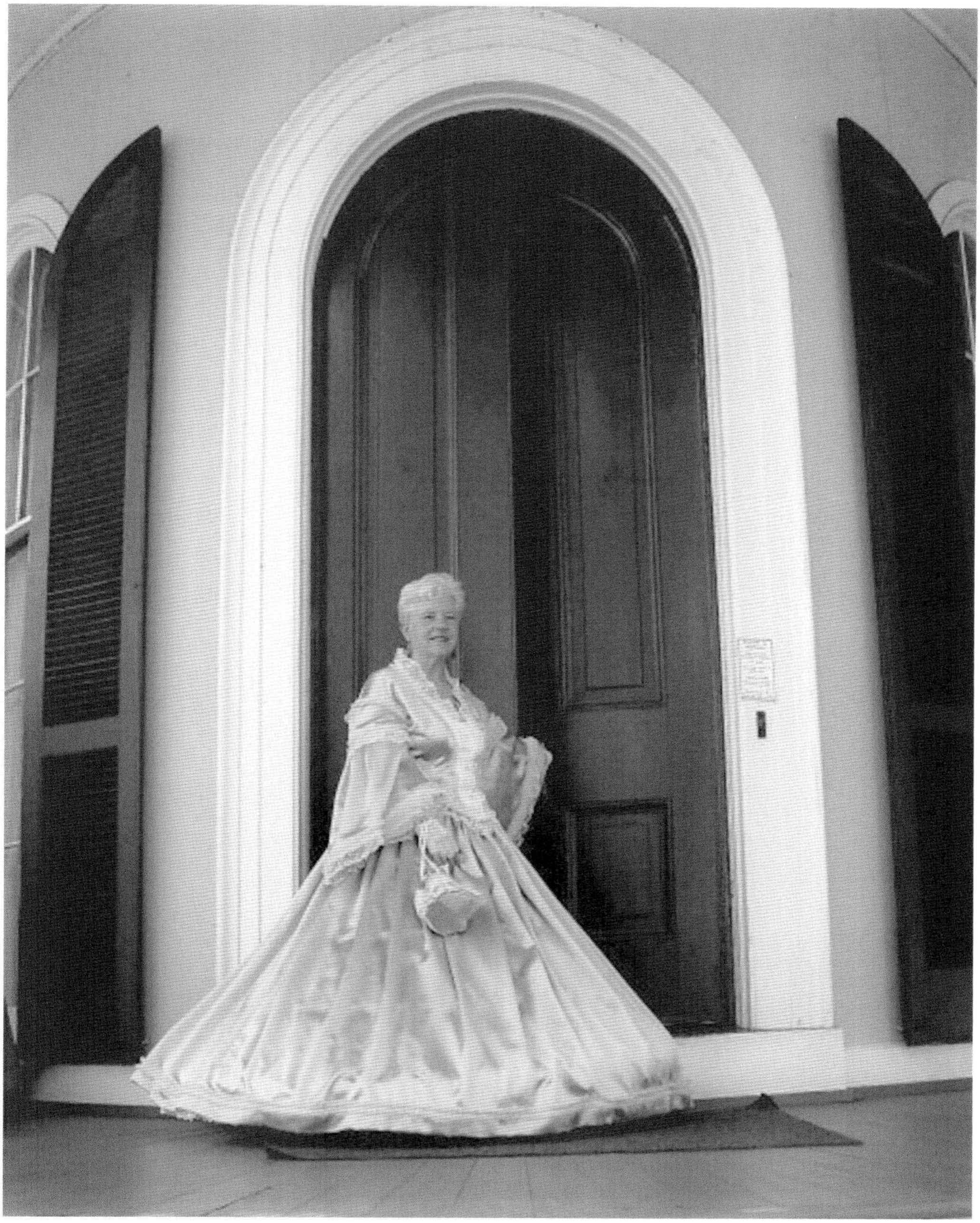

Suzanne (Schuler) Ullrich

Suzanne poses in period costume at the front doors of Hillforest House Museum. When she married her husband, Richard, she threw her wedding bouquet from the mansion's entrance balcony. She is the docent and volunteer coordinator at Hillforest House Museum and gives of her time for the betterment of Aurora. Suzanne studied at Edgecliff College of Xavier University. After teaching school for several years, she joined Richard at the Ullrich Drug Store. Suzanne works hard to preserve her family's rich heritage in Aurora. (Courtesy of the Hillforest Foundation.)

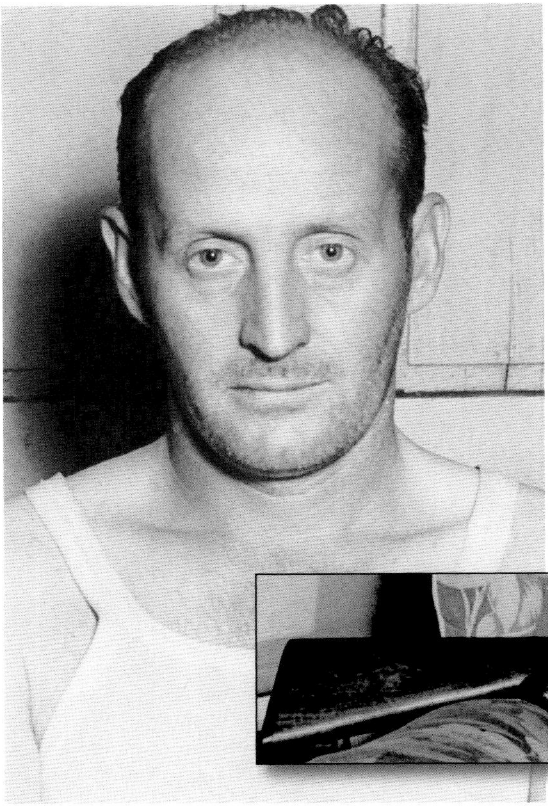

Virginius "Dink" Carter

It may have been Aurora's crime of the century. On May 16, 1941, Virginius "Dink" Carter (1908–1942) shot and killed five members of his wife's family outside of Aurora. The victims were Johnson Agrue, 59; his wife, Nina, 64; their sons Will, 33, and Leo, 23; and granddaughter, Mary Breeden, 12. Carter's wife, Leona, was a twin to Leo and not at the farm at the time.

After he shot Nina in the kitchen, the little girl tried to run away. In the photograph on the opposite page, an "X" marks the spot where Mary's body was found outside the barn.

Carter (pictured at left) hitchhiked back to Aurora, where at some point his father found him, and he told him about the murders. The

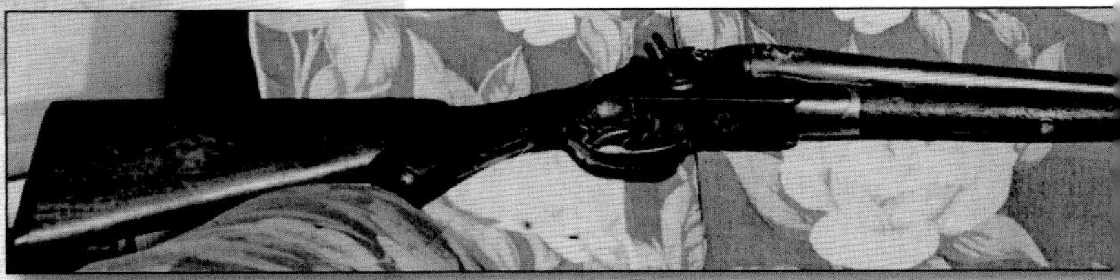

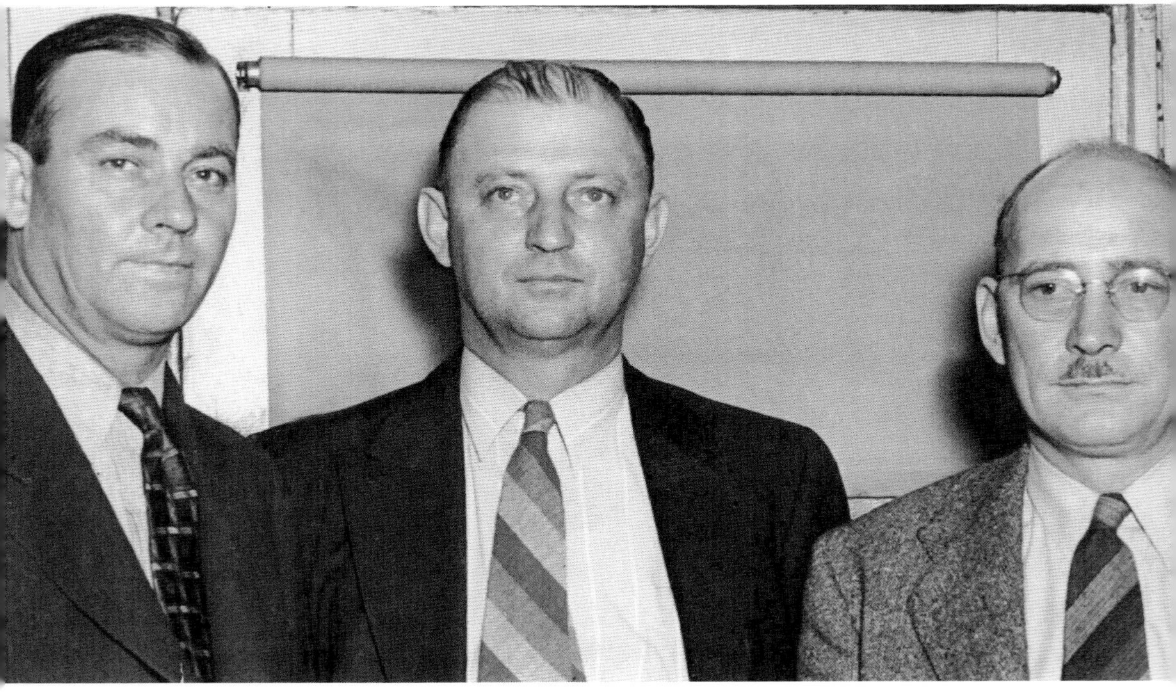

two of them drove back to the crime scene. Walking around with the police, Carter showed them where he hid the gun. He was escorted to a police car and sent to jail. Pictured at the bottom of the opposite page are the police investigators; from left to right they are Ted Cook (special deputy), Arch Voit (deputy sheriff), and William Winegard (Dearborn County sheriff).

Carter was put on trial and sentenced to death in the electric chair at the Michigan City State Prison; this was carried out on February 10, 1942. He was buried in Riverview Cemetery, his grave facing those of the family he murdered, to serve, it was said, as his reminder in the afterlife of his horrible crime. (Courtesy of DCHS.)

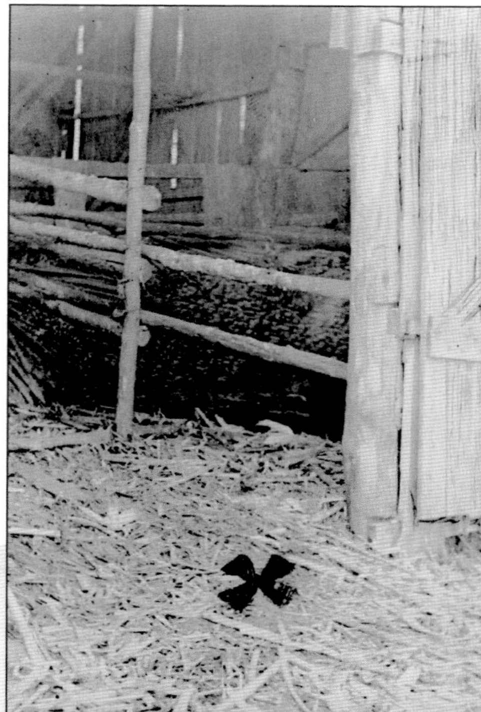

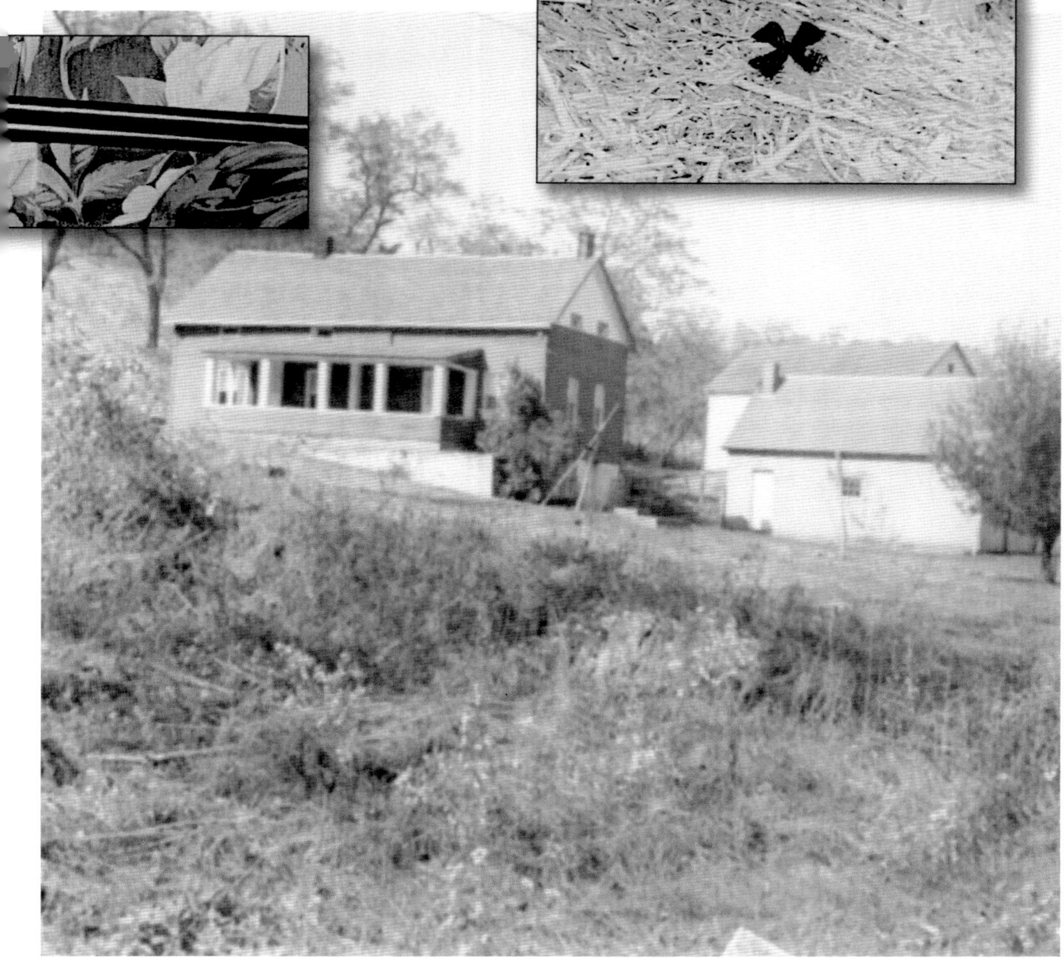

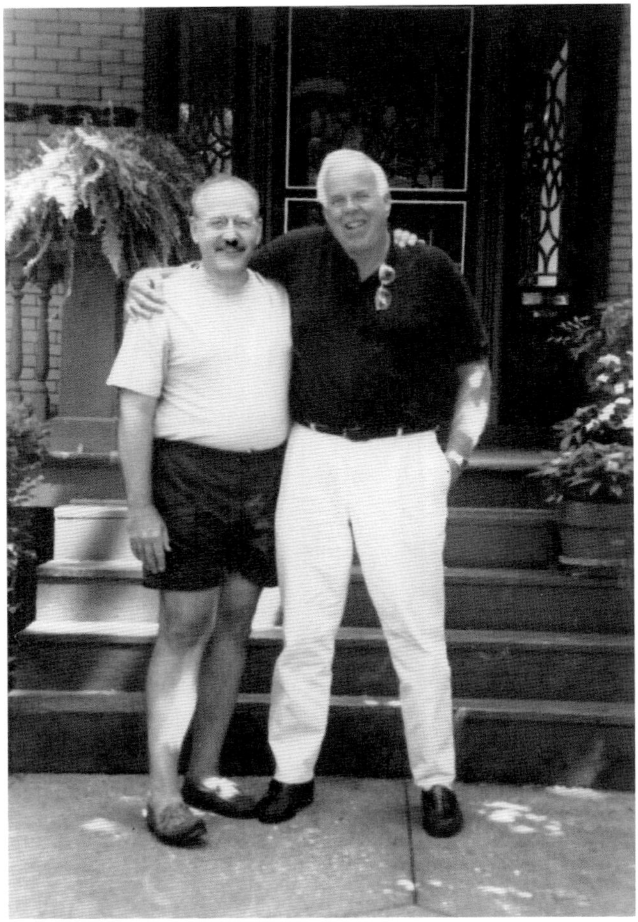

Frank Linkmeyer

Frank Linkmeyer is a legend in Aurora, but little is known about a major event in his life. One night in 1957, Frank—16 at the time—got off work at the bowling alley about 9:00 p.m. and decided to join his dad, Denton, and brothers Bob and Larry, who were camping on Laughery Island. The island is just off the Aurora shore on the Ohio River. At that time, the island was a popular camping spot, especially on this Labor Day weekend. Linkmeyer pulled up to the island and saw some commotion going on out on the river. Someone was shooting off bottle rockets and one had landed in a small boat. The people in the boat panicked and capsized the boat and, with no life vests on, were assumed drowned. Linkmeyer made his way over to the area in his boat, and someone yelled, "He's right by you, Frank!" Linkmeyer looked down and could see a flashlight beam coming out of the water and the top of a child's head. He reached in and grabbed the hair of a young boy, Don Dreffner. Once in the boat, Dreffner made praying hands and said, "Please save my dad." Linkmeyer had no idea that the father, Ralph Dreffner, had been just below the boy, trying to push him to the surface. The boy was taken to shore, and Linkmeyer never knew the child's name until a couple of years ago, when a friend found the father's coroner's report. Linkmeyer called information and found a Dreffner in Cincinnati. A young girl answered the phone and began crying when Frank told her he was the one that saved her father's life. Don Dreffner (left) and Frank Linkmeyer posed for this photograph at their meeting. Dreffner said, "Thank you for saving my life." Always an expert swimmer, Linkmeyer, now 71, swims back and forth across the river for exercise, just like he did when he was a boy growing up in Aurora. (Courtesy of Frank Linkmeyer.)

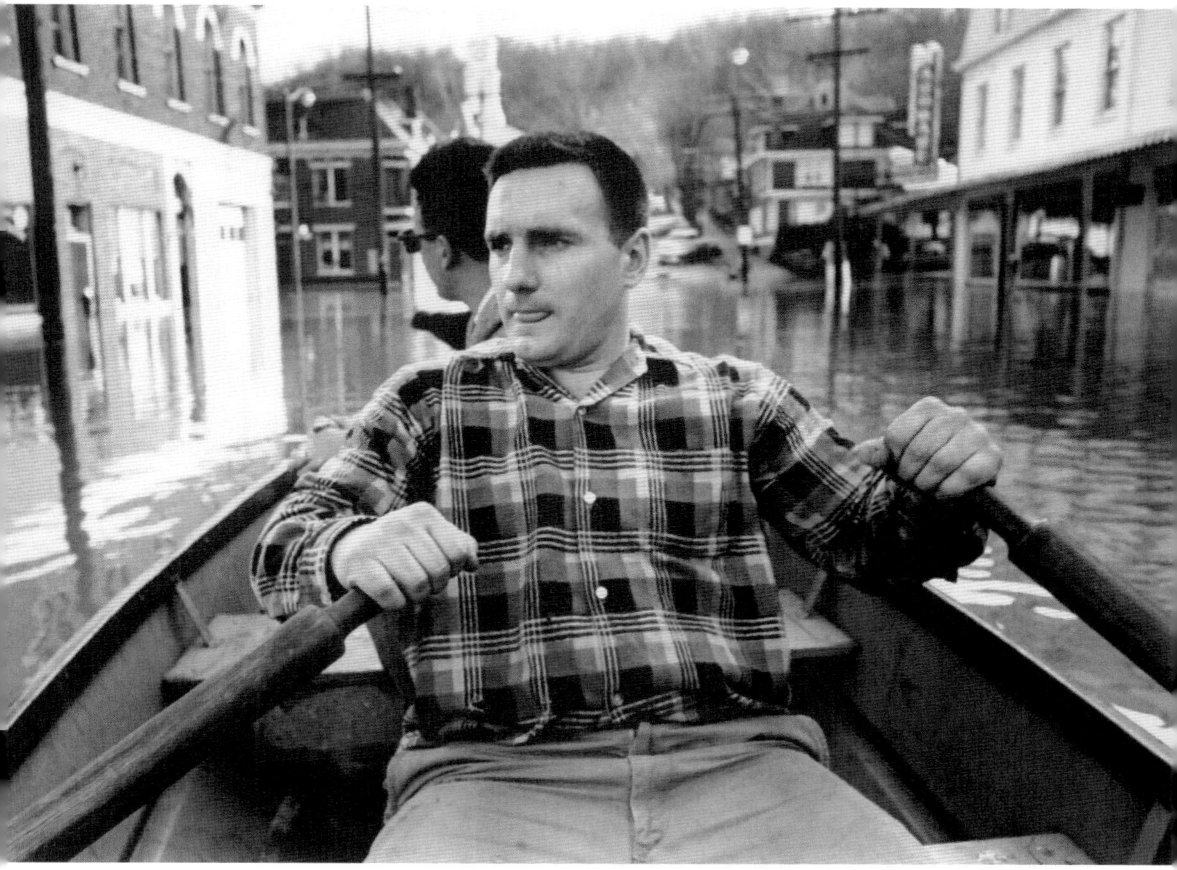

Richard "Dick" Ullrich Sr.

Growing up in Aurora, the Ullrich family has endured many floods. In this photograph, 23-year-old Richard is rowing south on Main Street toward Third Street. His first big challenge as a store owner came during this 1964 flood. Instead of moving merchandise to upper levels, as was done in the past, it was loaded into semitrailers and parked at the Hillforest Mansion driveway. Prescriptions could still be filled at his parents' home on upper Main Street near Hillforest. He is the son of Wilfrid and is a 1962 graduate of Purdue University School of Pharmacy. Richard is married to Suzanne Schuler. (Courtesy of the Ullrich family.)

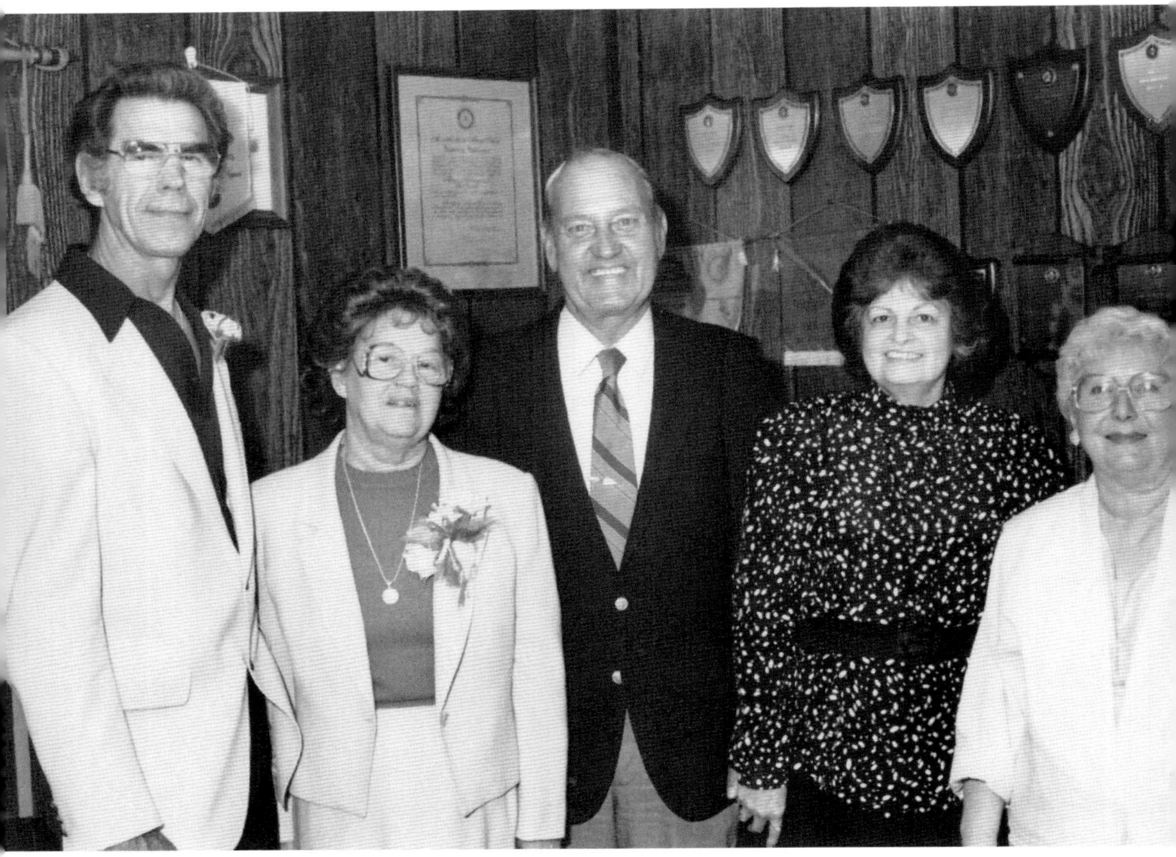

Aurora Ruiz Shuck

The native Cuban loved having the name "Aurora," and she loved living in Aurora. She married plumber Ray Schuck in 1948 and worked as a bookkeeper. The couple worked tirelessly promoting the city. She and Ray filled their store windows on Second Street with animated Christmas displays. This photograph was taken at a 1989 awards banquet held in her honor. From left to right are Ray Schuck, Aurora Schuck, Mayor Leon Kelly, Joy Kelly, and Francis Morgan. (Courtesy of Ullrich Studio.)

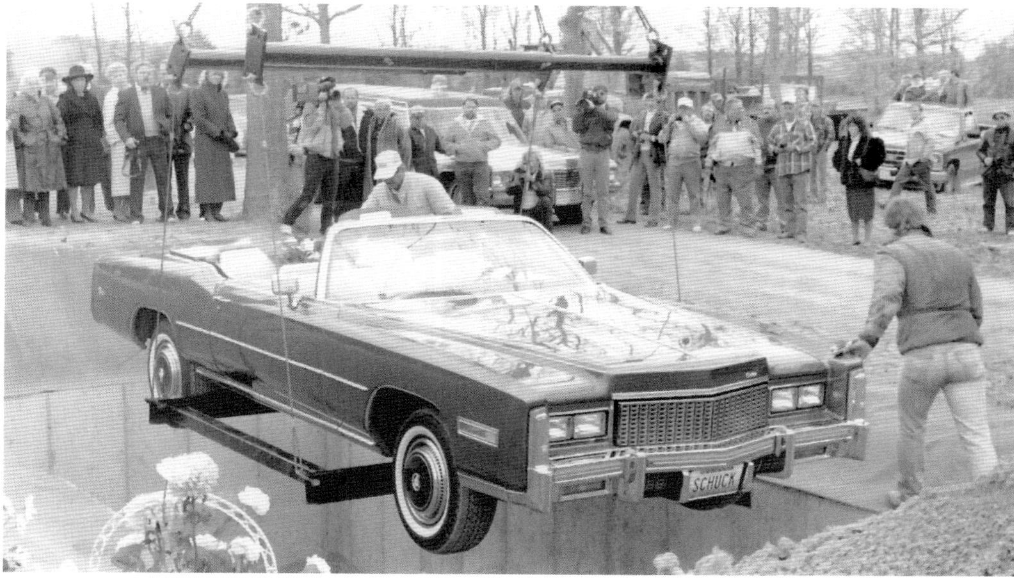

A Funeral for Aurora

In 1989, Aurora was fighting cancer at the age of 62. Her final request was to be buried in her Cadillac Eldorado, in Riverview Cemetery. A small wish became a big deal in the news world. A total of 14 plots had to be purchased and dug, and a concrete vault had to be poured. The Environmental Protection Agency (EPA) advised her husband, Ray, how to do the burial. The gas tank was removed. News cameras filmed as the sparkling car was lowered into the vault with the top down and the casket set atop the car. Ray would joke that he made sure the tank was full so that Aurora could ride around in heaven. Ray died in 2002 and was cremated, with some of his ashes put into the grave with his beloved Aurora. (Courtesy of Ullrich Studio.)

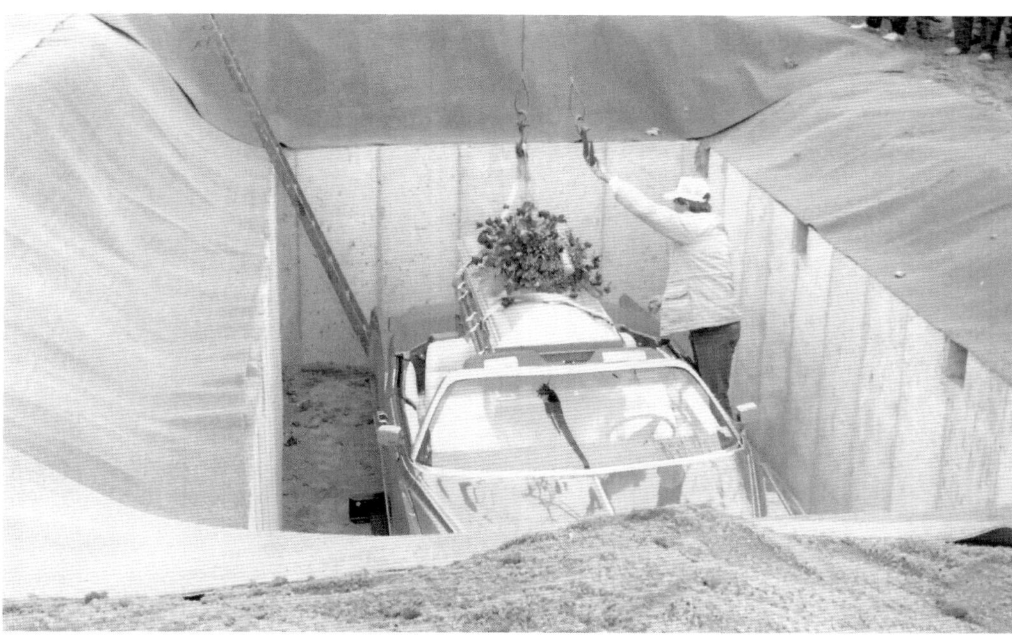

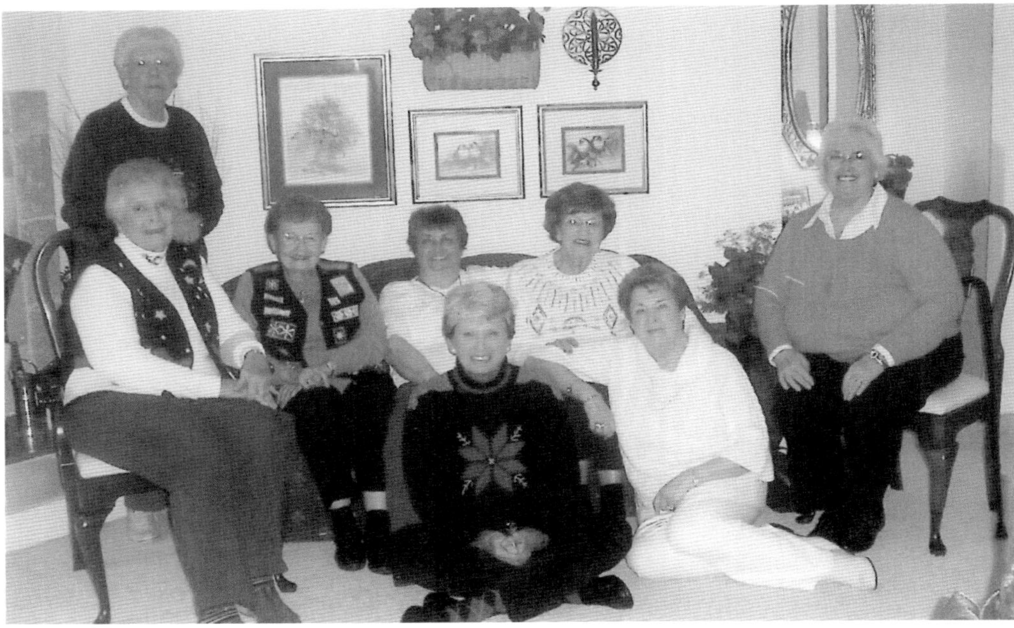

The Bridge Babes
The Bridge Babes play every second and fourth Wednesday of the month. Like clockwork, they have lunch at the Dearborn County Country Club then play Bridge. Shown are, from left to right, (first row) Phee Ellinghausen and Meg Harter; (second row) Shirley Morris, Tish Hopping, Sharon McClure, Marie Hizer, and Sabra Duerstock; Dixie Bowen is standing. (Courtesy of Phee Ellinghausen.)

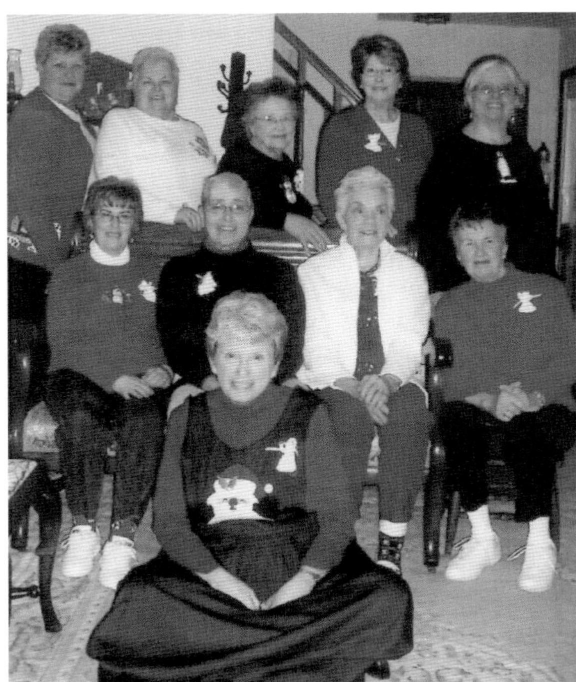

OBC Bridge Club
Together since 1986, this bridge club has traveled, since 1990, to summer bridge retreats in Kiawah, Hilton Head, Chincoteague Island, Kelley's Island, Black Mountain, Pigeon Forge, and Brown County, Indiana, among other destinations. The members of OBC are, Phee Ellinghausen (seated on floor); (second row)Patty Rullman, Cindy Strzynski, Marge Waldon, and Martha Kaiser; (third row) Charlotte DeVille, JoDell Steuver, Kay Raffignone, Janet Burton, and Laura Rolf. Shirley Meyer is not shown. They have played on floats in three Farmers' Fair parades. (Courtesy of Phee Ellinghausen.)

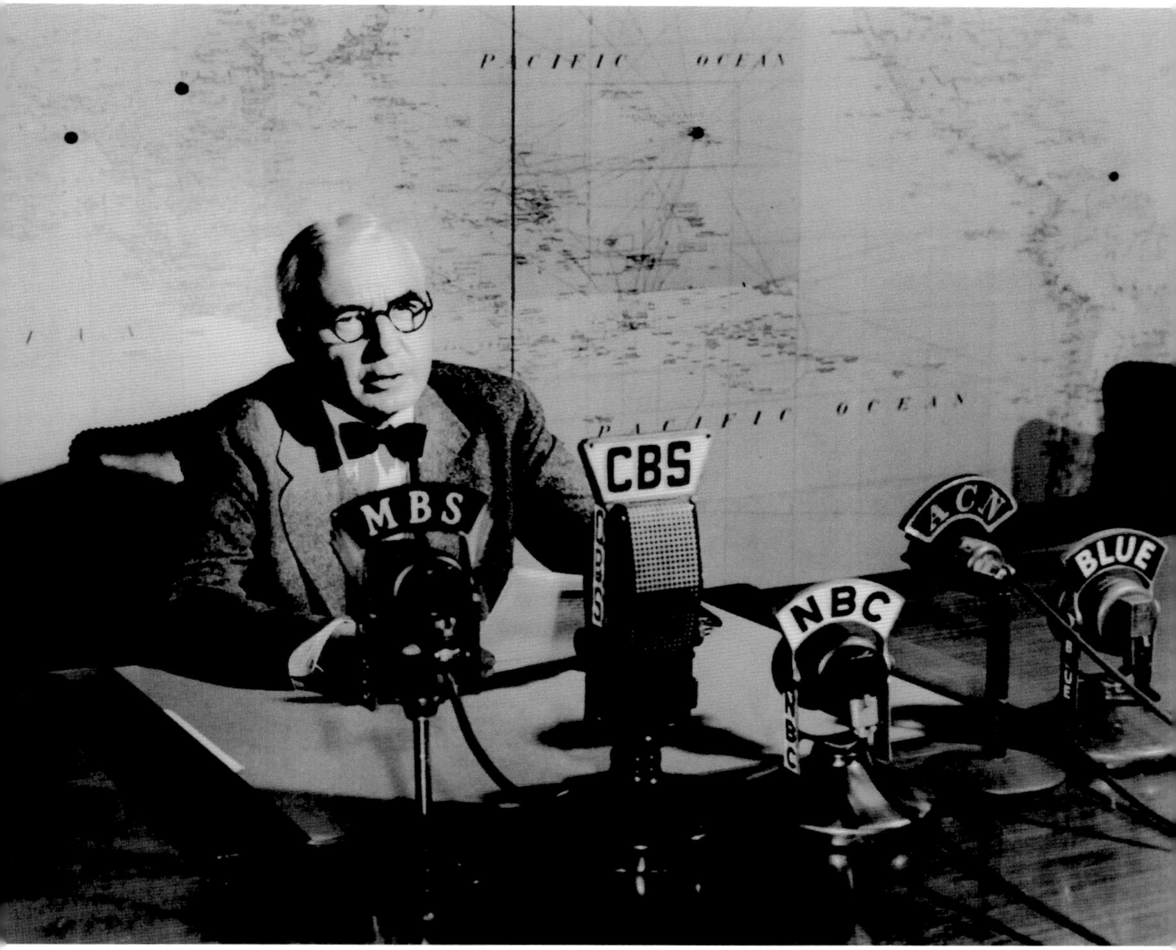

Elmer Holmes Davis

Davis (1890–1958) was a well-known news reporter, author, director of the US Office of War Information during World War II, and a Peabody Award recipient. He began his career in news after his freshman year in high school, when he started working for the *Aurora Bulletin* as a printer's devil. Davis was a small-built young man, and athletics were not his forté. But he had a quick mind and loved to write. His father was Elam Davis, a cashier for the First National Bank of Aurora. One of Davis's first professional writing jobs was with the *Indianapolis Star*, a position he held while attending Franklin College. A brilliant student, he was honored as the 398th Rhodes Scholar to Queen's College in Oxford in 1910. His stay in England was cut short when his father became ill and eventually died. Davis met his wife, Florence, in England. Upon his return to America, Davis became an editor for the pulp magazine *Adventure*, leaving after a year to work as a reporter and editorial writer for the *New York Times*. For the next decade, Davis reported on stories ranging from pugilist Jack Dempsey to evangelist Billy Sunday. It was his coverage of Billy Sunday that gained him notoriety. (Courtesy of DCHS.)

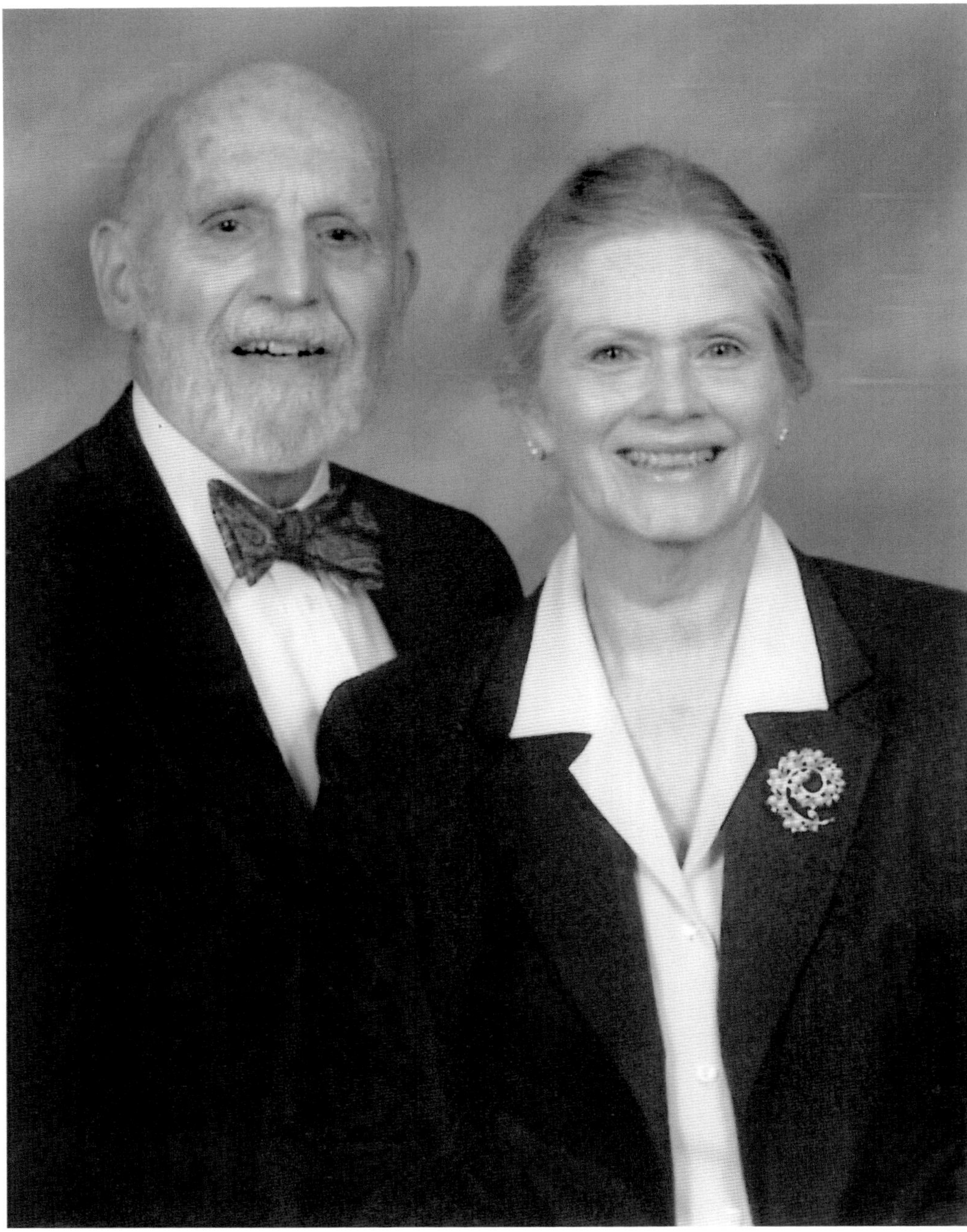

Rev. Jean and Dr. Frank Frable

Dr. Frable treated literally thousands of patients at the Dearborn County Hospital since he became a charter member in 1959. The doctor earned a reputation as a highly skilled and compassionate physician, and he became one of the founders of the Ludlow Hill Clinic on Bielby Road. He dressed each day for work in a suit and his signature bow tie. His wife, Rev. Jean Frable, is retired from the Richwood Presbyterian Church in Union, Kentucky. (Courtesy of the Frable family.)

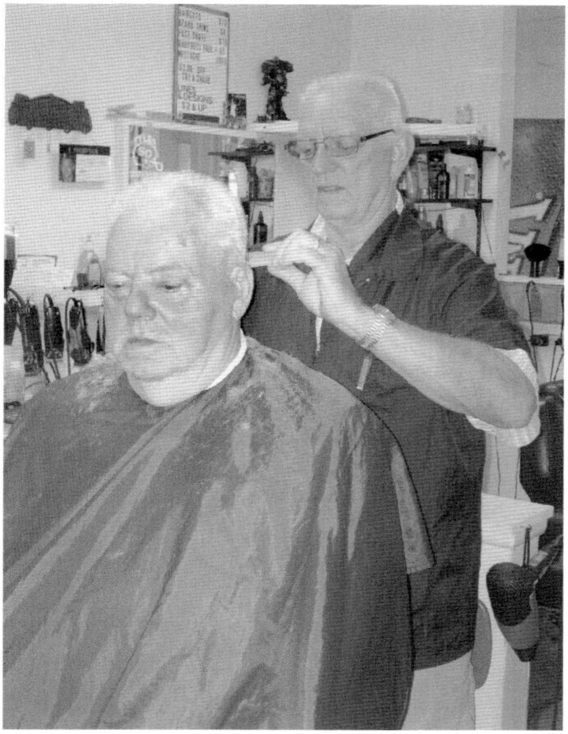

Tom's Barber Shop
Thomas Herndon (right) runs Tom's Barber Shop on Second Street. The building has been a barbershop for over 100 years. Tom's, one of two barbershops in town, was opened by Herndon after he retired from Monsanto several years ago. Getting pampered is Scott Goodpaster. (Author's collection.)

Ted Chipman
Ted Chipman has been a barber for 39 years and a real estate agent for 16 years in Aurora. Chipman's Barbershop is on George Street, just before the bridge into Aurora. Chipman jokes that his client Terry Block (seated) of Salem Ridge is from out of town. Block and Doug Whitaker are coowners of Tandy's IGA on Third Street. (Author's collection.)

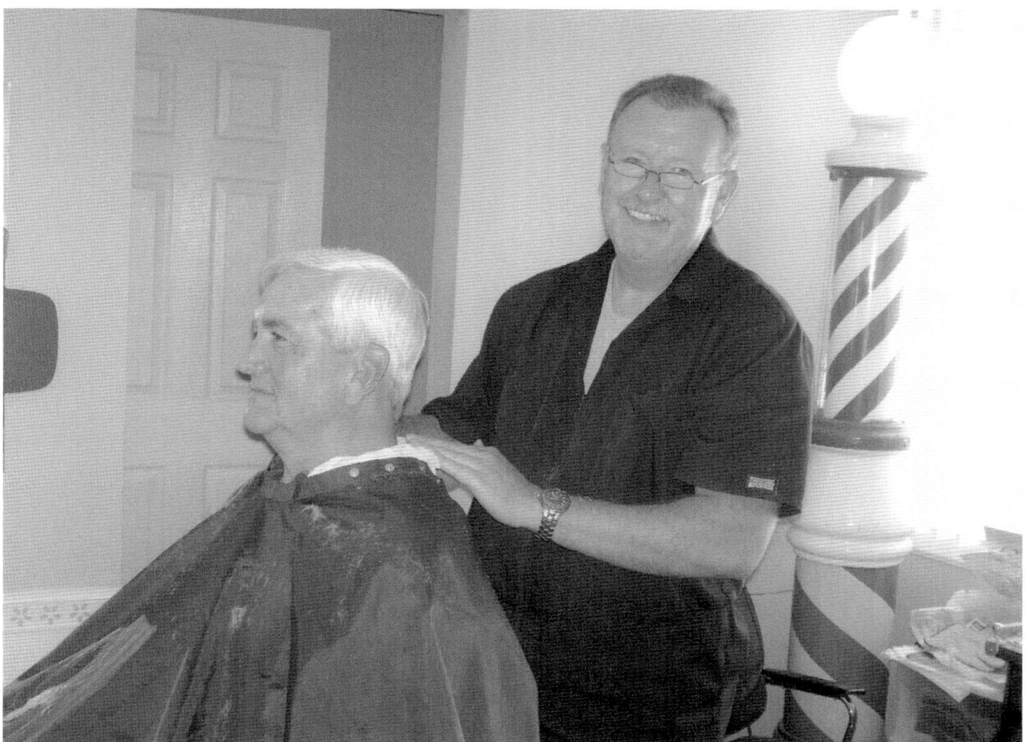

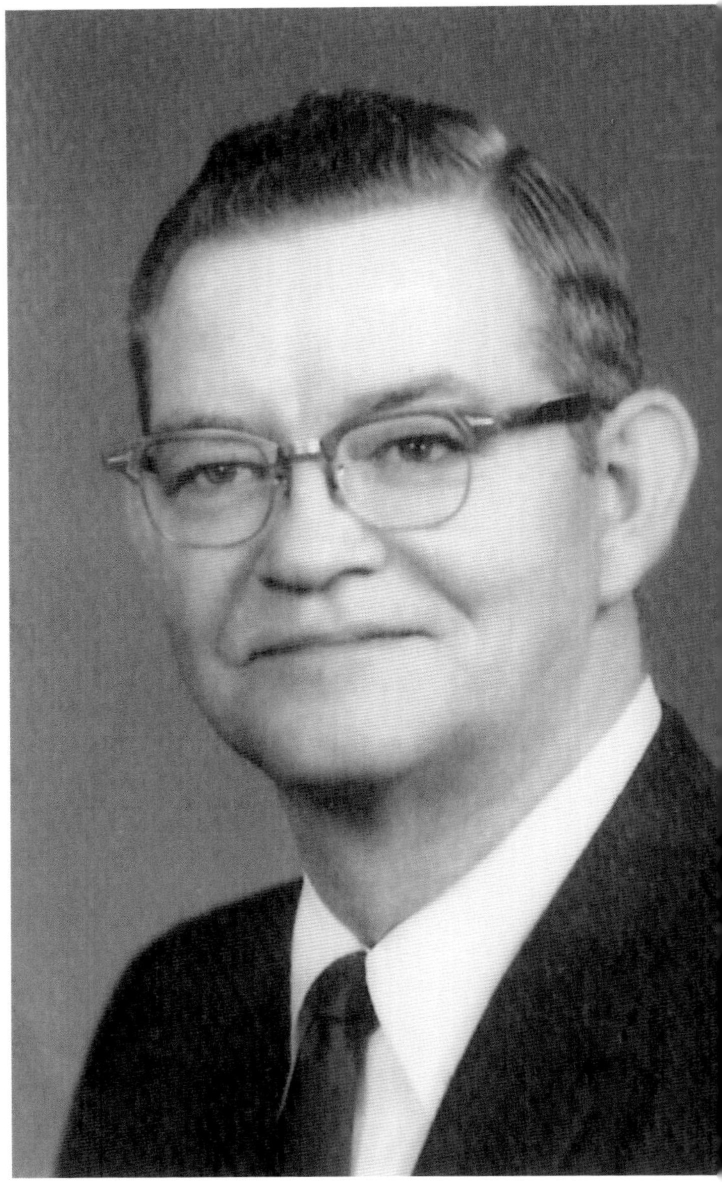

Judge Lester Gatch Baker
Judge Baker was born on July 11, 1914, and is the twin brother of Dr. Leslie Baker. He attended Aurora Elementary, Junior High, and High Schools before going to Indiana University. He began the practice of law in 1937, and began public service with two terms as prosecutor from 1940 to 1943 and from 1946 to 1948. He served as Dearborn circuit judge from 1948 until his death. His term as prosecutor was interrupted by military service in the US Army from October 1943 to June 1946. Judge Baker served as president of the Indiana Judges Association in 1970, and he was a life member of the Veterans of Foreign Wars, American Legion Post 231, Aurora Rotary Club, Masonic Lodge, Shriners, and the advisory and review committee of the Boy Scouts of America. He also was one of the figures instrumental in starting Dearborn County Hospital. He married Armada Janet Fisher in 1940. (Courtesy of the Baker family.)

CHAPTER FIVE

Artistic Legends

An artistic legend is a person who creatively expresses ideas and inspires people to see the beauty in their medium. The Southeastern Indiana Art Guild met the call of the city with its successful "Windows of Aurora" project. The group painted scenes onto unsightly, boarded-up windows, telling stories about earlier times. It also has an art gallery and teaches art at its location in the Schuck building on the corner of Second and Main Streets. Artist Tom Ward's work will bring a smile to one's face with sketches of his childhood on Hogan Creek. He not only paints the picture, he also tells a story with his colorful humor.

Almost everyone played an instrument in the 1800s. The various German bands marched in parades and entertained on Coulter's Store balcony. One person could have played in several bands.

On May Day, the residents would wake up to the sound of music coming from the hills, as a celebration of spring. One band would be on Sutton's hill and another one on Cheek hill. Boy Scouts stationed on the hills would signal each other with flags, letting the bandleaders know when to start the next song. Music was everywhere. The Schippers were wood carvers, painters, and musicians.

The Sangerbund was an early German singing society that met at the Nees Hotel. In the summer, windows would be open, and the city serenaded.

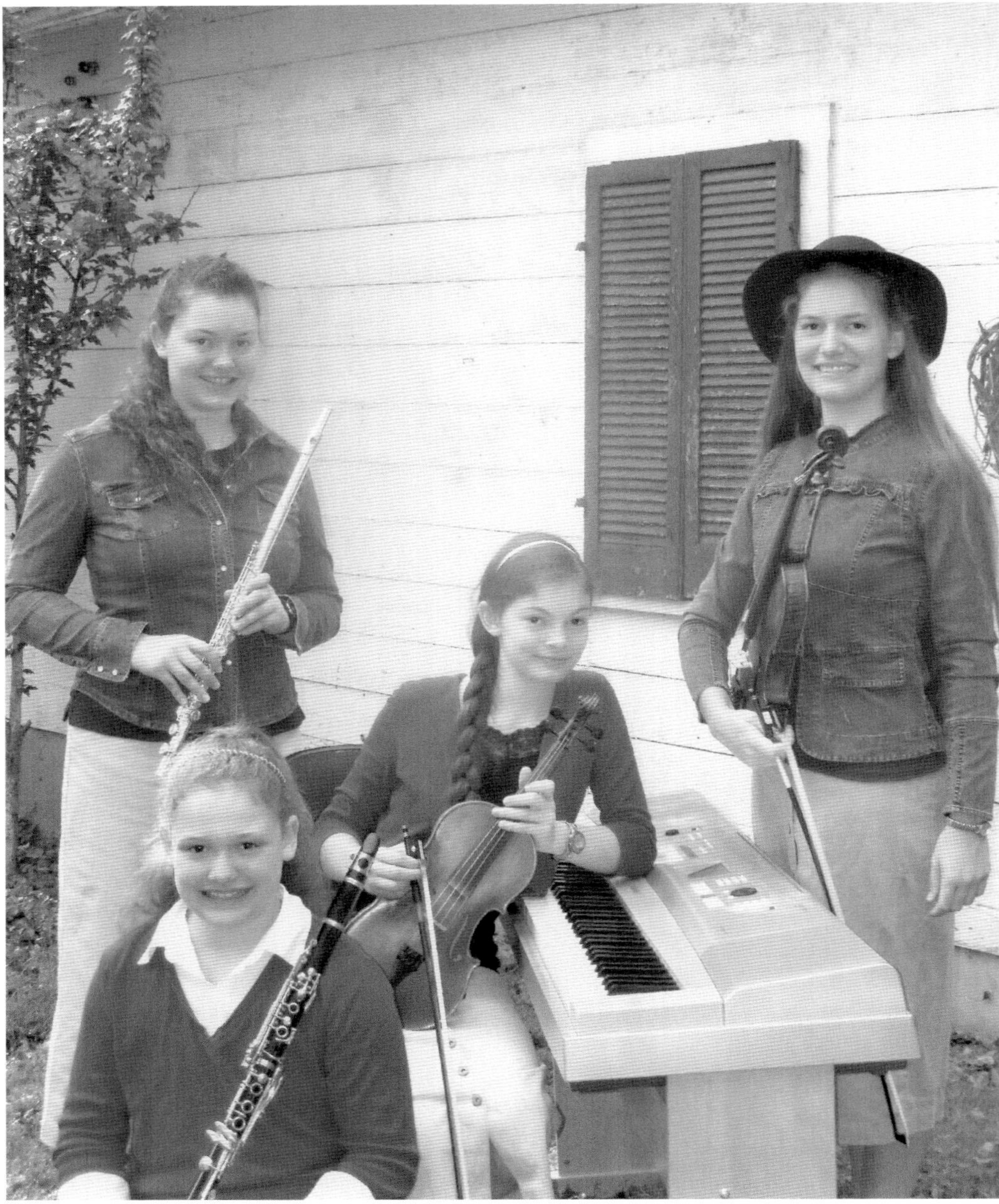

The Kessen Girls

Called "the Kessen Girls," they are usually seen all together. Each one started taking piano lessons at an early age from Mark Tanner of Greendale, Indiana. They are all accomplished musicians. Candace is pictured with the clarinet, Hollie with the flute, Heather is seated with the violin, and Crystal is standing with the violin. The girls all play several instruments and belong to the Young Voices Choir. (Courtesy of Crystal Kessons.)

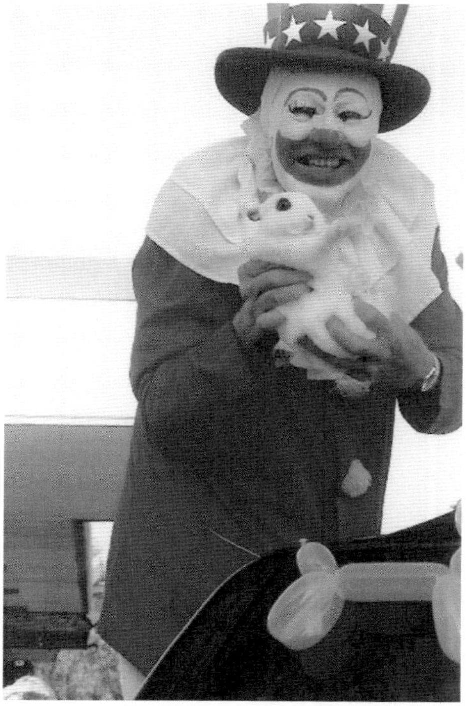

"Quacky"

For more than 36 years, Eugene Curtis of Toledo, Ohio, played the part of "Quacky the Clown" at the Aurora Farmers' Fair. The six-foot, seven-inch clown entertained several generations of children. Quacky had to retire in 2010 due to bad health. (Courtesy of DCHS.)

1976 Swing Choir

The high-stepping South Dearborn Swing Choir, directed by Steven Hedges, entertained at many events and programs. Shown here are, from left to right, (front row) Doug Baer, Geneva Fehling, Jana Miller, and Bobby Northcutt; (second row) Tony Bennett, David Schwegeman, Mary Jane Renner, Chris Lambert, Mary Jean Ward, David Cassidy, and Paul Bunnell; (third row) Carol Tyler, Cindy Billingsley, and Sue Harves. (Courtesy of Ullrich Collection and S. Hedges.)

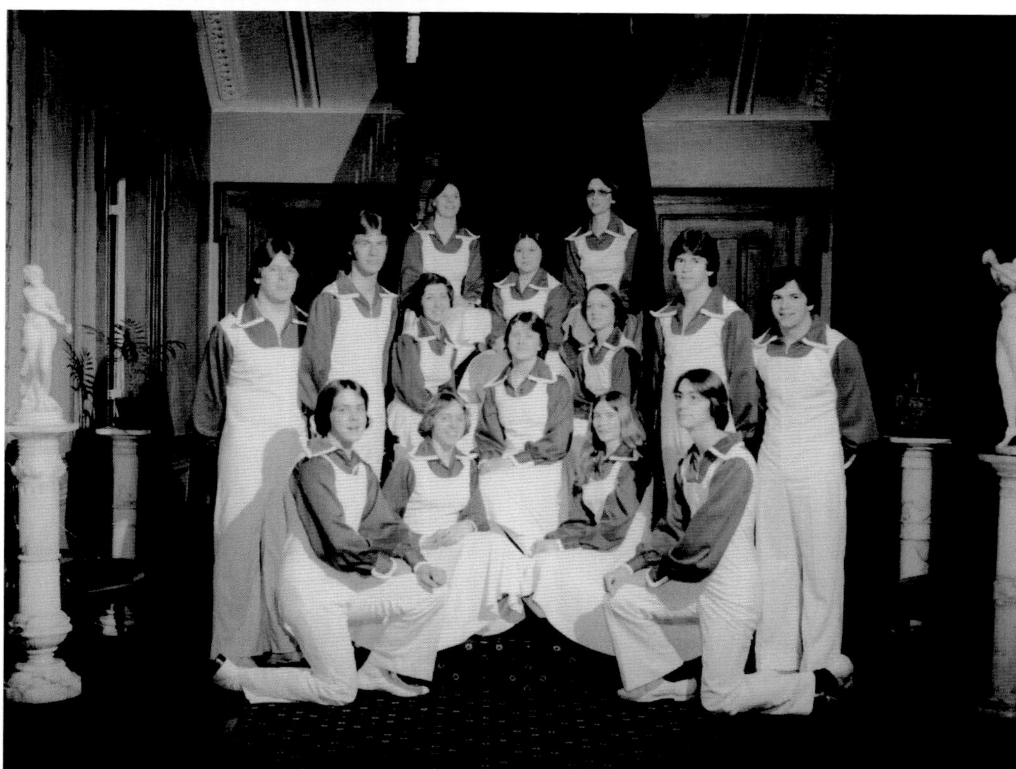

Tom Ward
Tom Ward once said that air-conditioning ruined the neighborhoods. When windows were open in the summer, everyone knew your business. Voices echoed. On warm evenings, people sat on their porches and visited with their neighbors, or went to the creek. Tom can be described as an artist, a public speaker, a would-be inventor, or, simply, a great dad. His humorous, public-speaking stories are about how he spent his youth on and in area rivers and creeks. Many of his paintings depict him reliving his boyhood. The action in his prints and paintings are a carryover from his job as a cartoonist. Ward has designed furniture and was the style promotion director for Aurora Casket Co., Inc., for 35 years. (Courtesy of the Ward family.)

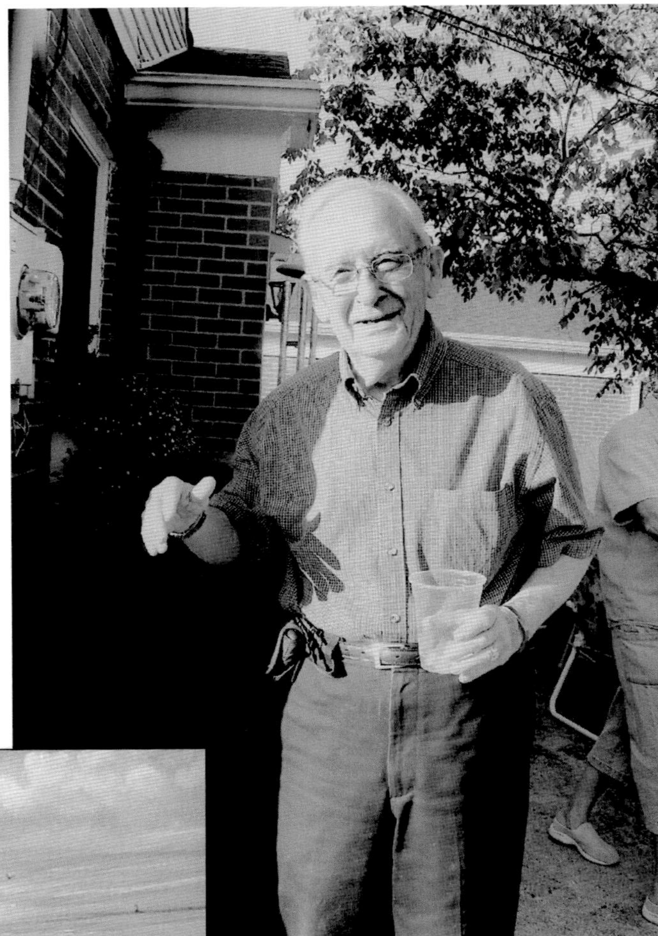

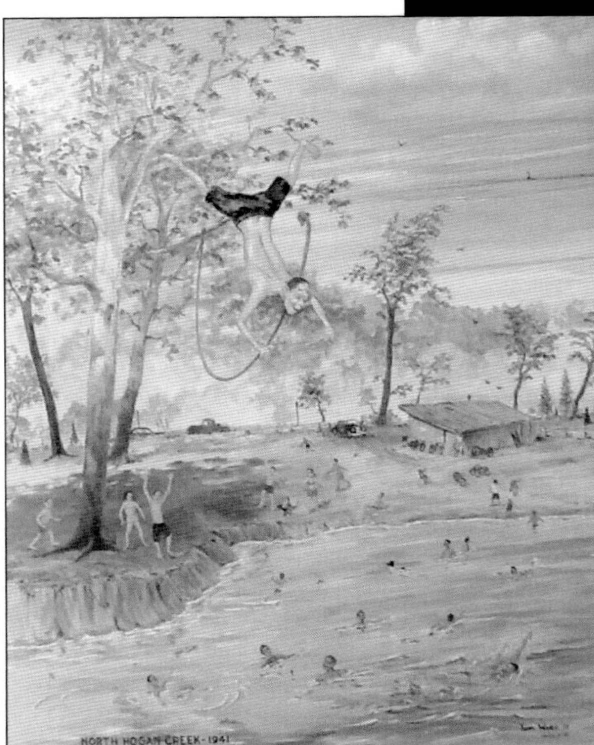

North Hogan Creek, 1941
Tom Ward grew up on Hanover Avenue, and the creek was right behind the house. In the big trees along the creek, one can still see remnants of old rope swings on their branches. (Courtesy of Tom Ward.)

Steve Pratt and Lonnie Mack

Steve Pratt (right) is shown here cutting up with his uncle Lonnie Mack. Pratt's career began when he started singing in church at the age of five. His first gig, performing for the local Rotary Club, paid $10. Not only a performer but a gifted songwriter, he has won the Kentucky Fried Chicken song-writing contest three times in a row. Pratt wrote songs for Owepar Publishing Company, owned by Dolly Parton and Porter Wagoner. In 1990, he earned an award from *Billboard* magazine for writing "If I Had a Million Dollars," and again in 1991 for writing "We Don't Love Here Anymore." In 1997, Pratt became a member of the Country Music Association in Nashville. Steve was inducted into the Southeastern Indiana Musicians Hall of Fame in 2006. Pratt and his band, The Oakey Avenue Band, hang on to their roots by playing at many local events.

Lonnie McIntosh was born in 1941 and began playing at the age of seven, using a guitar he traded for a bicycle. While still young, he was playing guitar for tips outside the Nieman Hotel. In 1958, he bought the seventh Gibson Flying V guitar from that model's first production run of 81.

Mack is a roadhouse blues-rock legend, one of modern rock's first true guitar hereos. His playing has influenced the course of rock and roll and has had an impact on many of modern rock's guitar heroes, including Eric Clapton, Keith Richards, Jimmy Page, and especially Stevie Ray Vaughan. His early music bridged the gap between 1950s rockabilly and the psychedelic blues-rock of the following decade, and, like the best rock-and-roll, his work continues to embody a mixture of white- and black-roots music. Rock, blues, soul, and country—Mack brings them all together for a sound that has been all his own for nearly 40 years. (Courtesy of Steve Pratt.)

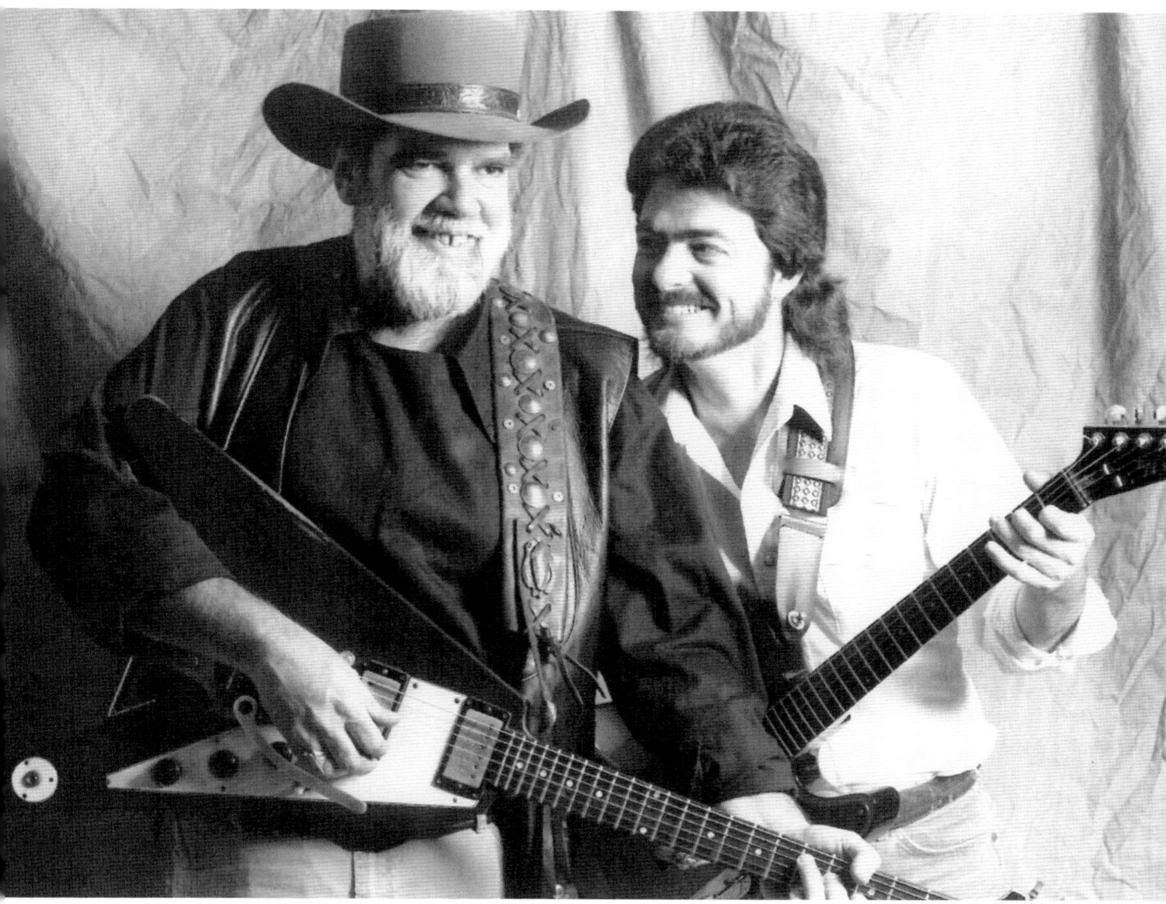

Albert Teaney

Albert Teaney (1873–1936) is shown with his wife, Edith (Bibenger), and son Gordon. He began his employment with Prudential in 1899, and by 1902, he was promoted to assistant superintendent of the Aurora Branch, Covington District. The company honored him as a member of the Prudential Old Guard. Teaney also served as a director of the Aurora State Bank and played in J.B. Coulter's Band. (Courtesy of DCHS.)

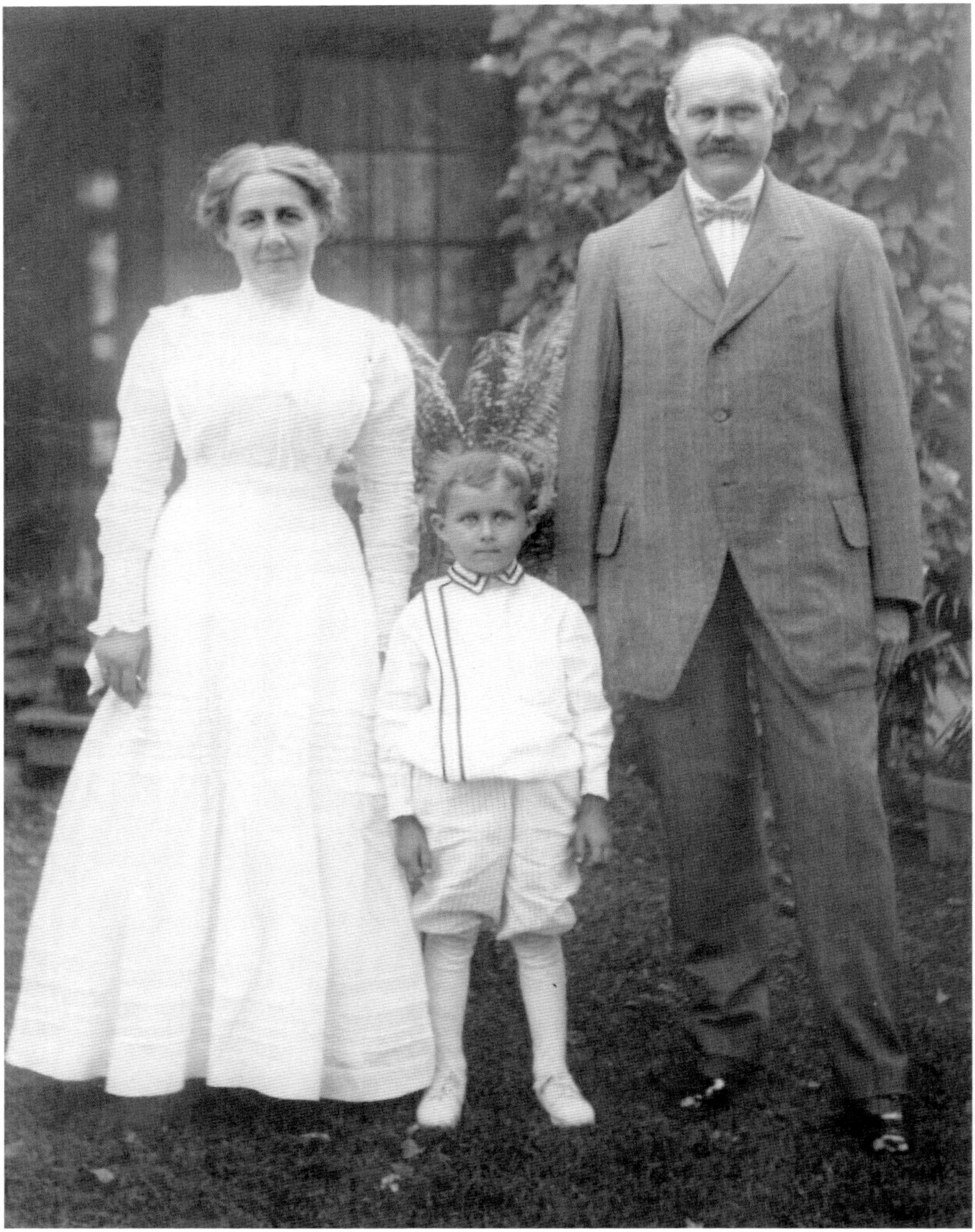

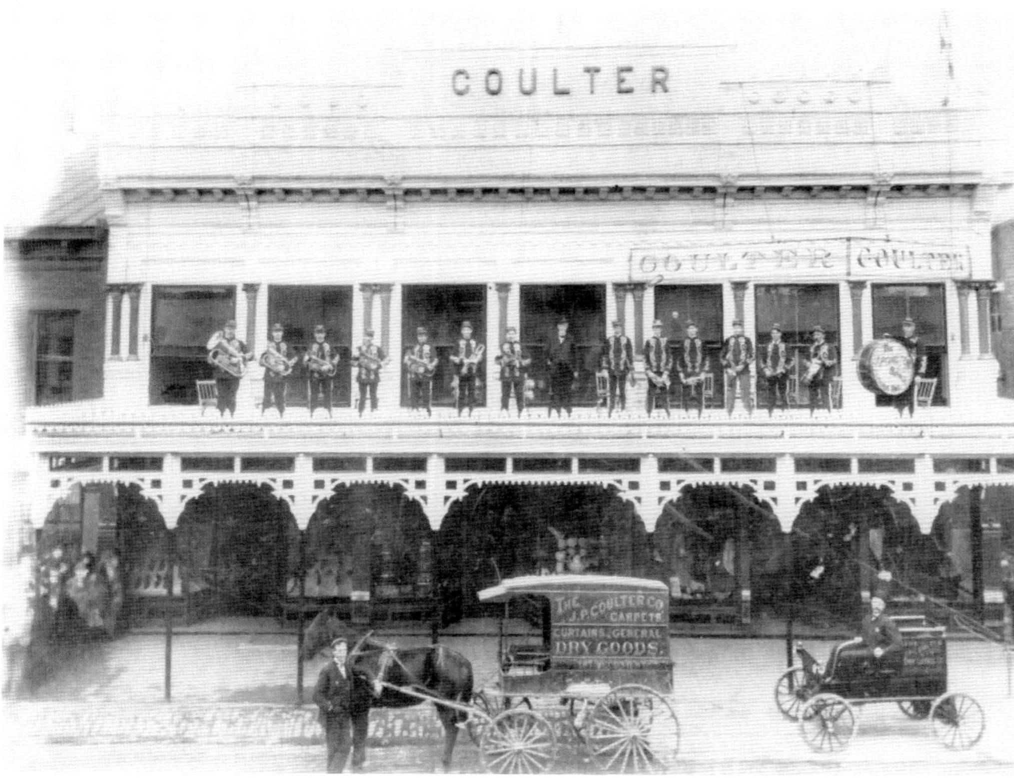

J.B. Coulter's Band

Coulter was a talented musician and a prominent businessman. The band practiced in a room above his store and would often give a free concert on the porch. Members of this band (in no particular order) were Frank Hubbard, Jim Martin, Gus Schipper, Gus Herzog, Charles Smith, Kelley Miller, Mooney Campbell, Louis Baker Sr., Elmer Johnson, George Taylor, Bunk Hubbard, John Van Osdol, Albert Teaney, Bieney Bienkamp, and Thomas Rice. (Courtesy of Aurora Public Library.)

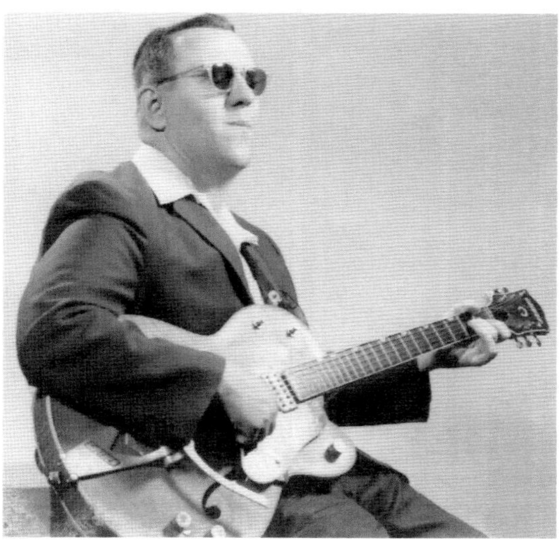

Ralph Trotto

Ralph Trotto was blind, but he never let it stop him. According to his sister Jessie Probst, Ralph was not born blind but went blind shortly after a surgery destroyed the cornea. Trotto is credited with helping to teach Lonnie Mack to play the electric guitar. At one time, Trotto and Mack lived across Moore Street from each other. The neighbors on the street would get to hear them play together on their porches. Other musicians would stop by for the chance to play with the guitarist. He would be amazed to know that in 2007, his 1960 D-18 Martin guitar was up for auction for $2,499 on the Internet. Ralph Trotto usually played an electric Gretch. (Courtesy of Jesse Probst.)

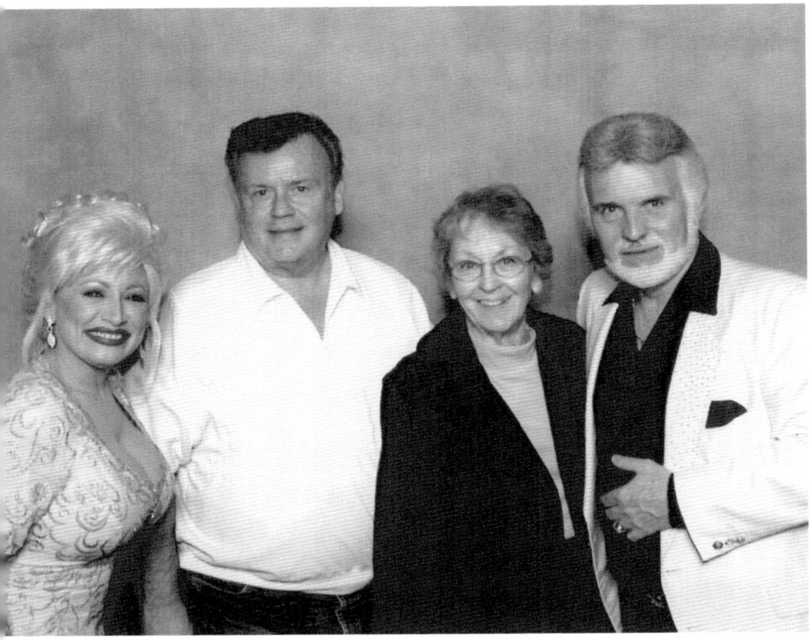

T. Steven Hedges
In his 32-year teaching career, Steve Hedges was a drama, music, band, and choral director in the South Dearborn school system. He has been named to the Southeastern Indiana Music Hall of Fame and actively promotes his nonprofit group, Ohio, Indiana, Northern Kentucky Regional Productions (OINK). Pictured from left to right are a Dolly Parton impersonator, Steven Hedges, Gerri Farrar, and a Kenny Rogers impersonator. (Courtesy of OINK.)

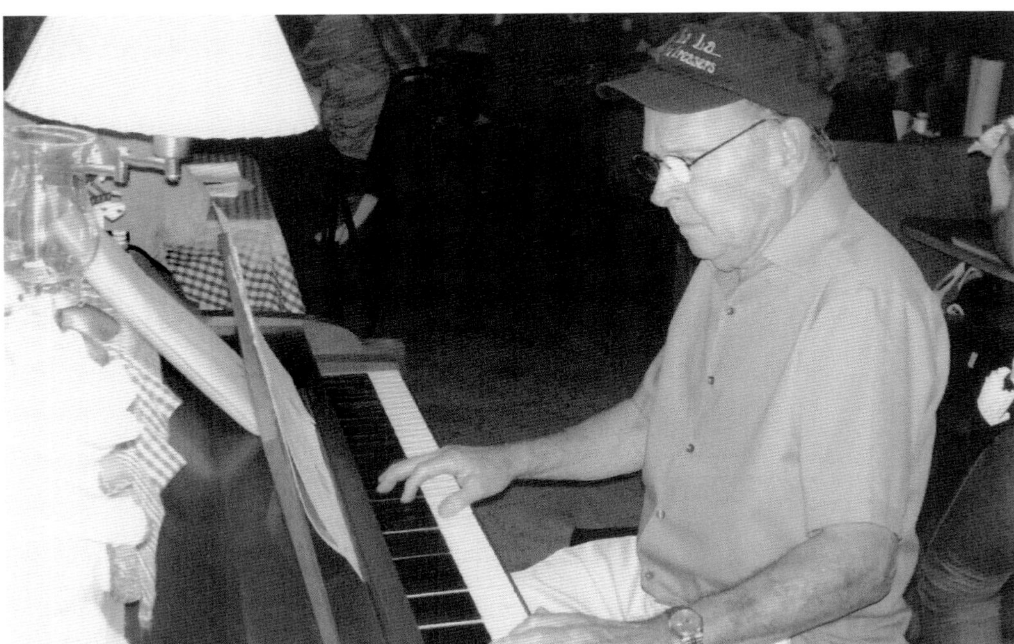

Landon Smith
In 1947, when Smith was 12, his mother sent him to study piano in downtown Cincinnati every Saturday for four years. He played piano with Nelson Elliott's Hi-Liter Orchestra and for 20 years played offertory for Trinity Christian Center. He now plays for fun and to help raise money for the Relay for Life organization. (Author's collection.)

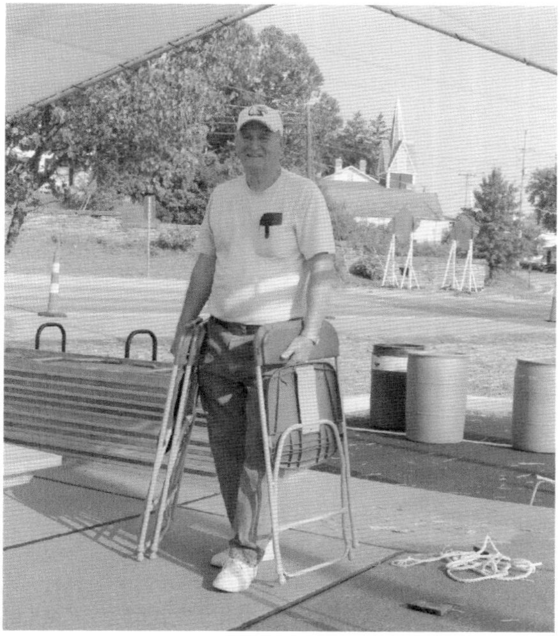

Southeastern Indiana Music Hall of Fame

Musician Ken Jackson and the Southeastern Indiana Music Hall of Fame board have found a way to honor area musicians. Jackson formed a board with eight musicians: Nelson Elliot, Bob Hudson, Bob Bischoff, Stafford Ripley, Clifford "Dutch" Hoffmeier, Bob Linkmeyer, Carolyn Leming, and George Smith. Upon receiving its nonprofit status, things started evolving. The first year, the organization inducted two members. Since that time, it tries to induct five living and five deceased members each year. The winners are revealed at Aurora's Farmers' Fair. Plaques line the walls of the Hall of Fame Museum, on Walnut Street in Lawrenceburg. Each contains the inductee's name and photograph. (Author's collection.)

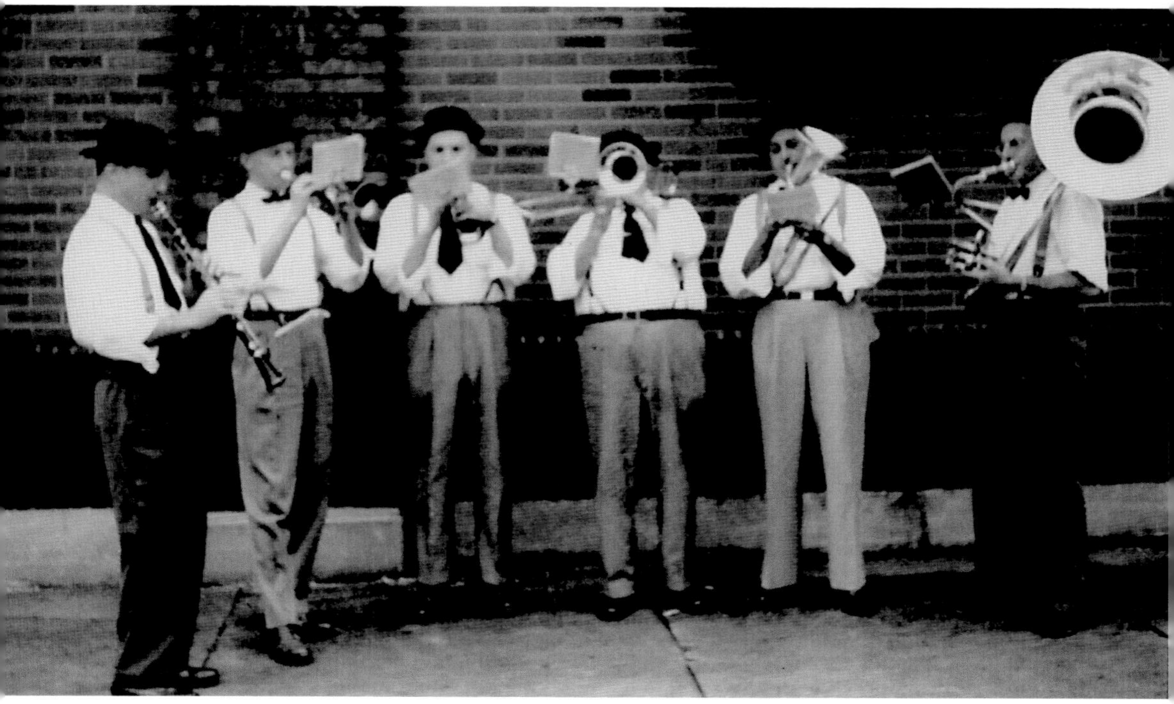

The Little German Band

It has been said that "the fun didn't start until the Germans got here." When German immigrants arrived, the city became a center of German culture, with bands, orchestras, and a theater. This group was called the Little German Band. Pictured are, from left to right, Paul Strassinger, Carol Sutton, Bill Kuebler, Fremont Bradley, Ray Hussung, and Ross Hussung. (Courtesy of DCHS.)

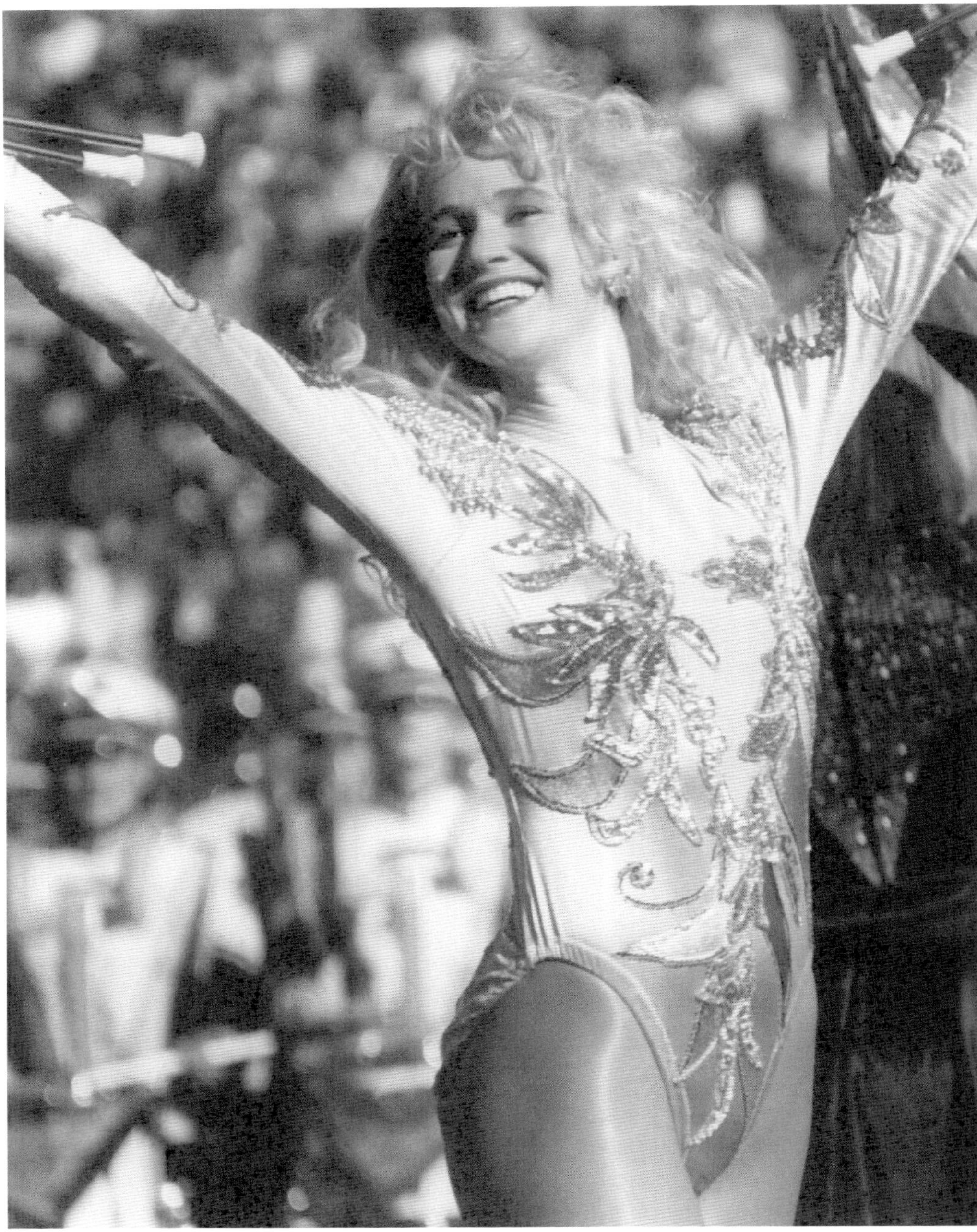

Holly Fehrman

Holly Fehrman started twirling at the age of nine. She was feature twirler at Aurora Middle School for two years and at South Dearborn High School for four years. She held the prestigious position of Purdue Golden Girl—something she had her eye on from an early age. As a twirler, Holly has traveled to five European countries and Singapore, and she led the Indianapolis 500 parade four times. Holly, a realtor for Fehrman Realty, is married to Scott Allen, and they have two children. Her golden cape and batons are on display at the Dearborn County Historical Society on High Street in Lawrenceburg. (Courtesy of Jan Fehrman.)

CHAPTER SIX

Future Legends

Since Jesse Holman came to Aurora, city leaders have been planning for the future, whether for the next day, the next week, or the next 100 years. While the pioneers worried about enough places to hitch or stable horses, a later generation needed plenty of parking spaces for automobiles.

An earlier generation shopped at bakeries and five-and-ten stores and utilized the services of icehouses and milk deliverymen. This generation finds that it does not need to step out of the house to shop. Technology has always made our lives easier. O.P. Cobb held patents for several of his inventions used at his iron and nail factory. His patents made life easier in his time.

Perhaps high-speed trains will replace a lane on US-50, and solar energy will power houses efficiently. The Main Street program works to entice new business and to promote tourism for the town. One thing is certain: the future legends will still be hardworking, everyday people.

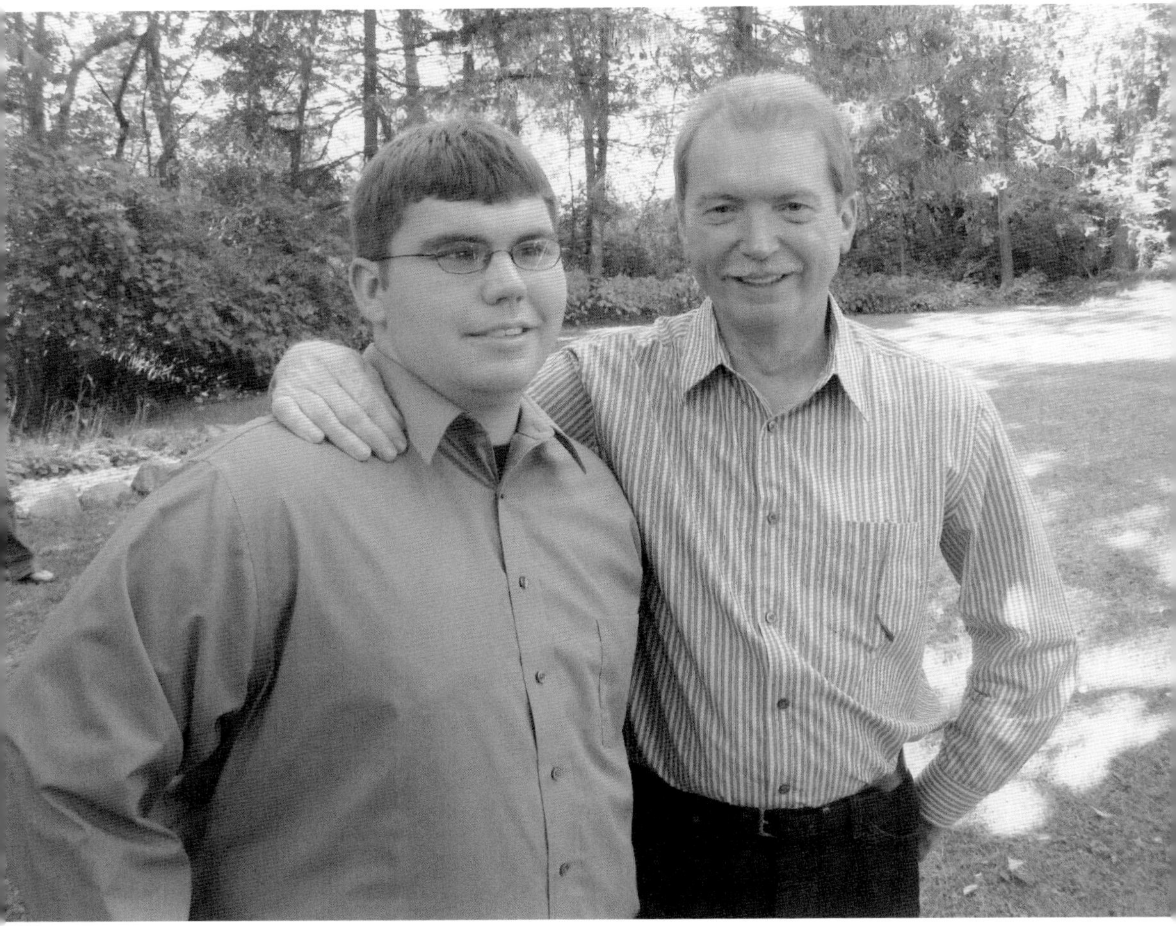

Like Father, Like Son
Jared (left) and Victor McPeek were not just father and son, they were best friends. They loved to tinker on Victor's red Corvette. "Team McPeek" always had a car project going on in their driveway on Hanover Avenue. Victor lost his battle with ALS, and his best friend, his wife, daughter, and his friends lost a great person. (Courtesy of the McPeek family.)

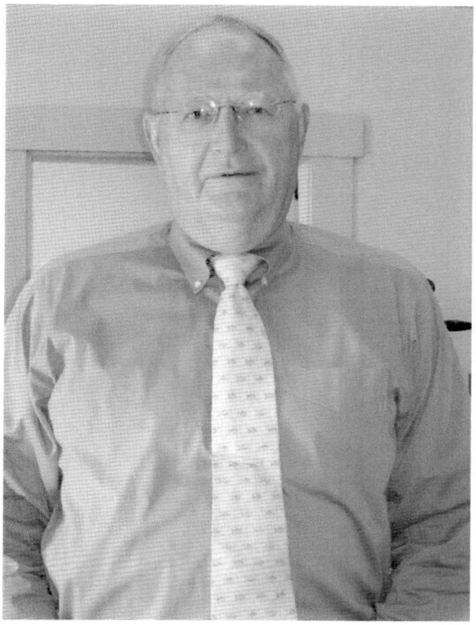

Dr. Frank L. Burton, OD
If going to the eye doctor on Third Street, one will be seen by Dr. Frank Burton. Burton began his practice on August 15, 1968. He and his wife, Janet, are active members in the community. (Author's collection.)

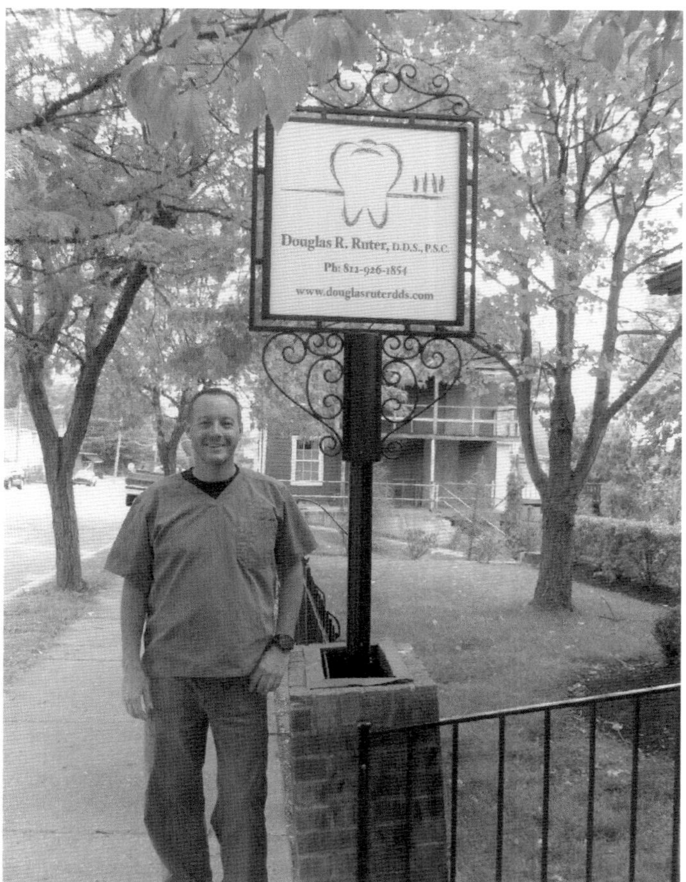

Dr. Douglas Ruter, DDS
Ruter attended St. Mary's School and graduated from South Dearborn High School in 1987. He and two others were the first to win a state competition for South Dearborn as part of the Hoosier Academic Super Bowl Science Team. Ruter started his dental practice in Aurora in November 1996. He has three boys, Luke, Zach, and Ben, all currently at St. Mary's. (Courtesy of D. Ruter.)

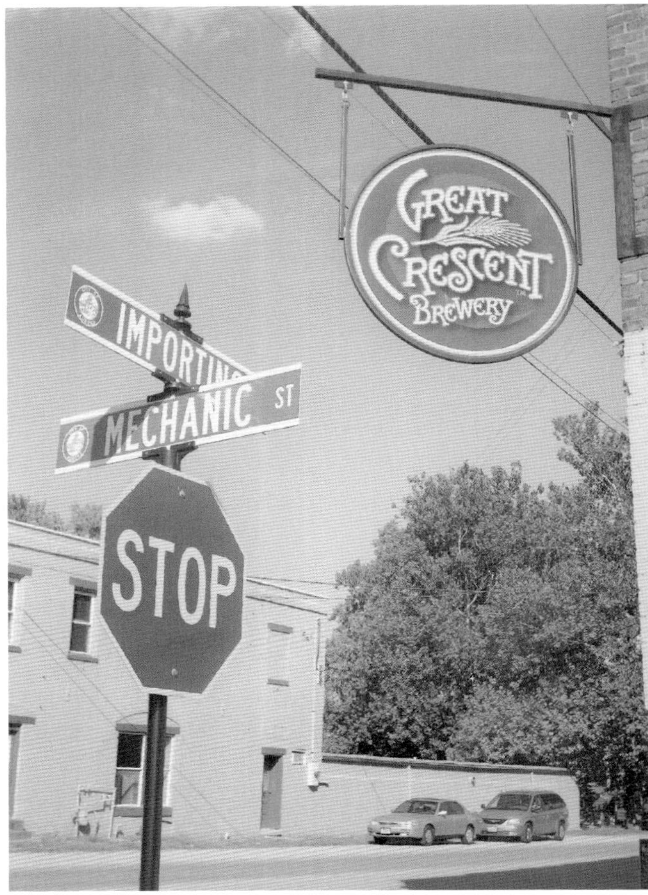

The Great Crescent Brewery

The Great Crescent Brewery was named for the once-popular Crescent Brewing Company that existed in Aurora from 1873 to 1899 (below). The present-day brewers, while not using the former establishment's recipe, offer a traditional, handcrafted ale and lager. The current microbrewery owned by Dan and Lani Valas, started out in a storefront on Second Street, then moved in early 2010 to its own building, the old Indianapolis Chair factory, located on the corner of Mechanic and Importing Streets (right). It operates directly across the street from the old Gaff. (Right, authors collection; below, courtesy of DCHS.)

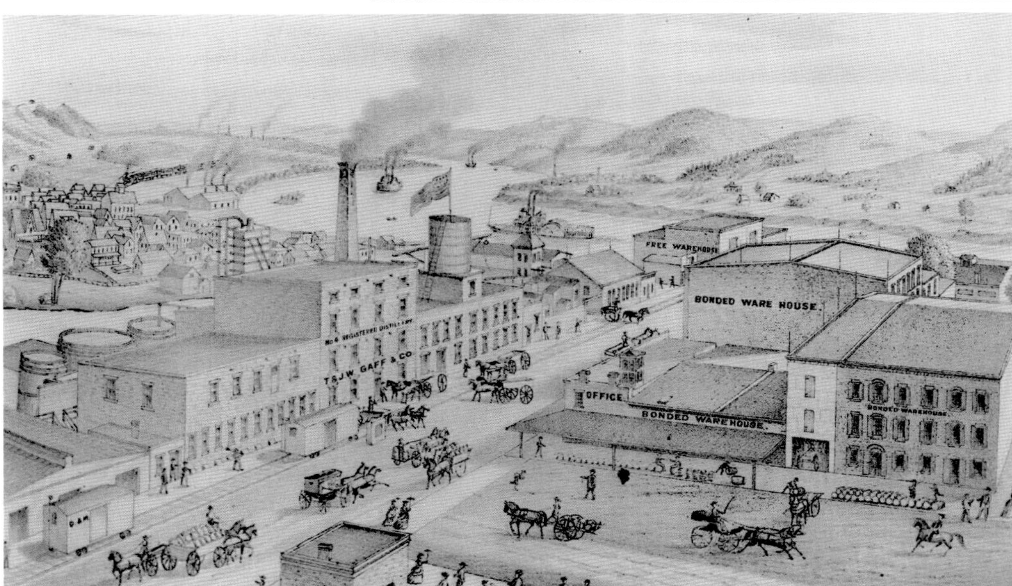

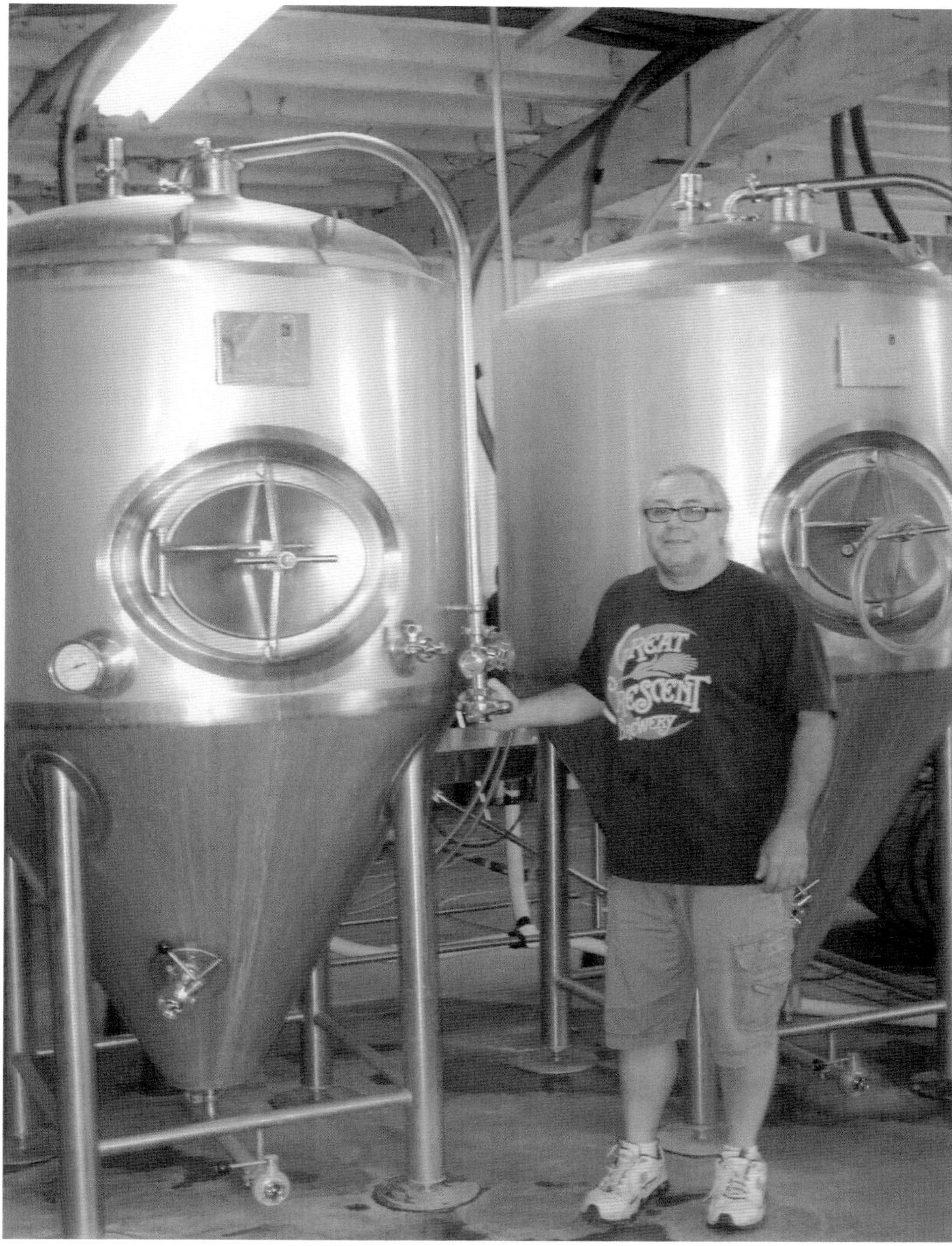

Dan Valas

Dan Valas, the owner of the Great Crescent Brewery, stands next to the distilling tanks. The Great Crescent Brewery completed an expansion in mid-2011 to include six new fermentors and a 10-beer barrel (BBL) steam-fired brew house. Each barrel of beer is 31 gallons and the tank will hold 10 BBL. (Author's collection.)

Ben and Nancy Turner
In March 1977, Aurora High School may not have won the semi-state basketball championship, but Ben Turner Jr. and Nancy (Fahey) Turner won each other. In 2008, after three sons—Benjamin Leo, Matthew Fahey, and Joseph Curry—and 30 years of marriage, the couple resigned themselves to the fact that they were never going to have grandchildren. A year later, Matthew's wife, Susan, gave birth to twin boys, William Matthew and Mason Wright Turner. Later that year, Braxton Avery Turner was born to Benjamin and Tabitha. In 2011, another set of identical twin girls—Mona Sophia and Lillian Fahey Turner—were born to Matthew and Susan Turner as well as two bonus grandchildren, Zoe Renee and Jayden Kai Ross. The total went from 5 to 14 in two years. (Courtesy of the Turner family.)

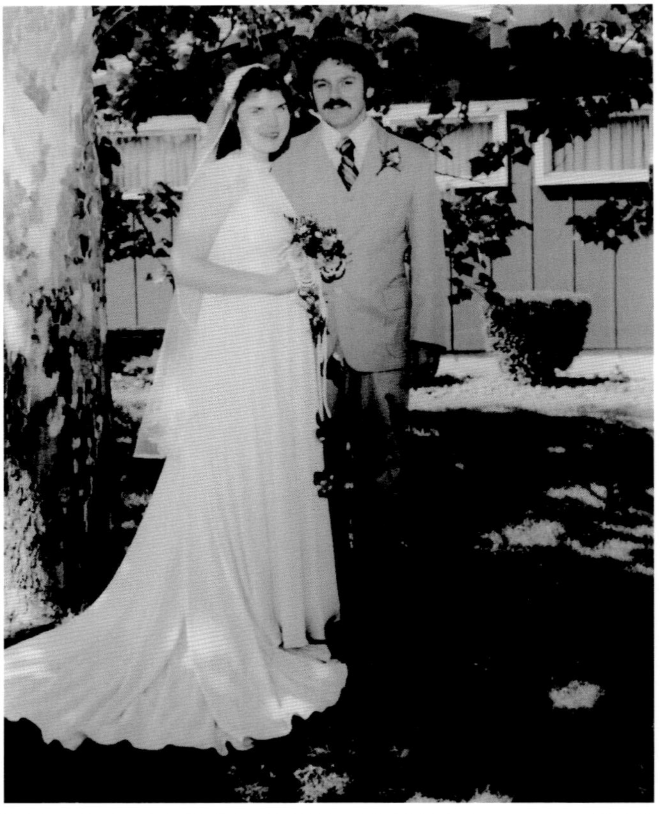

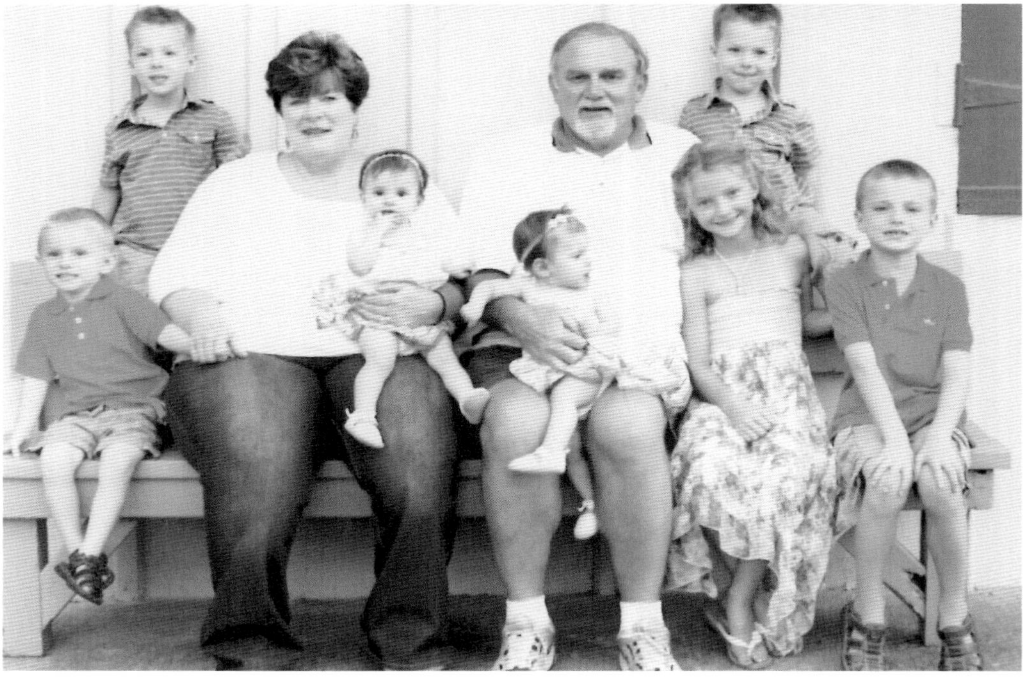

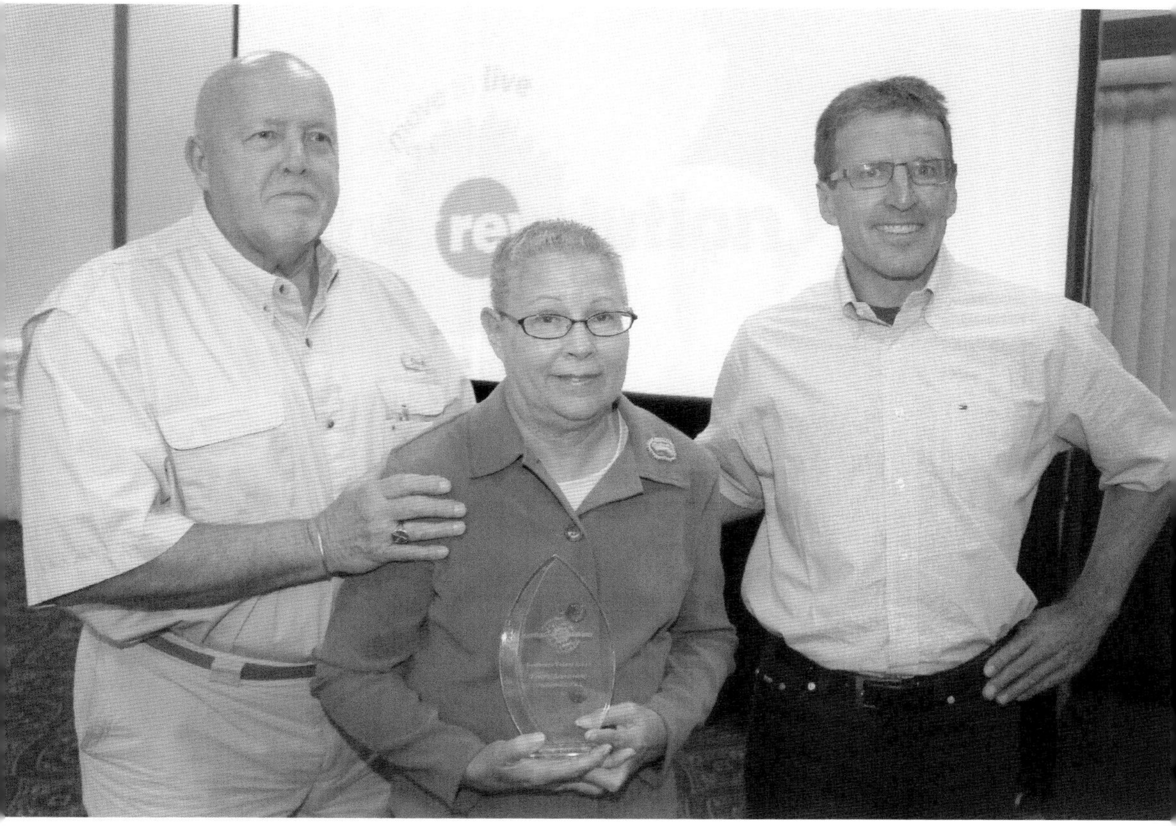

Linda and David Armstrong
Linda Armstrong (center) was diagnosed with Parkinson's disease in 2000, at age 54. She is active in support groups, fundraising, and advocacy. She is the southeast Indiana representative for the Parkinson's Action Network. Linda was honored with the 2012 Sunflower Victory Award at the Sunflower Revolution Symposium & Expo. She was praised for "representing the spirit and the 'Move to Live, Live to Move' philosophy of the Sunflower Revolution." The Sunflower symposium is an annual educational program of the Gardner Center, at the University of Cincinnati Neuroscience Institute. The Victory Award acknowledges those who inspire, empower, and give hope within the Parkinson's disease community.

When she is not speaking before Congress about the urgent need to find a cure for Parkinson's, Linda is creating beautiful necklaces, bracelets, and sea-glass pins, which she sells under the title "Beading for a Parkinson's Cure." All proceeds benefit the Gardner Center. Also shown in this photograph are her husband, David Armstrong (left), and Olympic athlete Davis Phinney, whose foundation sponsors programs that provide the information, tools, and inspiration to live well with Parkinson's today.

David Armstrong's handshake is strong, and his voice demands attention. His six-foot, muscular frame is almost too big for the chairs. For years, he spent his days training athletes. He was the strength and conditioning coach at Xavier University. He has traveled around the world as the Olympic USA weight-lifting senior international coach, and he has coached other sports, such as wrestling and football. Now semiretired, he works at the Aurora Public Library. (Courtesy of Tom Uhlman for the Garden Family Center.)

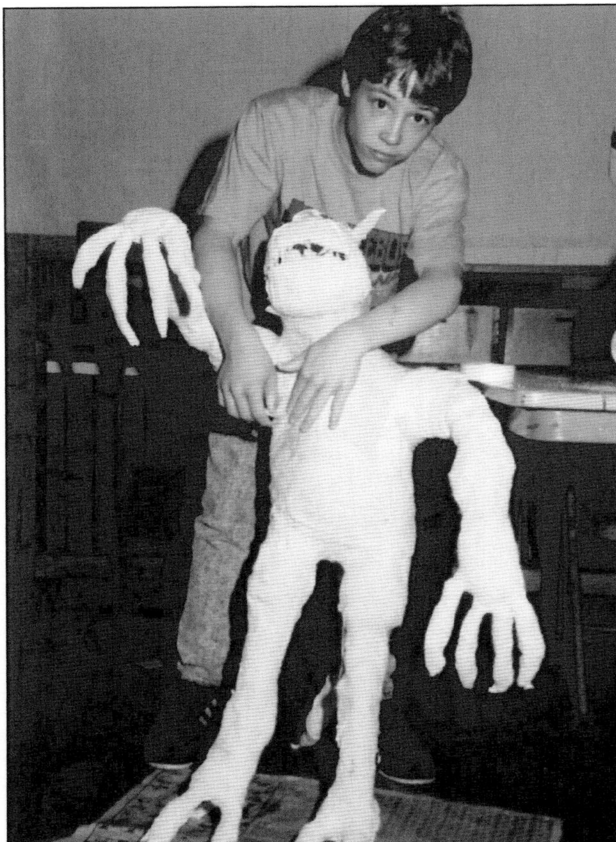

Take Me To Your Mummy

Jesse Schaefer is shown working on his art display for the Aurora Middle School art fair. Each year, the art fair gives the students a chance to show off their artwork and teach the process of creating their project. (Courtesy of the *Journal Press.*)

Got Mold?

This is the science fair project display of Jason Artrip of Aurora Middle School. During the fair, students showcase their work, usually including a poster to explain the project. For some science fairs, the actual project accompanies the poster. Projects and presentations are evaluated, and grades or awards are given. (Courtesy of the *Journal Press.)*

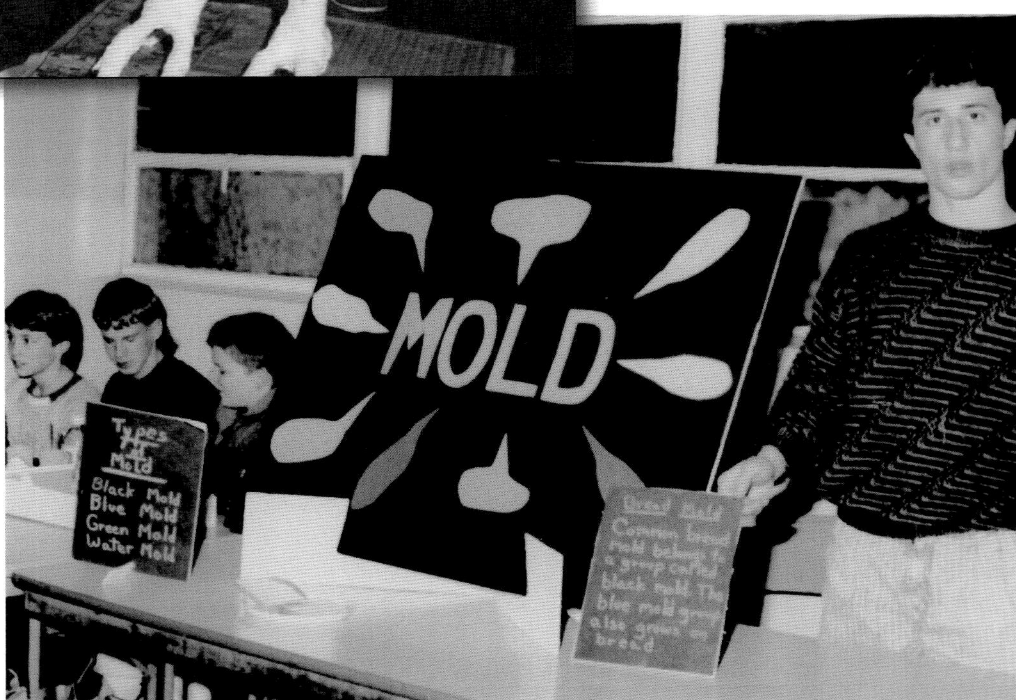

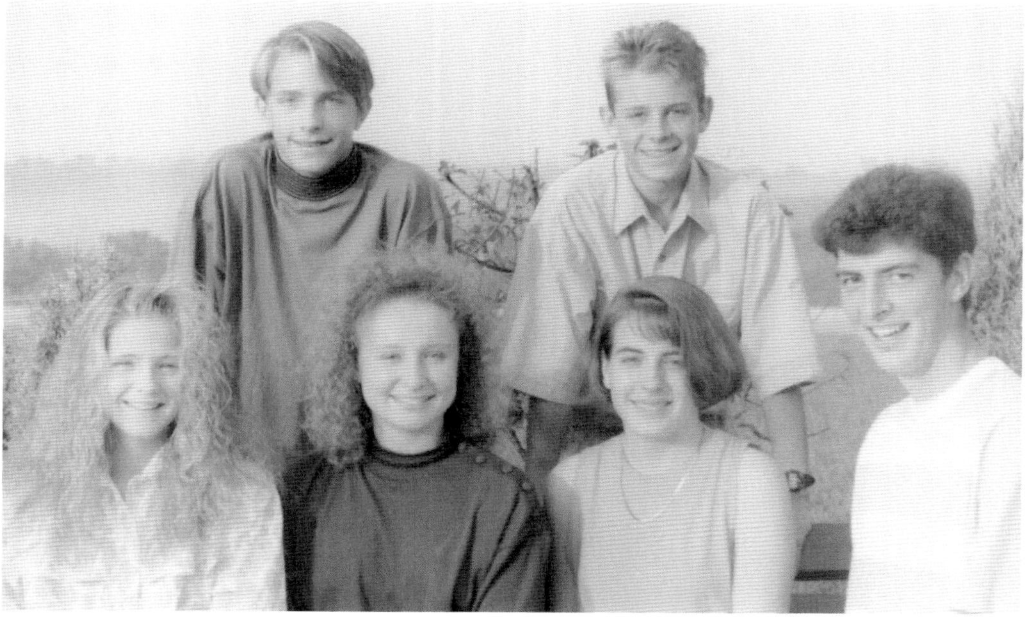

1990 Football Prince and Princess Candidates
The Aurora High School homecoming prince and princess candidates for 1990 were, from left to right, (first row) Crystal Dicus, Chris Sneed, Renee Fogle, and Jason Thies; (second row) Matt Herzog and Matt Stewart. (Courtesy of DCHS.)

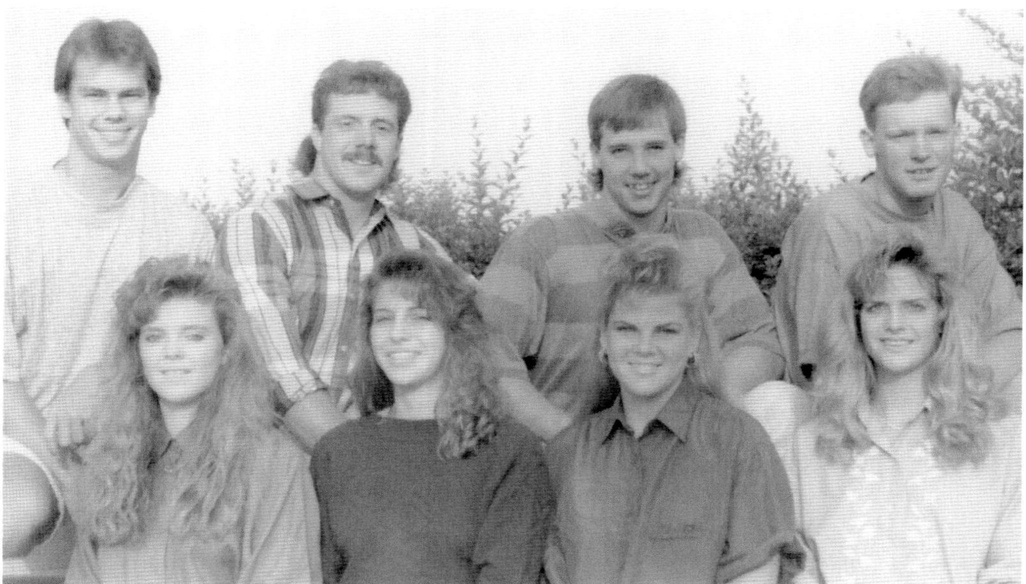

1990 Football Homecoming Candidates
The Aurora High School homecoming candidates for 1990 are, from left to right, (first row) Kristie Banschbach, Jamie Black, Mia Gray, and Lisa Mueller; (second row) Heath Howard, Mike Kervin, Danny Ochs, and Matt Petty. (Courtesy of DCHS.)

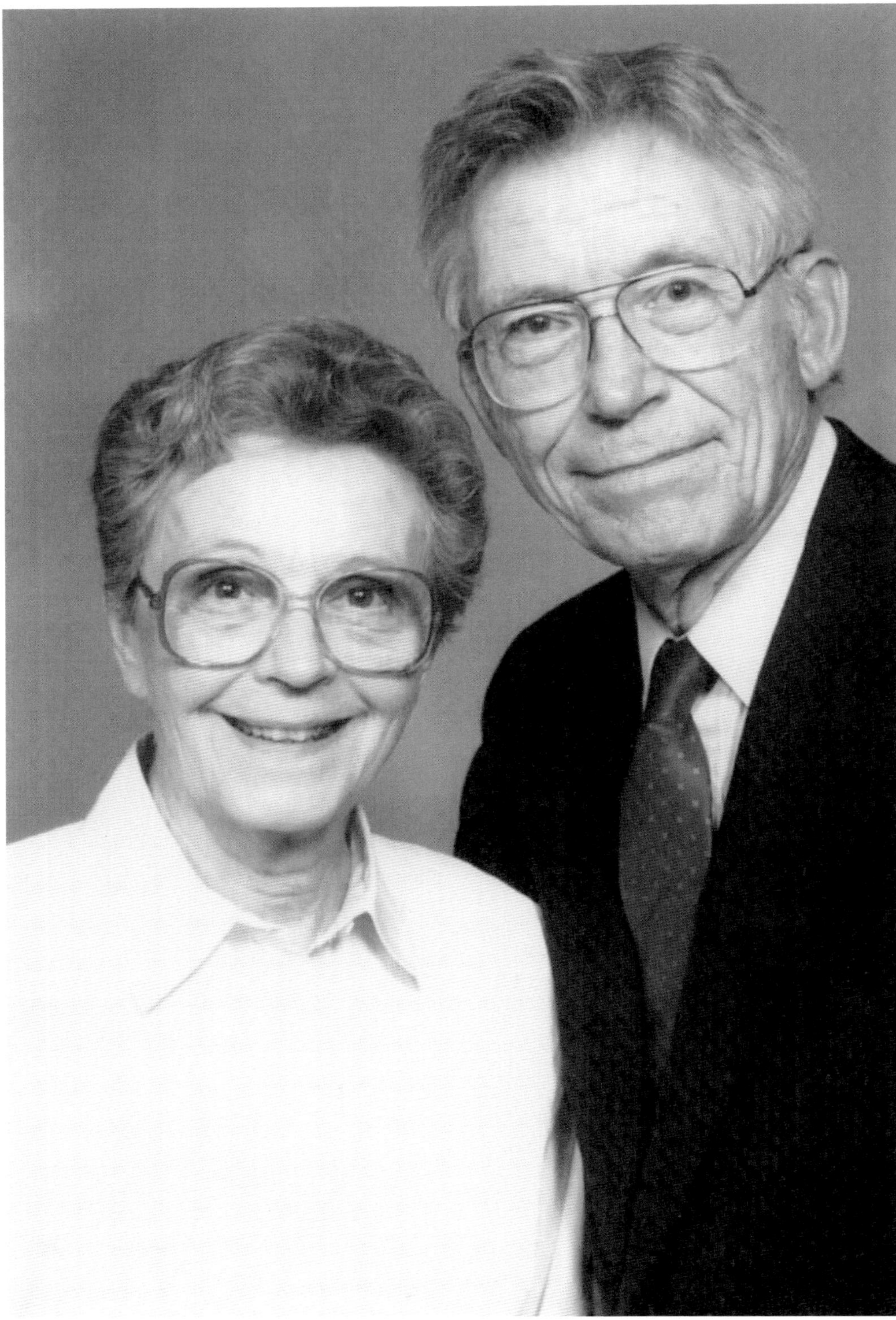

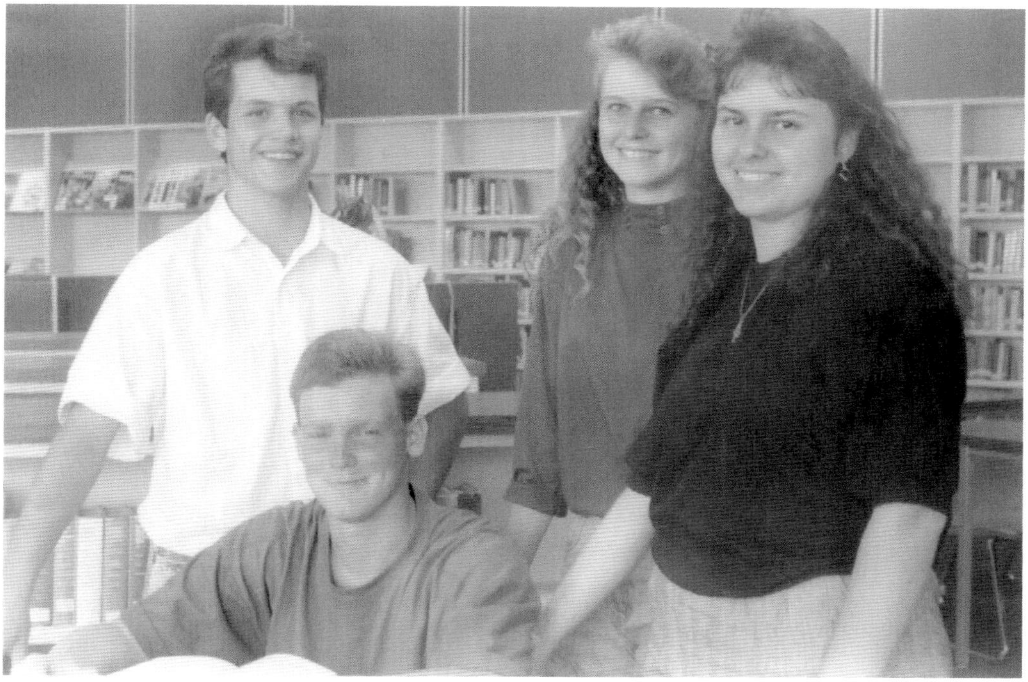

Student Government

The South Dearborn High School student government class officers for the 1990–1991 school year are, from left to right, (standing) vice president Cory Lyon, (seated) president Matt Petty, secretary Sandy Ante, and treasurer Georgeann Miller. (Courtesy of DCHS.)

Dr. Leslie and Dodie Baker (OPPOSITE PAGE)

Leslie M. Baker (1914–1999) was a noted physician, the first Eagle Scout in southeastern Indiana, and a recipient of the state's highest civilian honor. In 1941, he was called to active duty in the Army. He became a member of the 437 Medical Battalion of Gen. George Patton's Third Army during its drive from Normandy across the Ardennes, Belgium, Rhineland, and Central Europe. For his outstanding service, he received the Bronze Star and attained the rank of lieutenant colonel. Dr. Baker delivered more than 3,000 babies and continued making house calls even after he retired in 1993. With his twin brother, Judge Lester G. Baker, he pushed for the creation of Dearborn County Hospital, where the intensive care unit bears their name. "He believed the people of southeast Indiana were entitled to the same quality of care as other places," said his son, Judge John G. Baker.

When Dolores "Dodie" Baker (1916–2003) took on a project, she was relentless. She was a wonderful mother to four children, was involved in Aurora schools' parent-teacher organizations, and taught Sunday school and Boy Scouts. In the late 1950s, she and her husband were among a group of locals finding the funds to purchase Hillforest and restore it to its former grandeur. In the late 1960s, after the determination of mental health needs, there was no such thing as mental health treatment. Dr. Baker had to be a part-time psychologist as well as a physician. Dodie Baker fought hard to establish the Community Mental Health Center in Lawrenceburg and New Horizons in Batesville. The Bakers loved Dearborn County. It is reflected not only in what they said, but in what they did. They left a legacy and believed that if everyone does a little bit, everybody benefits. (Courtesy of the Baker family.)

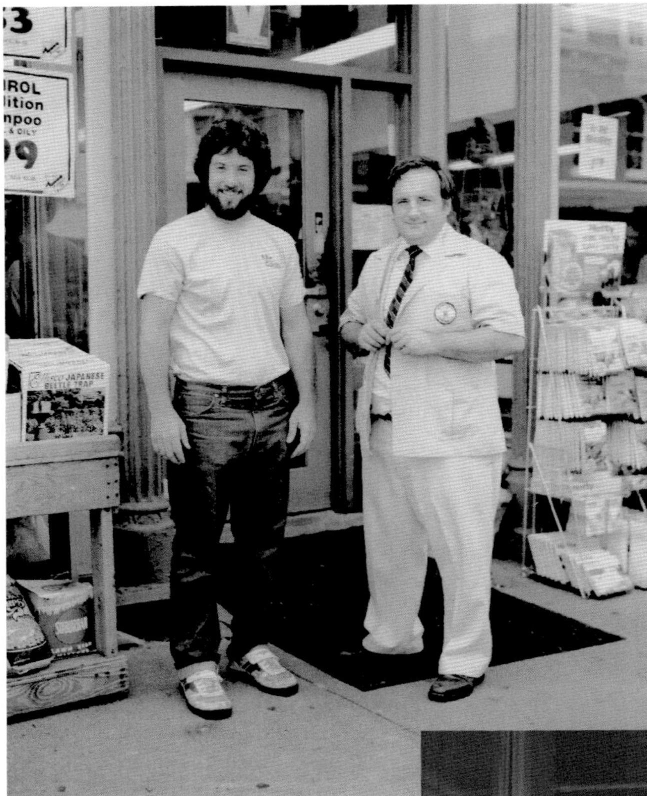

Ullrich Drug Store
The Ullrich Drug Store has reinvented itself to keep up with the times during its century-long existence. Richard Ullrich Sr. (right) initiated Ullrich Electronics, Ullrich Health Care, and reorganized the store departments. Standing with Ullrich in front of the building in 1983 is his son, Richard. John Ullrich purchased this building in 1883. (Courtesy of Richard Ullrich.)

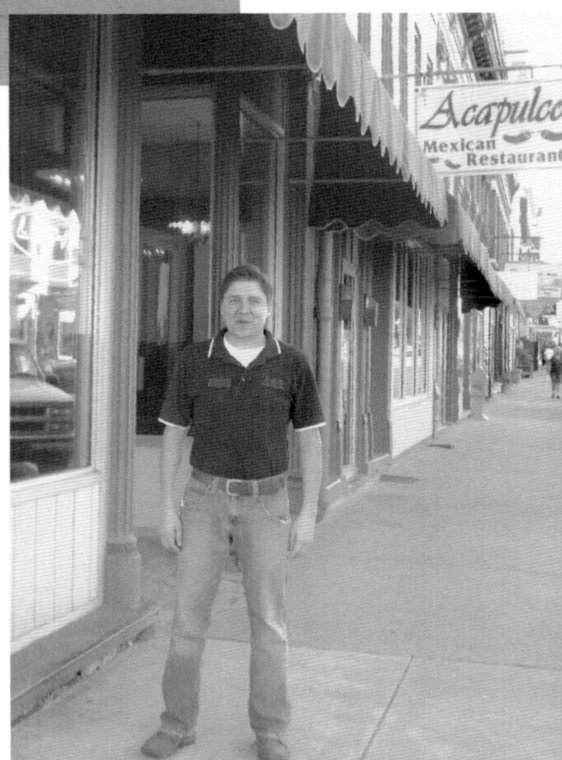

Ullrich's Corner
When the Ullrich family closed their drugstore on the corner of Second and Main Streets, the building was sold and transformed into a restaurant. Today, it is the home of the popular Acapulco Mexican Restaurant. Standing in front of the old facade is Efrain Rodriguez, manager. Rodriguez began with the Alcapulco Restaurant chain in 2006 and has managed the Aurora location since 2008. (Author's collection.)

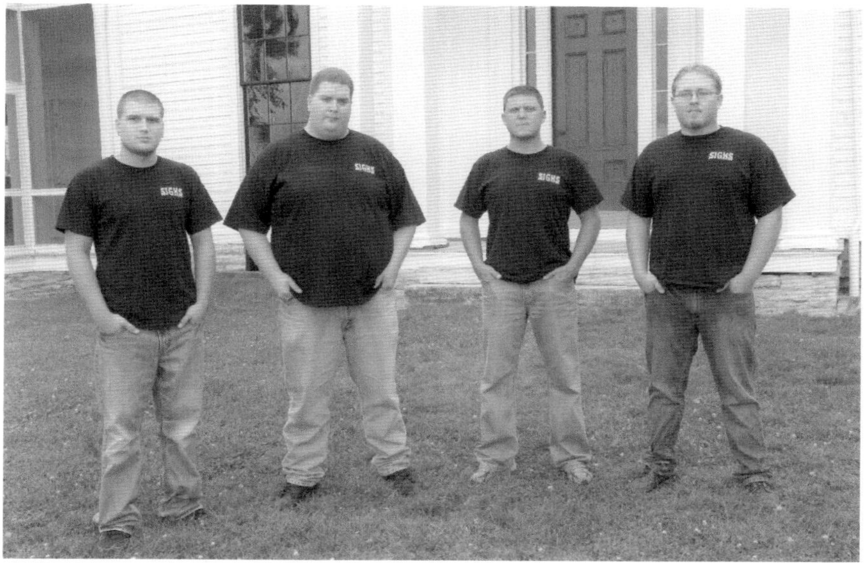

Southern Indiana Ghost Hunting Specialist (SIGHS) Paranormal Investigators
Standing in front of Veraestau, once the home of Jesse Holman, are, from left to right, A.J. Hastings, Brad Dietrich, Yancy Craig, and John Johnson. "When trying to find the most haunted place in Aurora, it is a hard choice," says Dietrich. The ghost hunters believe there is much history in small river towns such as Aurora. Based on local stories and personal experiences, the investigators believe that Hillforest and Applewood Restaurant are extremely active. (Courtesy of SIGHS.)

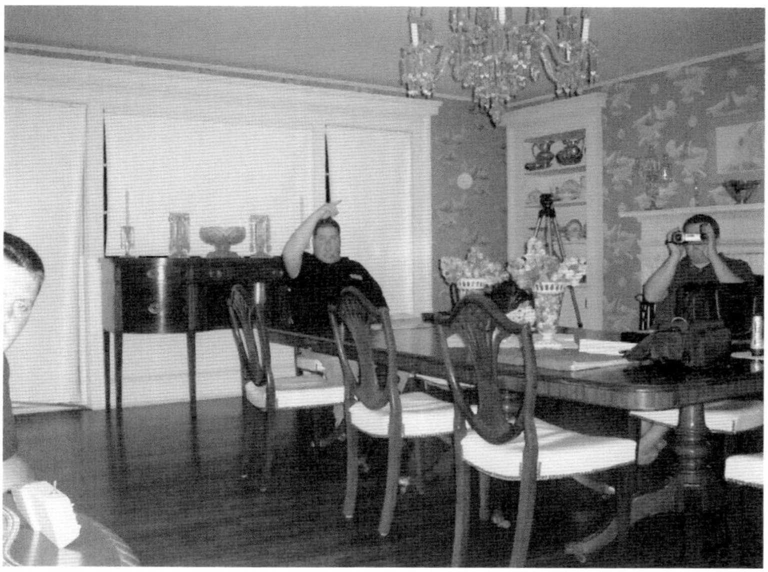

Ghosts A-Plenty
A SIGHS investigator points to an orb in the dining room of Veraestau. The old home has been investigated several times for ghosts, including instances in which footsteps were heard and hair was pulled. A little girl in the music room and an African American slave who stays in the basement are believed to be haunting the old house. (Courtesy of SIGHS.)

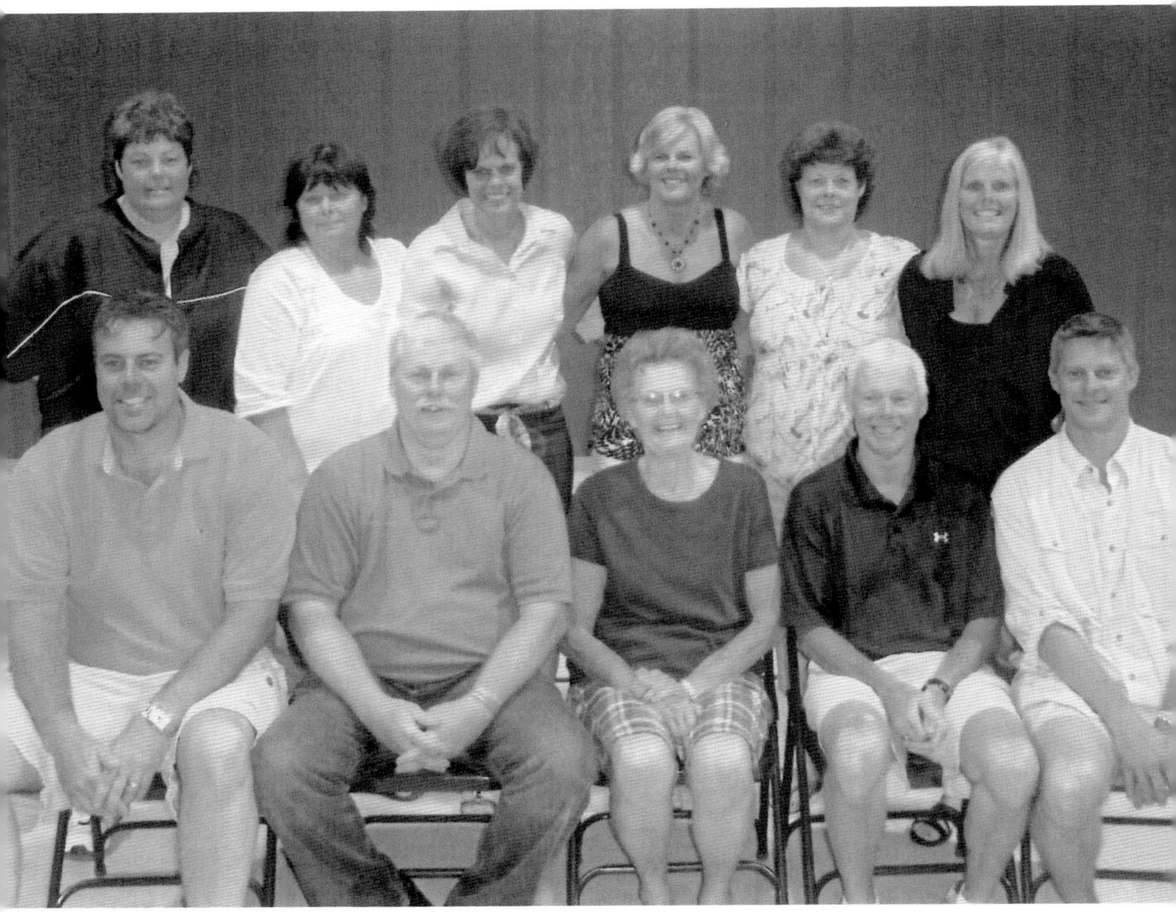

Betty Lou Tyler

Betty Lou Tyler (first row, center) will thoroughly entertain with her outgoing personality. This 85-year-old may lead a cheer at a basketball game or dance the worm on the floor with her grandchildren. She and her sisters would go to nursing homes and entertain for the patients. Tyler and her husband, William, were blessed with 10 children. William ran "Bill's Shoe Repair" in Lawrenceburg, which his son, Randy, still owns. Betty retired from Anchor Glass. All of these tall, good-looking Tylers were excellent athletes and set school records. Shown here are, from left to right, (first row) Chad, Randy, Betty Lou, Tim, and Bradley; (second row) Lisa Tyler, Kim Hamilton, Lori Becker, Carol Jean Bowling, Rindy Phillips, and Janie Fehr. (Courtesy of the Tyler family.)

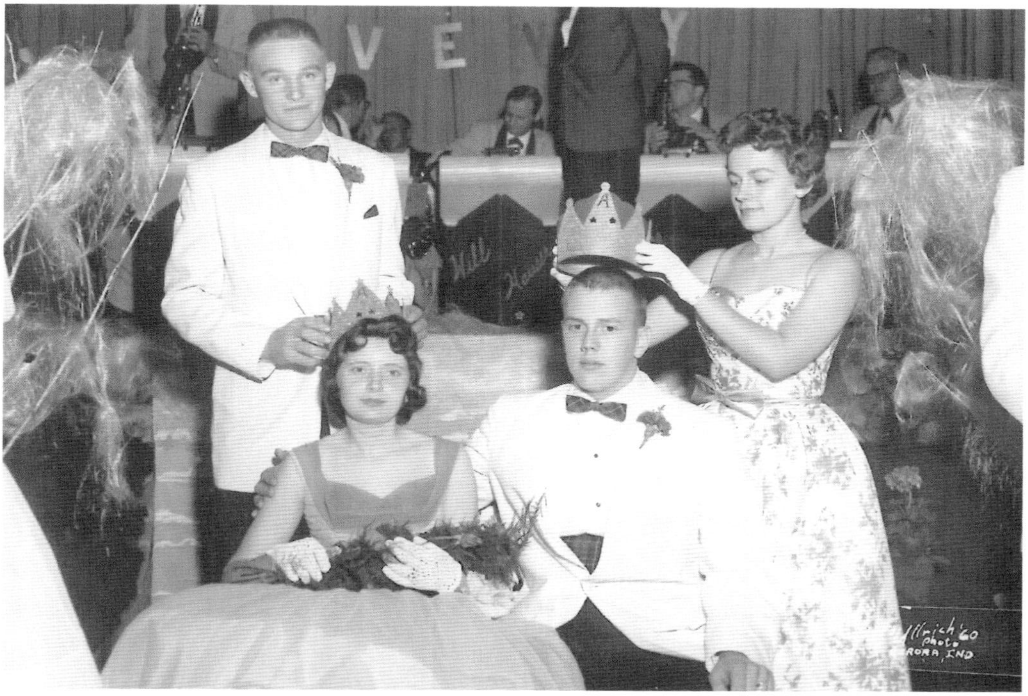

Charlene Lockwood and John Reid
The junior and senior prom has always been a major event closing out a school year. In 1960, junior Charlene Lockwood (front left) was crowned queen by Larry Rumsey (back left). John Reid (front right) was crowned king by Carolyn Kremer. (Courtesy of Ullrich Studio.)

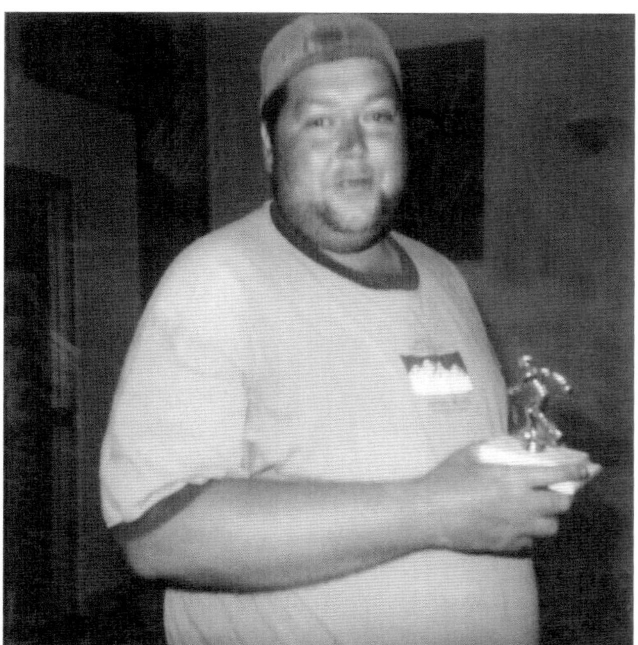

Chris Sechrest
Sechrest proudly holds a bowling trophy he recently received at a local tournament. He has worked at Walmart for 10 years checking carts. He lives on Hanover Avenue with his mother Judy and stepfather Jeff Muncy. His father is Jerry Sechrest of Aurora. (Courtesy of Chris Sechrest.)

John F. Ullrich Studio

John Ullrich (left) was the son of William and Irene Ullrich. For many years, John, his sister Mary Rita (center), and his son Roger (right) operated the photographic studio from the second floor of the Ullrich Drug Store. Thousands of professional photographs were taken by the family, recording the history and people of Aurora, one photograph at a time. (Courtesy of Ullrich Studio.)

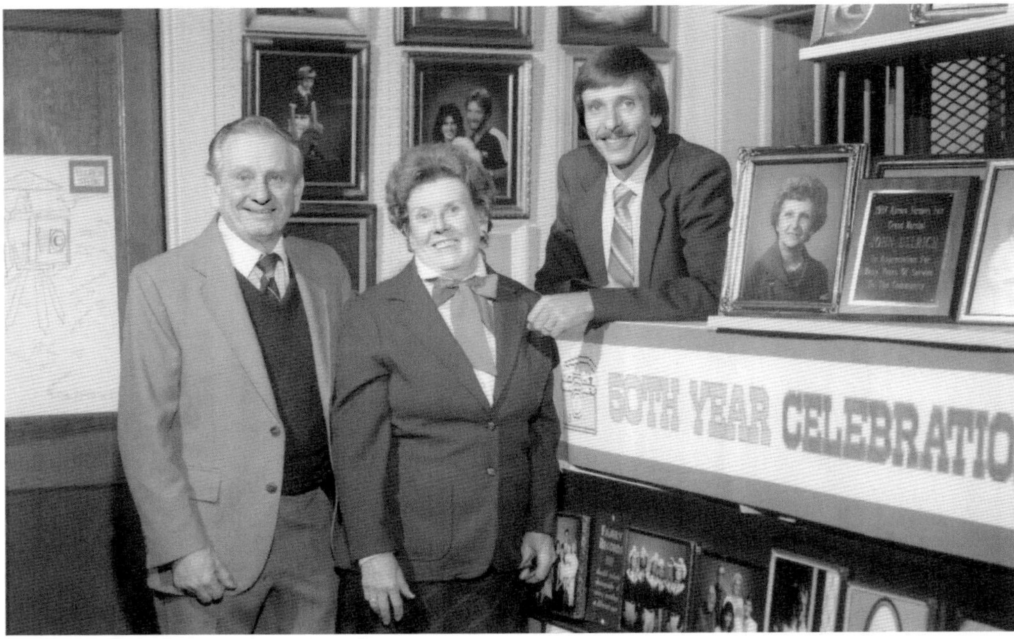

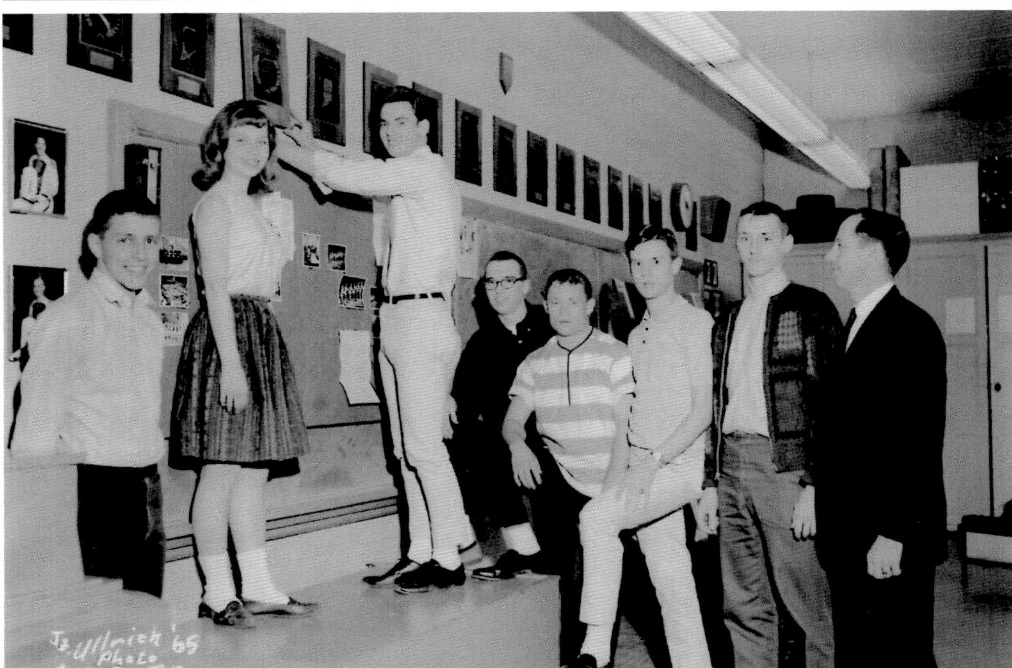

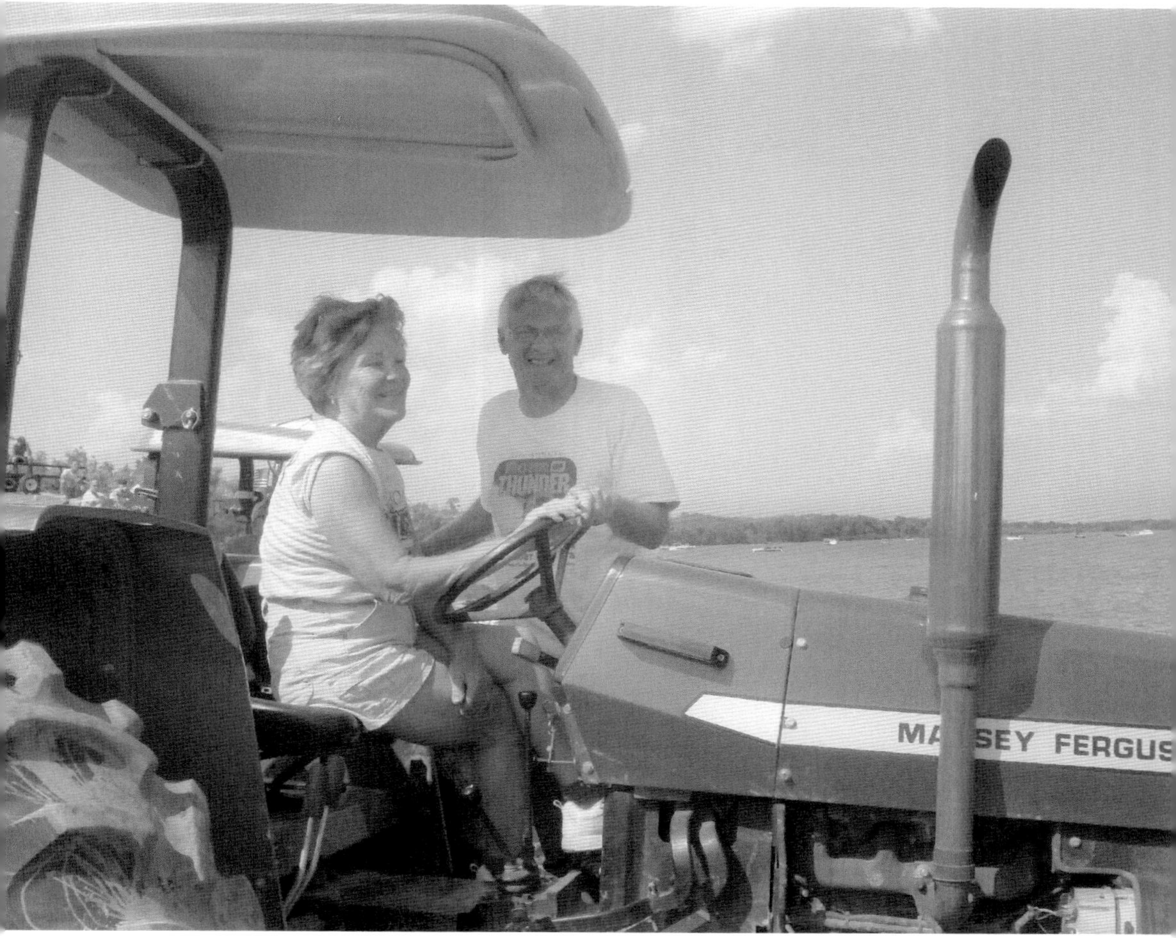

Charlotte Peters Hastings
Charlotte (Peters) Hastings is the owner of Aurora Floral and Gifts and was owner of the former Coachlight Inn Restaurant, both downtown Aurora businesses. Charlotte's grassroots approach to volunteerism has created four events that bring in more than 50,000 visitors to Dearborn County annually. She has three children, Debbie Walters, Donnie (the current mayor of Aurora), and Billy. Pictured on the tractor with her is "A Roar of Thunder" boat regatta volunteer David Kyle. (Author's collection.)

1965 Aurora High School Band (OPPOSITE PAGE)
In 1965, the Aurora High School band won first place in its division. The first thing the members did was hang their award on the band room wall. Shown here are, from left to right, Bill Longcamp, Karen Schaich, Clyde Fairfield, Dan Rice, G.R. Honchell, John Rullman, Ray Kuhlmeir, and teacher Bill Platt. (Courtesy of Ullrich Studios.)

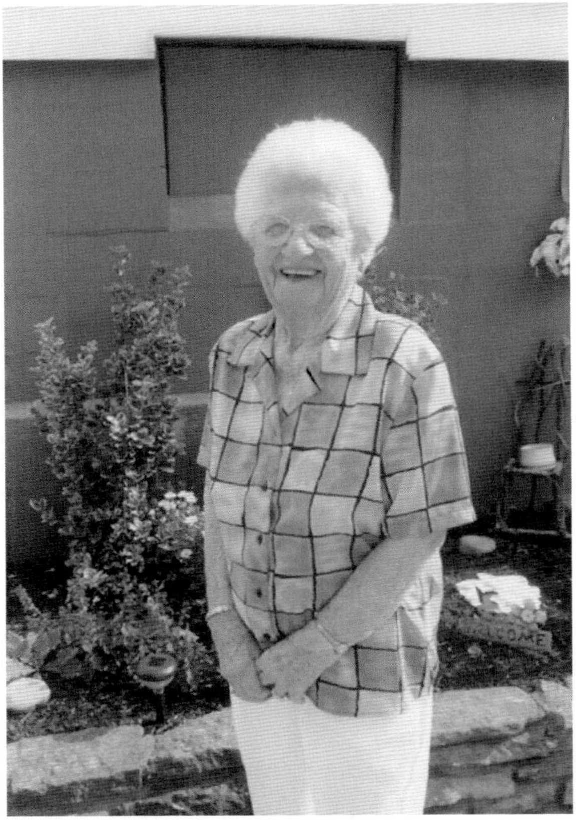

Irene Peters Hicks

Irene loves to keep busy. When she signed up for unemployment benefits at the age of 85, they told her she was in the wrong line. She worked for years as a waitress at Ullrich's sandwich bar and later at Coachlight Restaurant. She is now 94, and things have not changed much. She attends mass faithfully at St. Mary's Church, gardens, plays cards, and lives independently. She still hosts family holiday events where 60 or 70 family members show up. For 82 years, she has had a "real" Santa on Christmas Eve. Irene married Elmer Hicks several years after her first husband Raymond passed away. She passed on her strong work ethic to her children, who are pictured below. Seated are Irene Hicks and Patty Carter, and standing, from left to right, are Donna VanOstrand, Kenneth Peters, Linda Smithers, Mike Peters, and Charlotte Hastings. (Courtesy of the Peters family.)

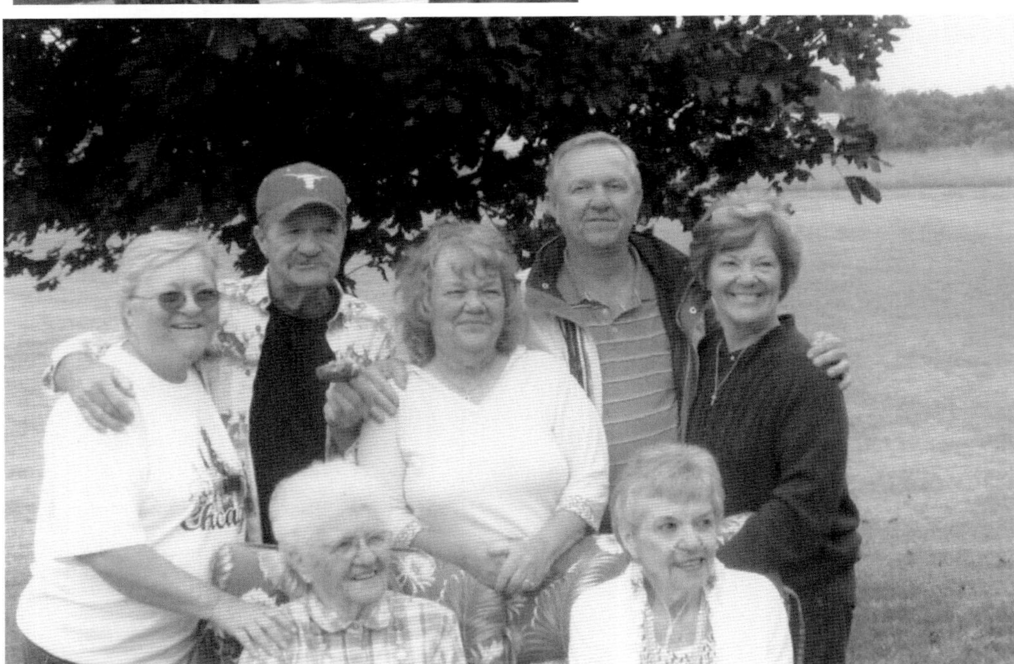

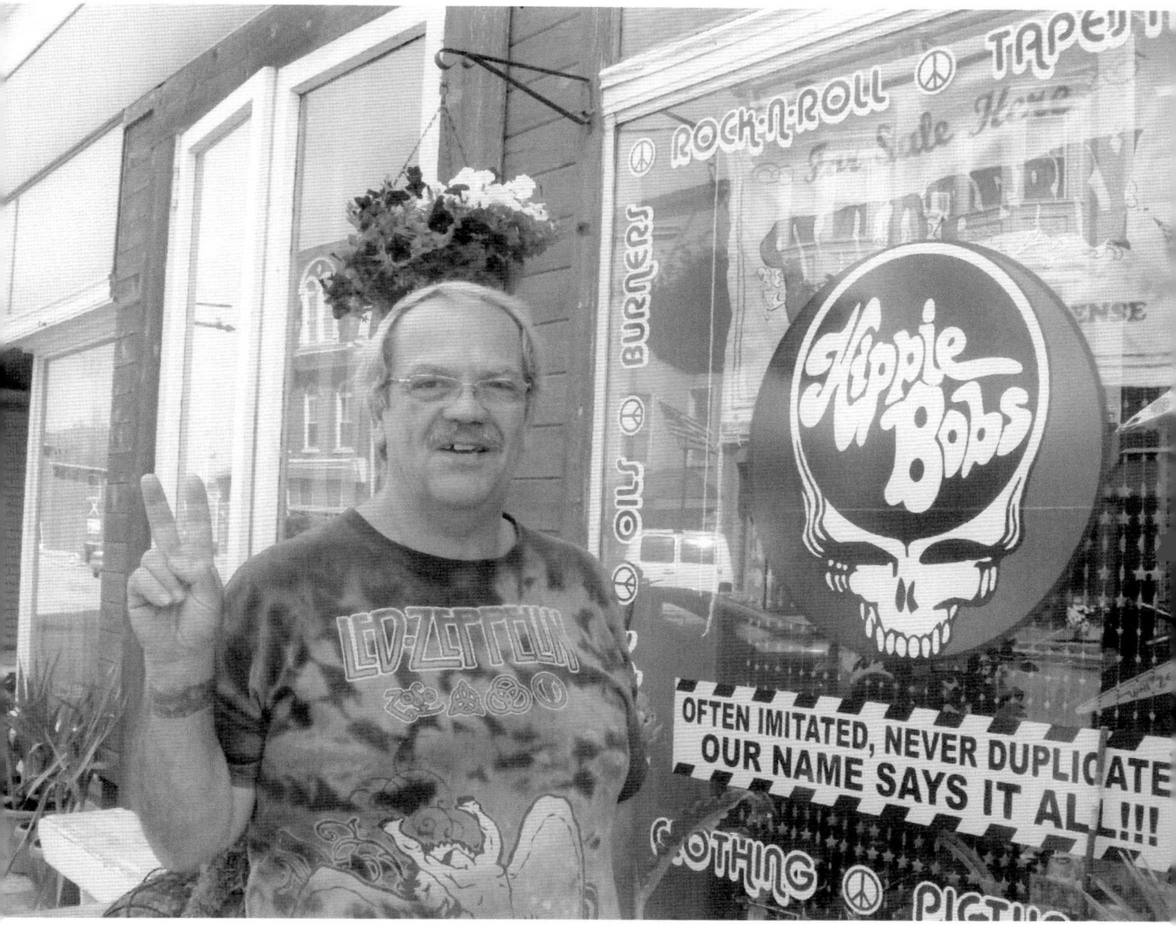

Hippie Bob

Jim Lee is often called "Hippie Bob," after his store on Second Street. He says he only wears tie-dyed shirts because he can get them at cost. Jim has a love of flowers and trees and has been known to grow an artichoke on the storefront sidewalk. He has raced motorcycles for 43 years. In 2010, he won first place in the 50-and-over class at the Vintage National Race and goes around the track more out of habit now. He has a son and a daughter, but most of his family lives in Italy where his plans are to one day retire. (Authors collection.)

Joshua Sweeney

Owner and chef Joshua Sweeney (right) brings a "high quality and contemporary cuisine" to his new establishment, Third and Main Restaurant. The old building, with its beautiful antique bar, has had several owners and name changes, including Pelgens, Coachlight, and Red Feather. Seen with Sweeney is Bruce Silber, barkeep. (Author's collection.)

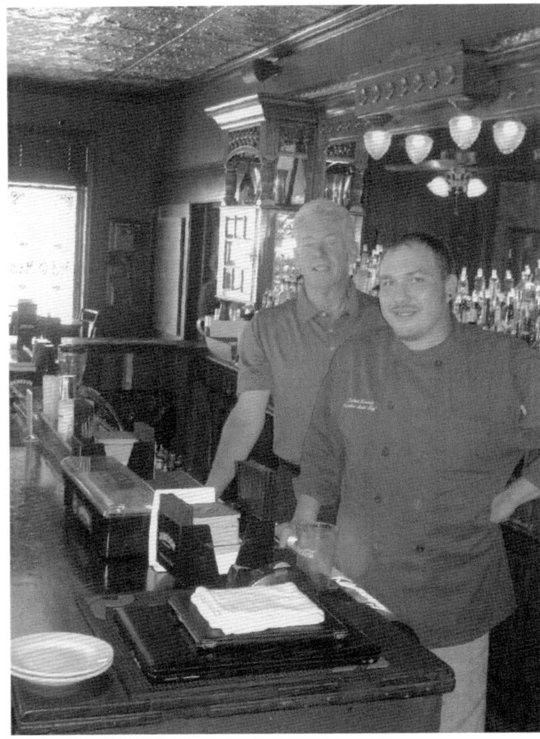

Tina and Thomas Cheek

Tina and Thomas Cheek are shown at their campaign headquarters in Aurora. Tom is running for state representative in house district No. 67. He was born in 1958, the youngest of five children. Tom's ancestors were some of the first settlers in Aurora. He has served as Dearborn County councilman and on the Community Mental Health Center board of directors. He married his high-school sweetheart, Tina Guss, and they are the parents of two and grandparents of three. (Author's collection.)

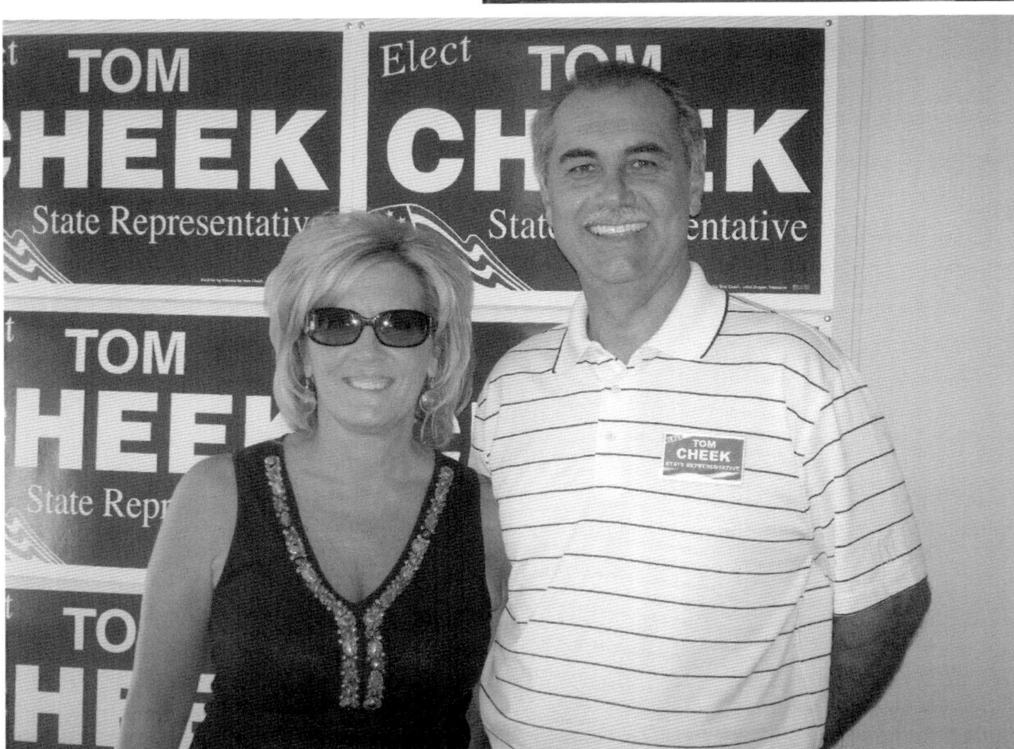

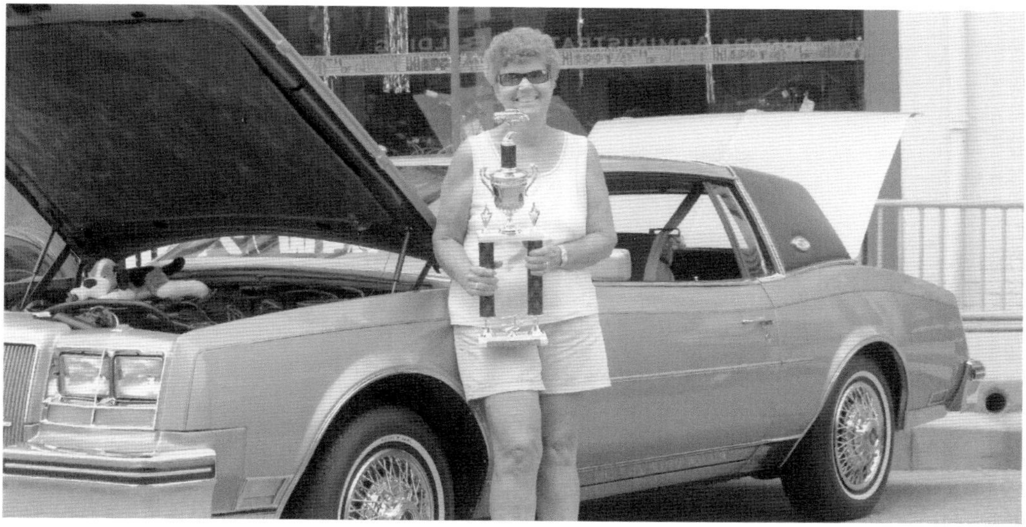

She's a Winner

When Ester Stoll goes to a car show, it is with her all-original, 1985 Buick Rivera. She started showing the car after local car enthusiast Fuzzy Meyer told her she should be taking the Rivera to shows. She has been a winner ever since. (Courtesy of McKenna Murray.)

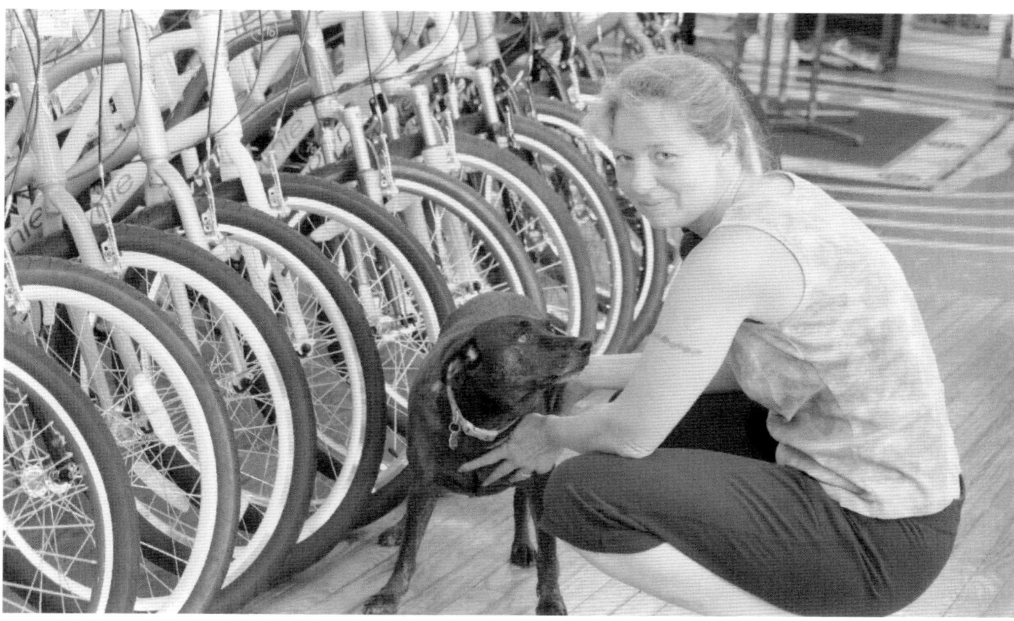

Machell Werning and Beau

Beau is seen here with his owner, Machell Werning, the manager of Weber Sports, located on the corner of Third and Main Streets. About eight years ago, another local store owner came into the bicycle shop with a black lab puppy, and Machell fell in "puppy love." A previous manager had a dog, and they found it was good for the store. Beau comes to work every day and considers the sidewalk in front of the building his personal territory. Kids stop in the shop after school to pet Beau. Tim Weber owns Weber Sports, which is in its 10th year in business. (Author's collection.)

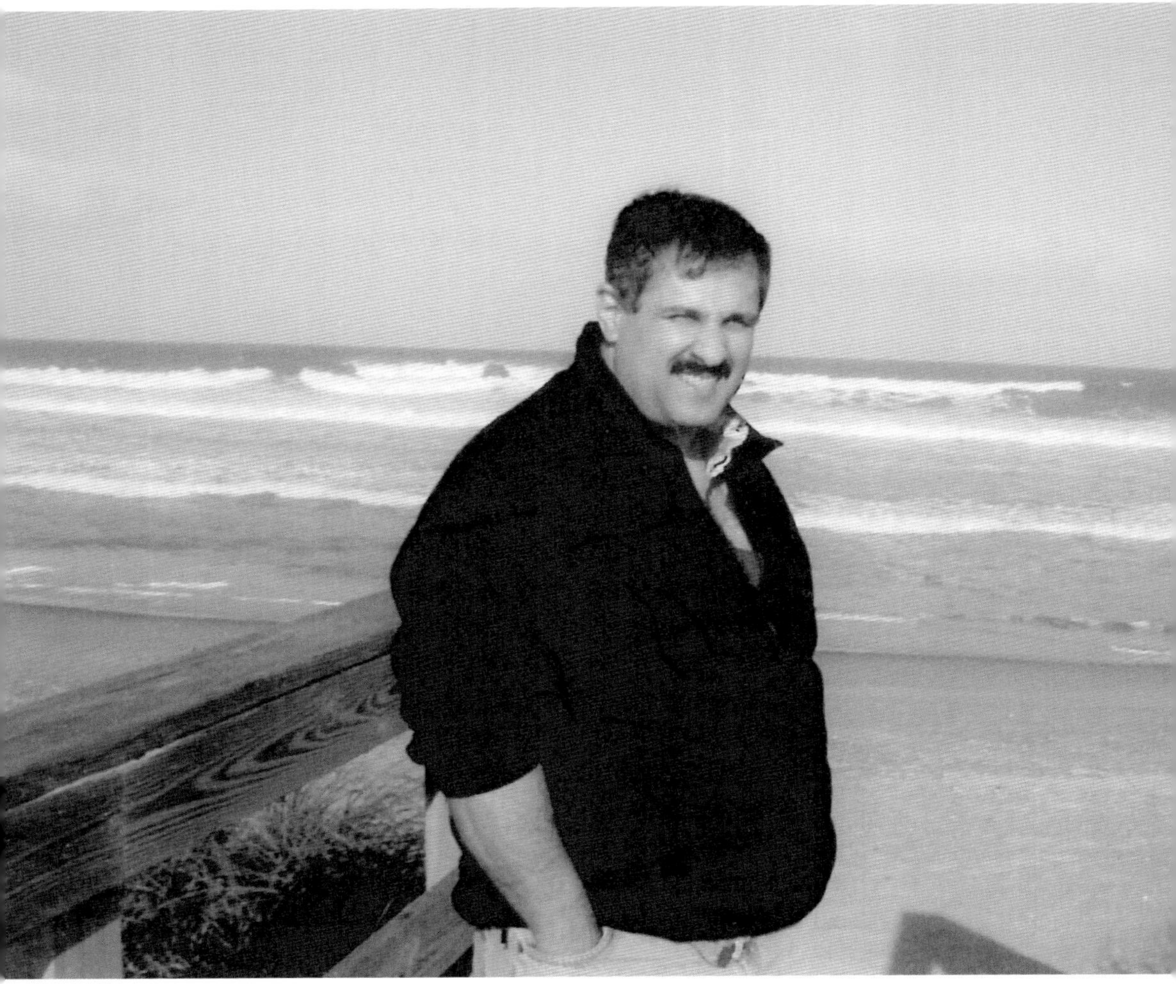

Joseph Awad
Awad has a love for the "hometown" community newspaper. While in college at the University of Cincinnati, he received the Inaugural Freedom Award. He has won more than 30 first-, second-, and third-place Hoosier State Press Association awards. Awad is editor of the *Harrison Record* newspaper and is former publisher and editor of the *Dearborn County Register*, *Aurora Journal Press*, and *Rising Sun Recorder*—all owned by the *Delphos Herald* newspaper group. He is past president of the Hoosier State Press Association (HSPA). He is a first-generation Italian American. (Author's collection.)

Charles Hill (OPPOSITE PAGE)
After 50 years, Charles Hill is still known as the fastest man at Aurora High School. Hill has held the record of a 4.434-minute mile since 1962. In 1978, Aurora High School consolidated with area schools and became South Dearborn High School. Hill, a Methodist minister, and his wife, Martha, have been the owners of the Golden Rule Book Store at 411 Second Street for 39 years. (Courtesy of Ullrich Studios.)

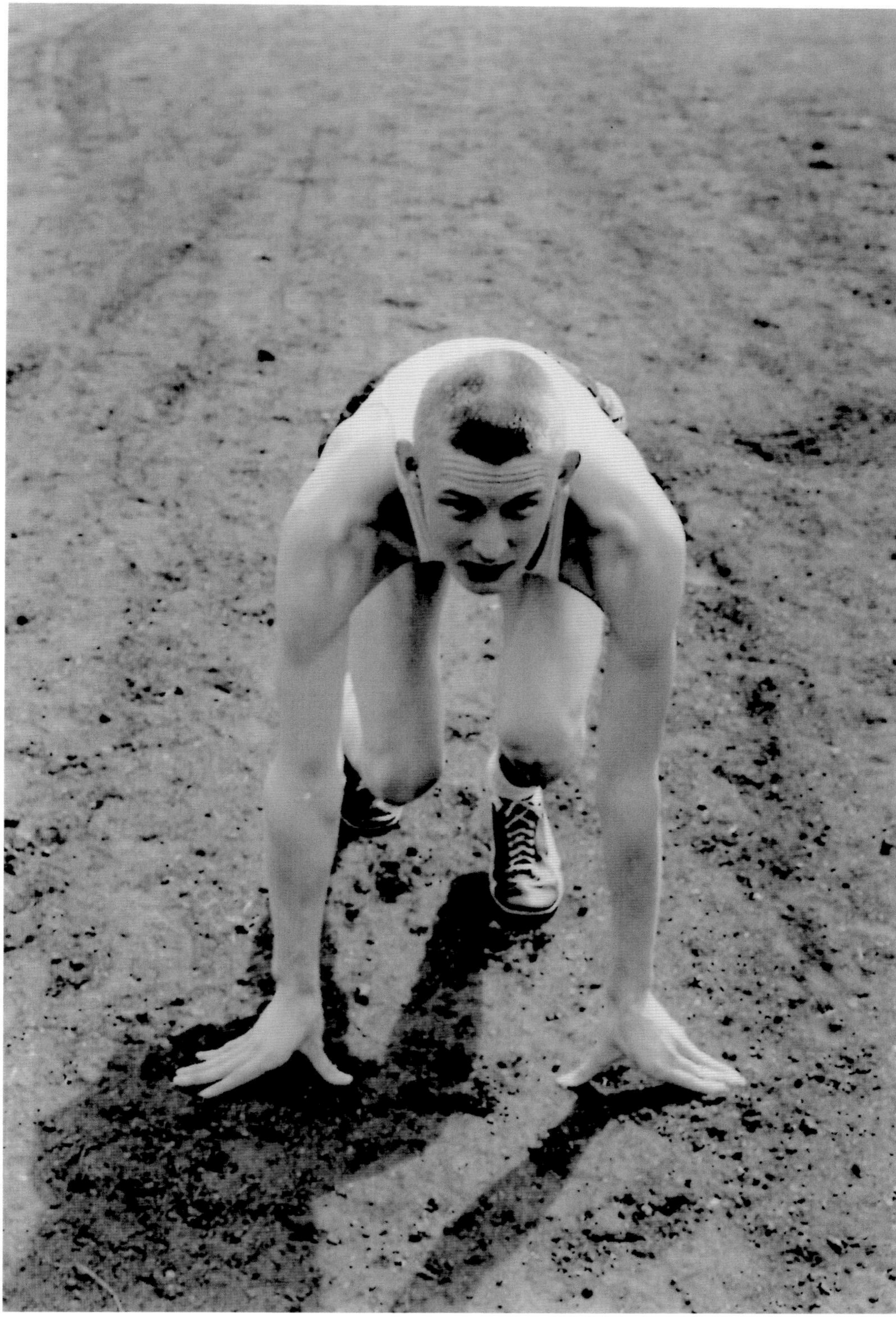

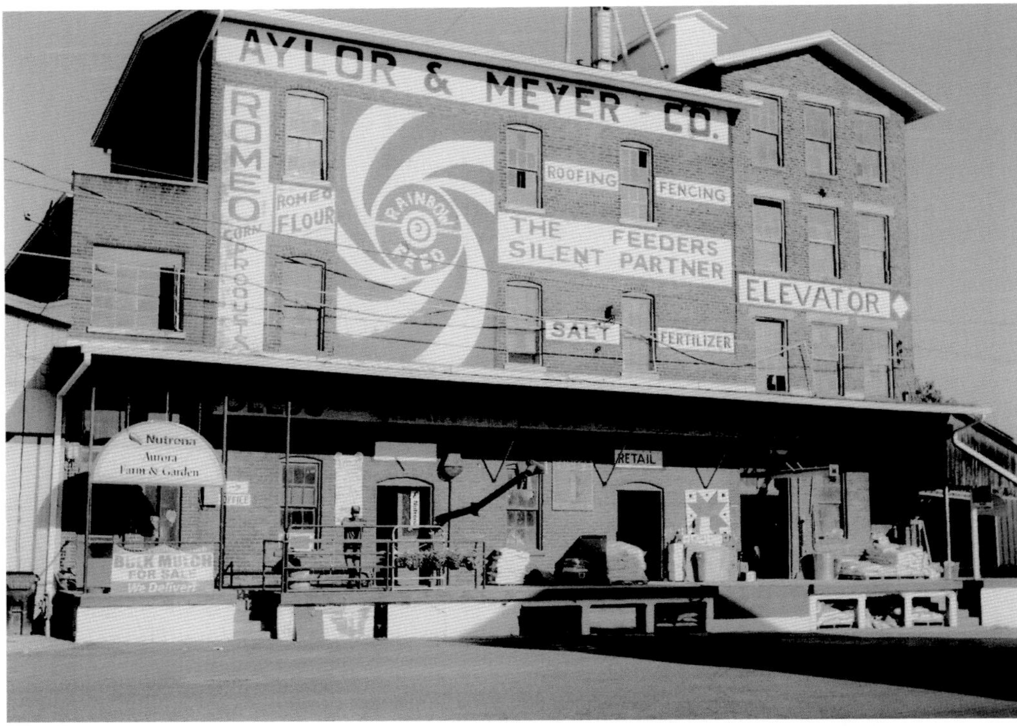

Aurora Farm & Garden
The 1864 Aylor & Meyer feed mill on Exporting Street bears years of colorful, painted advertising. It was originally called Acme Milling. In 1940, it was purchased by Anthony B. Meyer and Wilford H. Aylor and renamed Aylor & Meyer Co. It is one of the city's most photographed buildings. Wayne and Adam Kennett now own this colorful gem. The farm and garden store operates much like it did 148 years ago. (Author's collection.)

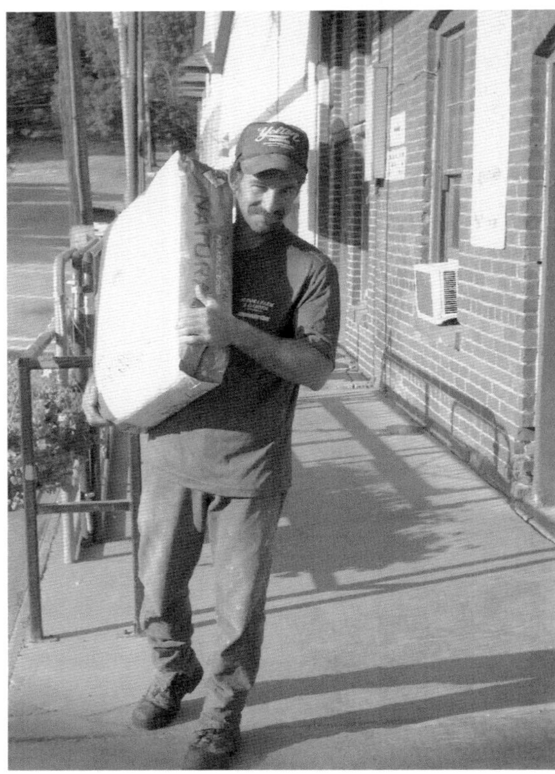

Bobby Schmale
At Aurora Farm & Garden, employee Bobby Schmale almost knows every customer's name and what the reason is for his or her visit. Bobby likes to sing karaoke in his spare time. (Author's collection.)

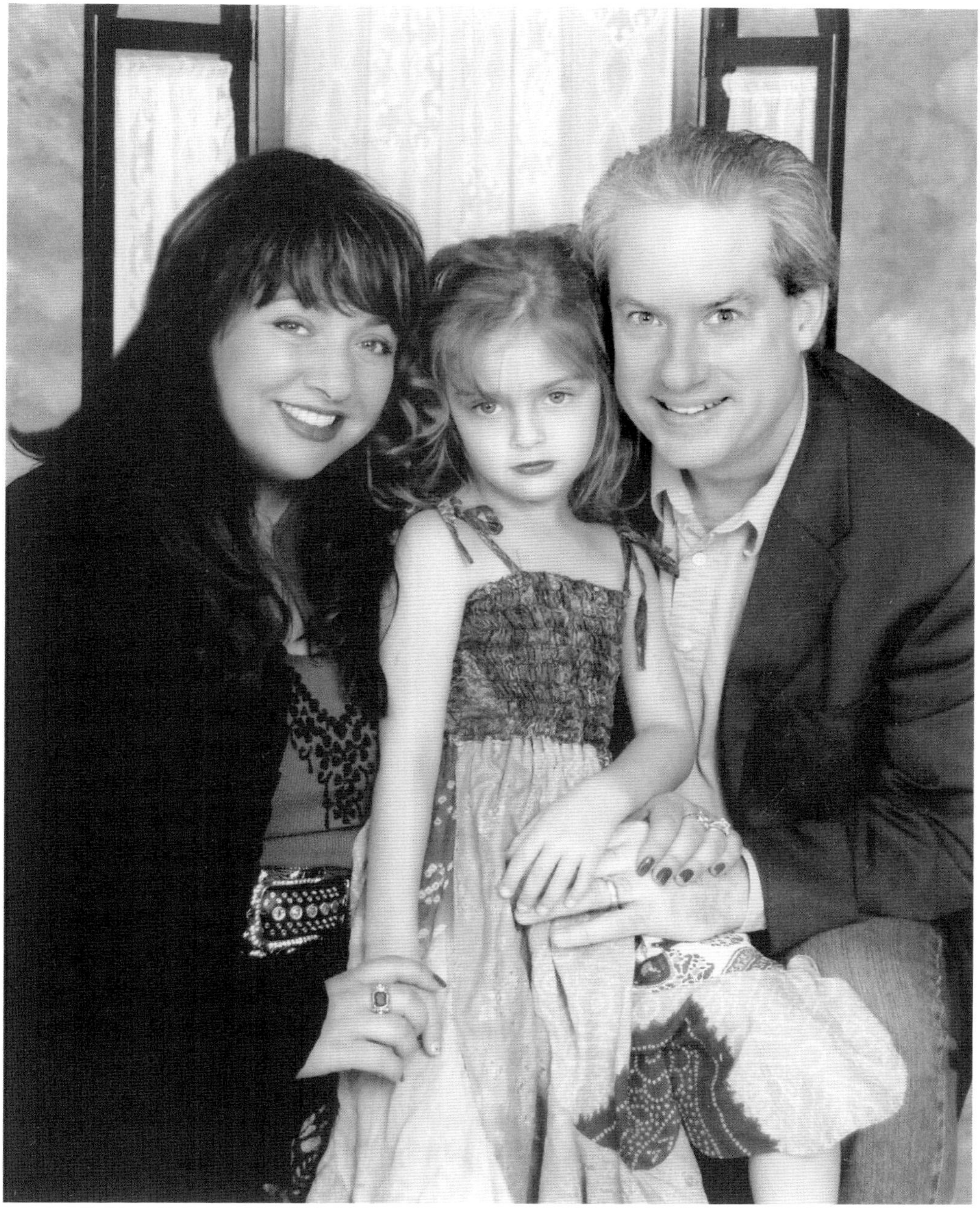

Richard Ullrich Jr.
Richard Ullrich studied Culinary Arts at Northwood University. The son of Richard and Suzanne Ullrich, he has proudly walked in his family's footsteps by becoming the 43rd mayor of Aurora. Richard, his wife, Lala, and daughter Ana live on Main Street in his grandfather Wilfrid's home. Lala grew up in Russia, where she studied international marketing at the Peoples' Friendship University of Russia. A busy woman, she works for a medical translation company, translating for Russian-speaking patients. (Courtesy of Richard Ullrich.)

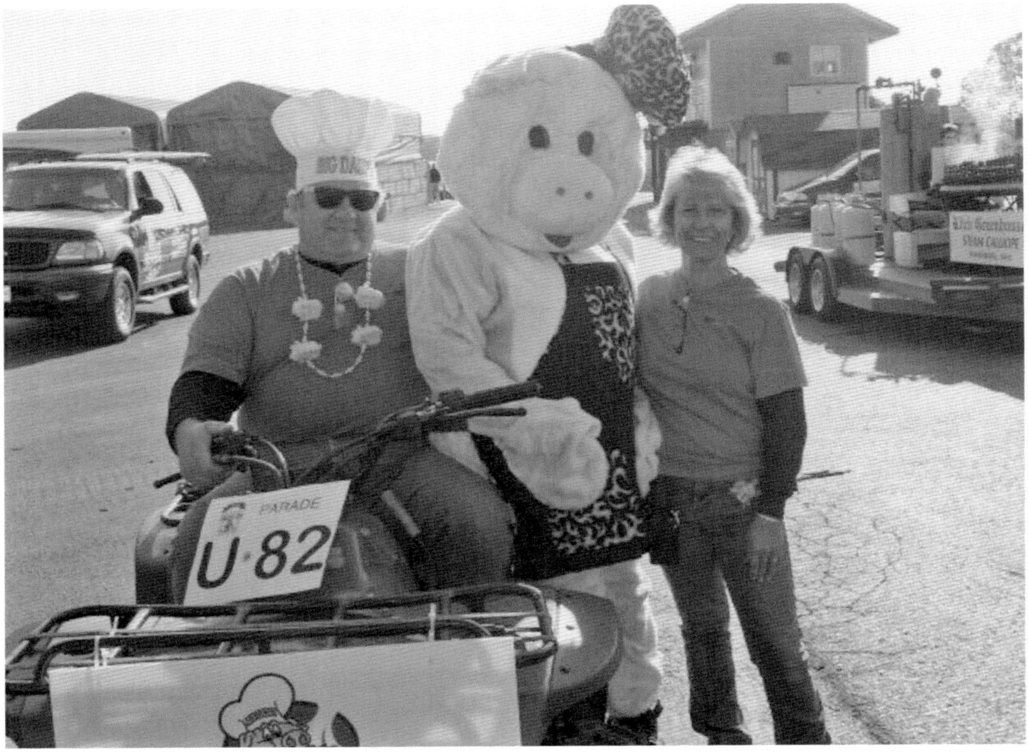

Best BBQ in Town
Robin Willoughby (right) knew she was in trouble when her husband, Victor, brought home a trailer with a barbecue smoker on it. He is a plumber by trade, not a cook. They began catering and, after some successful smoked butts and Robin's side dishes, the couple opened a restaurant called Big Daddy's Bar-B-Q & Lil' Momma's Fixin's on Broadway Street. On Friday night, it is a gathering place for karaoke and chicken dinners. It also hosts the "round table of knowledge" where, every morning, the local guys meet for coffee. (Courtesy of Robin Willoughby.)

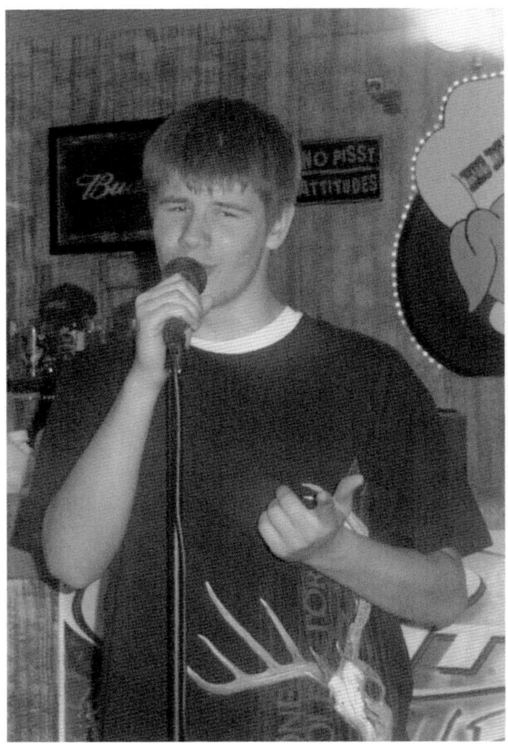

D.J. Adkins
As a young child, D.J. Adkins loved to sing. In this photograph, he is singing at Big Daddy's Bar-B-Q. The talented 16-year-old now travels back and forth to Nashville, Tennessee, and is auditioning for the big time. Karaoke is a favorite pastime in Aurora. Just about every night during the week, one only has to stop in at the Eagles, the Moose, or Big Daddy's to sing a few songs. (Author's collection.)

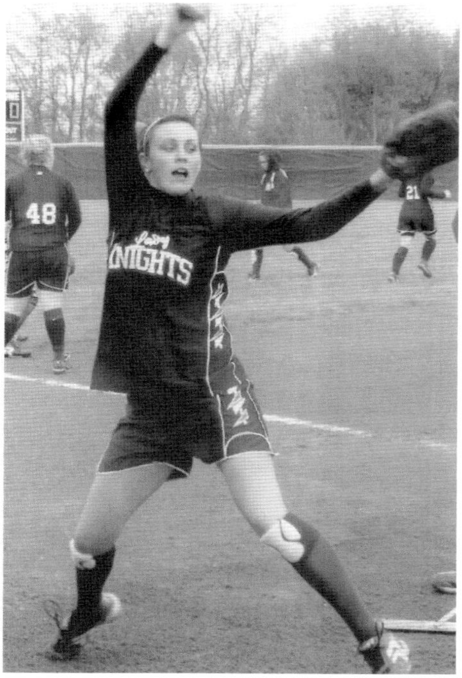

Kooper Vertz
As a fastball pitcher, Kooper Vertz can turn the tide of any game. The five-foot, eleven-inch 17-year-old can deliver a softball at 60-plus miles per hour. Kooper is a junior at South Dearborn High School and has been playing softball for 10 years. Her parents are Joe and Veda Vertz. (Courtesy of Joe Vertz.)

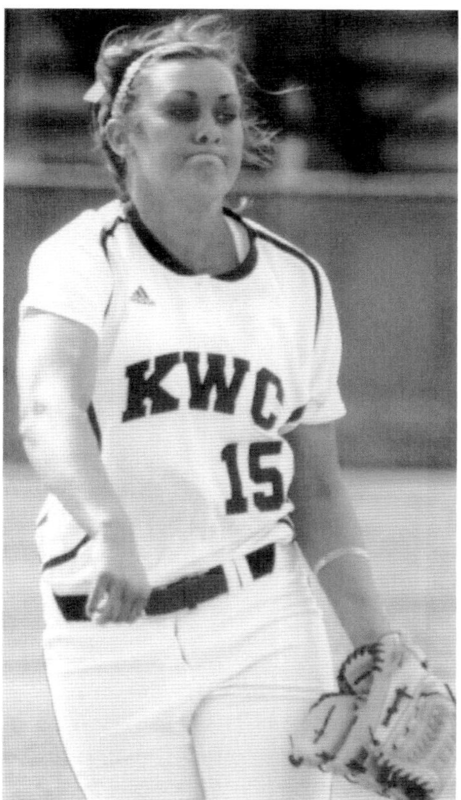

Jordan Vertz
When Jordan went to college and was told to knuckle down, she did—on a softball. She received a full scholarship to Walbash Junior College for two years and now attends Kentucky Wesylan College. Her career statistics show that she holds the record for the most no-hitters and struck out 18 batters in one game. She is studying marketing and communications and is the daughter of Joe and Veda Vertz. (Courtesy of Joe Vertz.)

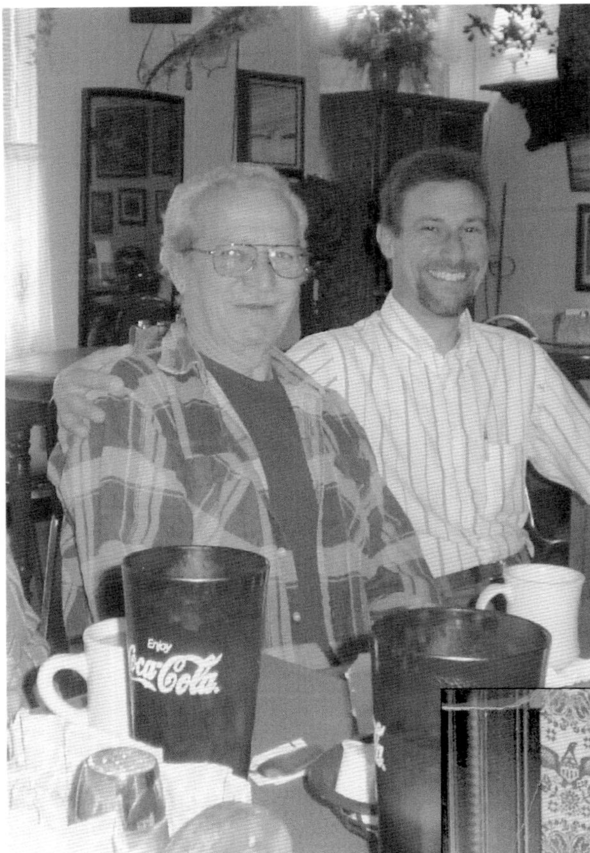

Bobby Kincaid and Pat Meyer
Bobby Kincaid (left) and Pat Meyer (right) loved to aggravate each other over coffee every morning. Friendly bets were made about their weekly NASCAR picks. Kincaid enjoyed restoring old classic cars, car shows, hunting, fishing, and riding his quad. He passed away in 2011. Meyer works in sales and owns the Motorpool Consignment car lot. His business is housed in a renovated caboose near the George Street bridge. (Author's collection.)

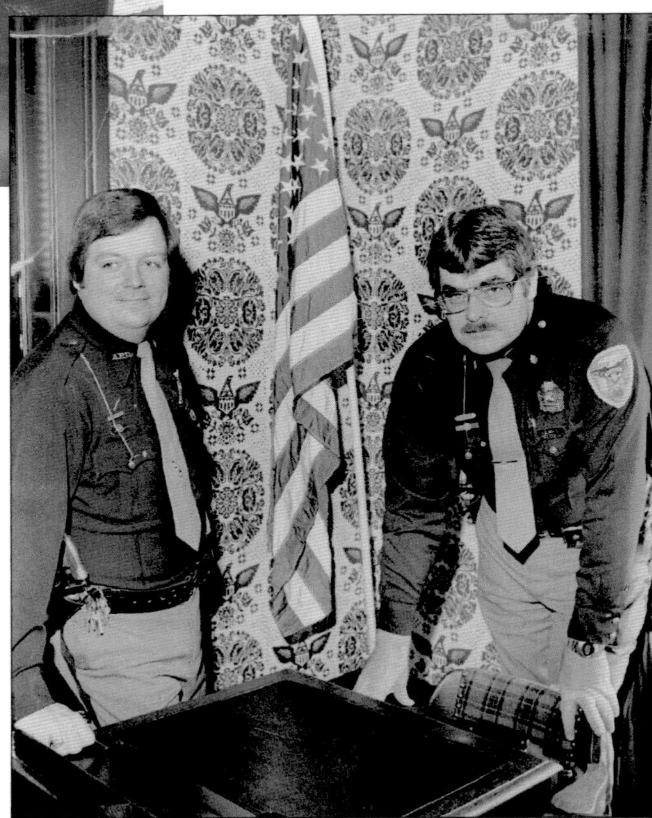

David Fogle and Gary Watts
If calling for the police in 1979, longtime friends and coworkers Assistant Police Chief David Fogle (left) and Police Chief Gary Watts would have answered the call. Watts often wore a Batman T-shirt under his uniform. Fogle eventually became chief deputy of the Dearborn County sheriff's office, retiring in 2009 after 23 years. Officer Watts passed away in September 2001. (Author's collection.)

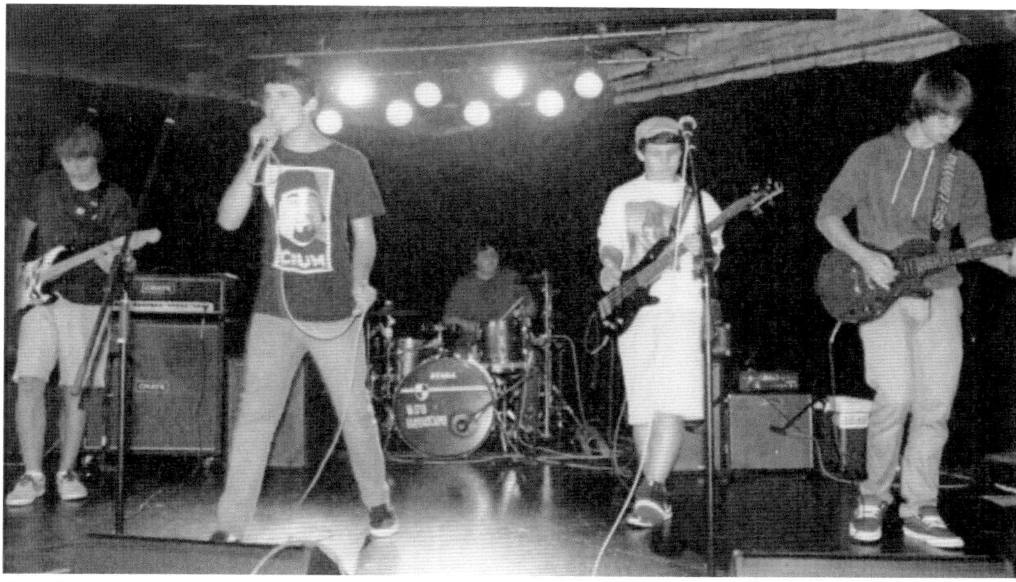

The Dugongs

The Dugongs are a group of musically talented teens. The group consists of, from left to right, Justin Riddell, Lucky New, Daniel Lunsford on drums, Noah Moses and Devin Sandlin. The Aurora band plays mostly their own music and very few cover songs. Their video and CD came out in 2012. The band named themselves after a photograph of a dugong (sea cow) that was hanging on the wall of a family member's home.

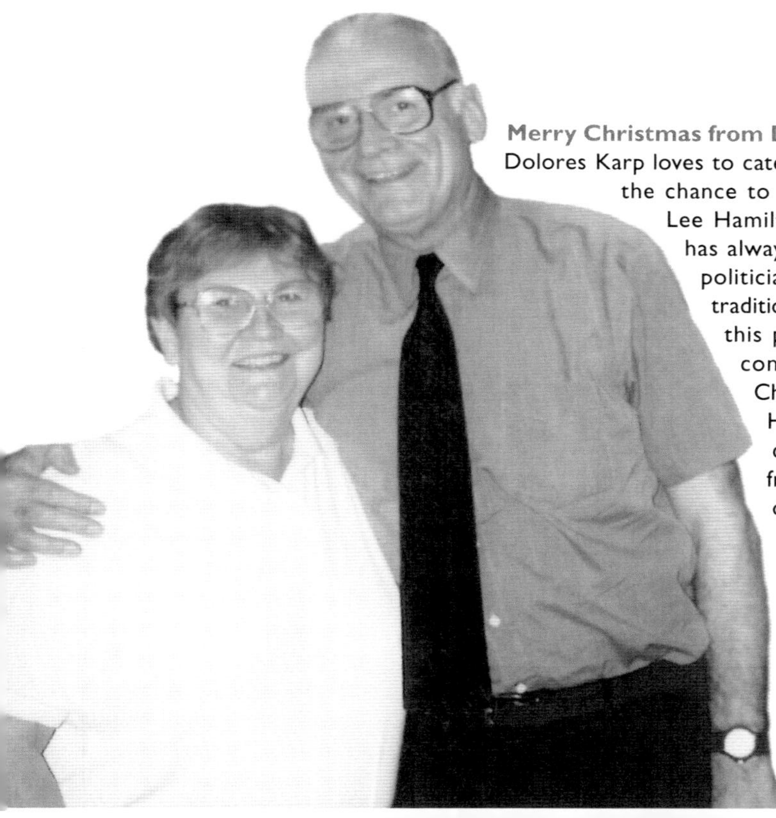

Merry Christmas from Dee and Lee

Dolores Karp loves to cater events. So, when she had the chance to cater for US congressman Lee Hamilton, she took it. Hamilton has always been one of her favorite politicians. In 1997, instead of the traditional Christmas card, she sent this photograph of her and the congressman, signed, "Merry Christmas from Dee and Lee!" Hamilton represented the 9th congressional district of Indiana from 1965 to 1999. (Courtesy of Debbie Acasio.)

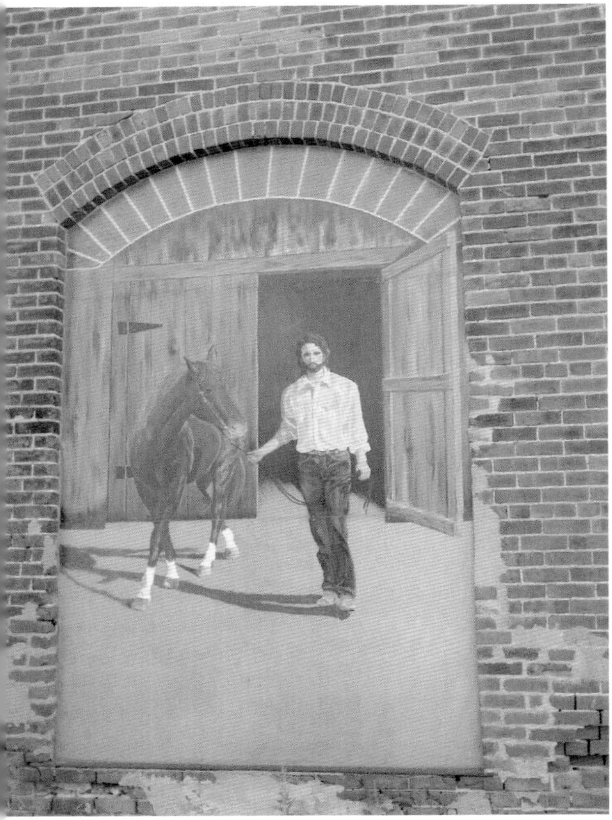

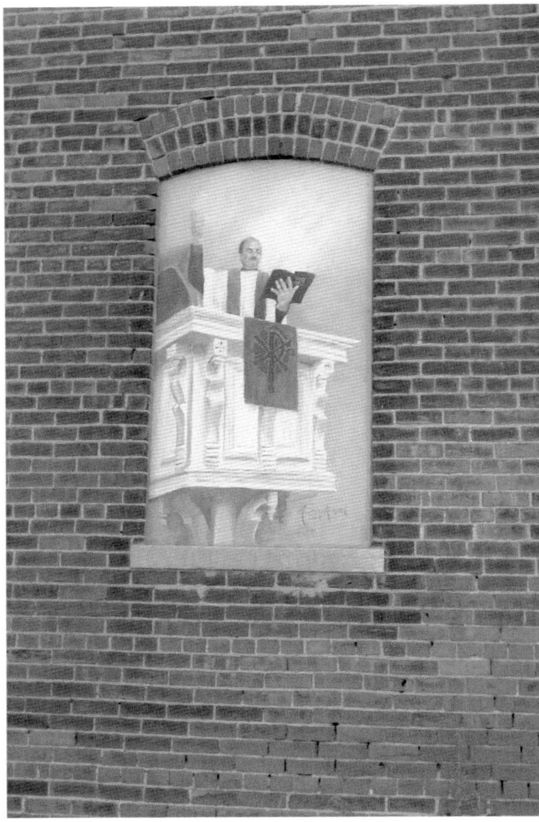

Windows Of Aurora

Boarded-up windows on empty buildings have become featured pieces of artwork about town. The life-sized painting above of a man and a horse depicts a blacksmith and livery stable that was once housed in this building.

Aurora is known for its churches. The painting above right depicts a minister preaching from the pulpit. The "Windows of Aurora" project portrays scenes that people in the early 1900s might have seen as they looked into or out of windows in town. The scenes have been painted by various artists and are installed at their designated locations in historic Aurora. "Windows of Aurora" is a Main Street project and is being funded in part by a grant from the Rising Sun Regional Foundation. The artists of Southeast Indiana Art Guild, the primary muralists of this project, are honored to have been chosen to participate in this project. The Southeast Indiana Art Guild is located in the Schuck building, on the corner of Second and Main Streets. Walking tours are available, and folks are welcome to tour on their own. (Photograph by McKenna Murray.)

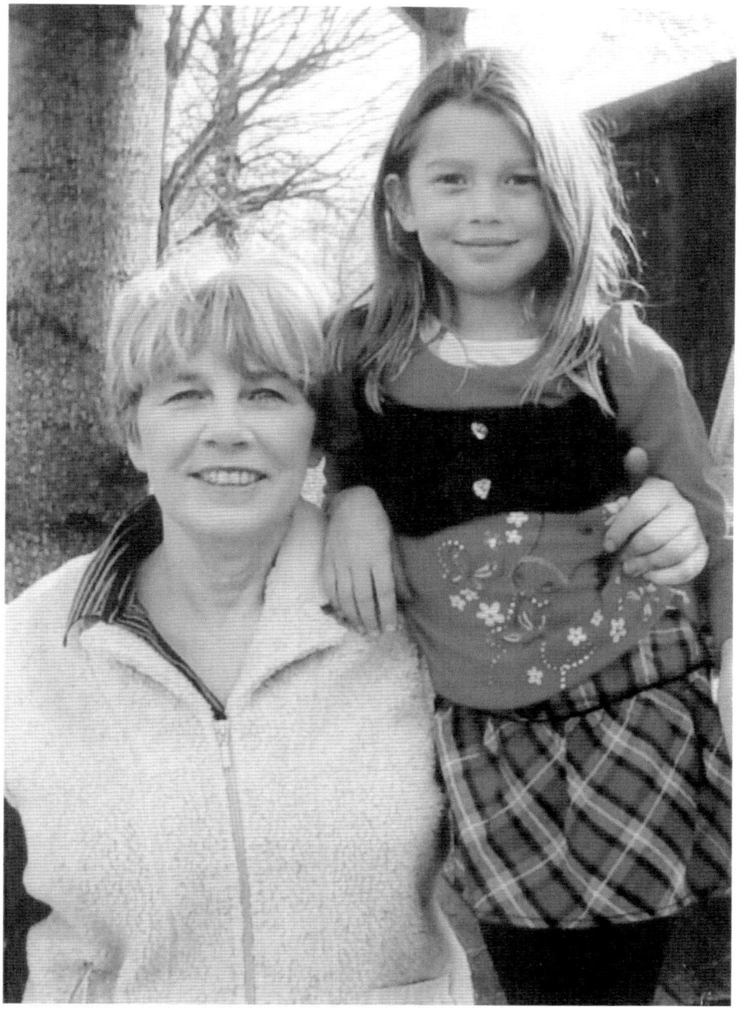

Author Jenny Awad

Awad (left) was the first boys' varsity soccer coach at Lawrenceburg High School. After years of coaching the boys' Soccer Association for Youth team, she was able to bring the team into the high school level at the beginning of sanctioned soccer in Indiana. She sits on the board of the Dearborn County Historical Society, and is the coauthor of three books, *Legendary Locals of Aurora*, *The Pictorial History of Dearborn County*, and *The First 100 Years of the Aurora Farmers Fair*. She also was a columnist for the *Aurora Journal Press* for eight years. While freelancing as a photographer at the Dearborn County newspaper, she took first place in the "1991 Best Feature Photo" competition from the Hoosier State Press Association. For 11 years, she served as cochair and treasurer for Aurora Riverfront Beautification (ARB). As a member of ARB, she helped to organize the "A Roar of Thunder" regatta boat races on the Ohio River in Lesko Park, Aurora. She sat as a commissioner on the Aurora Historic Preservation board for six years. Awad has been a resident of Aurora for 20 years. She is married to Joseph Awad and is vice president of sales and marketing for Ammbusher, Inc. Her granddaughter McKenna Murray (right) attended her first Aurora city meeting when she was one month old. Murray enjoys giving her friends tours of Riverview Cemetery. Photography and riding horses are her favorite hobbies. Several of her photographs were used in this book. (Author's collection.)

INDEX

LEGENDARY LOCALS

AN IMPRINT OF ARCADIA PUBLISHING

Find more books like this at
www.legendarylocals.com

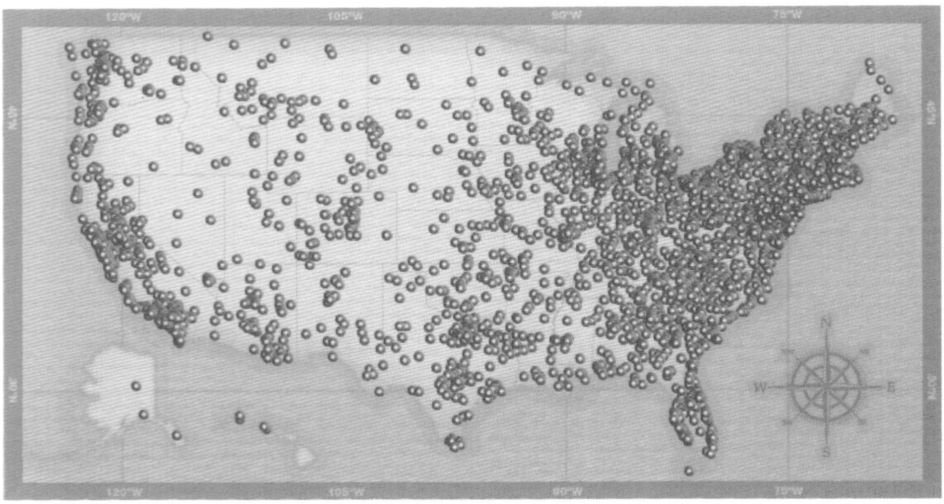

Discover more local and regional history books at
www.arcadiapublishing.com

Consistent with our mission to preserve history on a local level, this book was printed in South Carolina on American-made paper and manufactured entirely in the United States. Products carrying the accredited Forest Stewardship Council (FSC) label are printed on 100 percent FSC-certified paper.

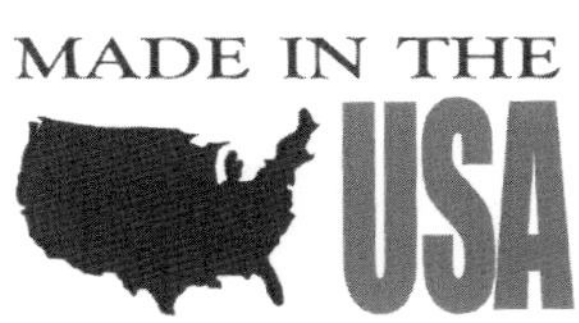